Sex Goes to School

Sex Goes to School

Girls and Sex Education before the 1960s

SUSAN K. FREEMAN

UNIVERSITY OF ILLINOIS PRESS

Urbana and Chicago

© 2008 by the Board of Trustees
of the University of Illinois
All rights reserved
Manufactured in the United States of America
1 2 3 4 5 C P 5 4 3 2 1
∞ This book is printed on acid-free paper.

Library of Congress Cataloging-in-Publication Data
Freeman, Susan Kathleen.
Sex goes to school : girls and sex education before the 1960s /
Susan K. Freeman.
p.   cm.
Includes bibliographical references and index.
ISBN-13 978-0-252-03324-7 (cloth : alk. paper)
ISBN-10 0-252-03324-8 (cloth : alk. paper)
ISBN-13 978-0-252-07531-5 (pbk. : alk. paper)
ISBN-10 0-252-07531-5 (pbk. : alk. paper)
1. Sex instruction—United States—History—20th century.
2. Sex instruction for girls—United States—History—
20th century.
I. Title.
HQ57.5.A3F74   2008
306.7082'09730904—dc22   2007045218

Contents

Acknowledgments

As an adolescent in the early 1980s, I had a lot of questions about sexuality that I never dared to voice. I recall not even having the courage to check out the library books by Judy Blume that spoke frankly about sex. A lot has changed in a few decades, and my interest in history and the kinds of feminist questions I ask about sexuality reflect the influence of numerous people. With gratitude to many supporters, teachers, and friends, I would like to acknowledge their direct and indirect contributions to the production of this book.

I began studying sex education as a graduate student at Ohio State University, where I was fortunate to receive a Graduate School Alumni Research Award, a grant from the Elizabeth Gee Fund for Research on Women, and a Woodrow Wilson–Johnson and Johnson Women's Health Dissertation Award. In graduate school I enjoyed the encouragement of many. Special thanks go to my dissertation advisor Leila Rupp; my committee members Susan Hartmann and Birgitte Søland; colleagues and friends Kirsten Gardner, Pippa Holloway, Heather Miller, and Stephanie Gilmore; and history department staff members Joby Abernathy and Gail Summerhill. Susan Cahn and Joan Catapano's interest in my book helped bring it to life, and I had the good fortune to spend an enjoyable year as a postdoctoral fellow in women's studies and history at Florida International University, mentored by Suzanna Rose and Aurora Morcillo. In the Department of Women's Studies at Minnesota State Mankato, where I have worked since the early 2000s, Maria Bevacqua, Cheryl Radeloff, and Jocelyn Fenton Stitt have contributed to an environment conducive to feminist research. As I completed revisions for the book, I enjoyed research assistance from graduate students Beatrice Quist, Adriane Brown, Kim Burrow, and especially Shelly Owen. Copyeditor Mary Giles and assistant managing editor Angela Burton at University of Illinois Press have been a pleasure to work with as well.

In my travels to archives around the country, many librarians and archivists assisted my work, and occasionally I had opportunities to speak with the people whose lives inform my research. Outstanding among these contacts was Elizabeth Force, responsible for the Toms River family relationships course. I regret that although she lived to be 104, she did not have a chance to see the book in print. After ending up in Mankato, I had an opportunity to learn from a graduate of San Diego's sex education programs, Carol Perkins. In addition to obtaining the job created by her retirement, I gained a very dear friend whose personal history and interest in my project has been tremendously important to me. She and Cy Perkins graciously shared their yearbooks and recollections about their high school experiences, which enriched my understanding of teenaged life in the 1950s.

My home and community while writing and completing the book has shifted from Ohio to Florida and finally to Minnesota. A constant source of love and support has been my parents, Jane and Bob Freeman, and my sisters, Alice Batson and Robin Freeman. I am grateful for their questions and interest along the way. Perhaps no one was prouder of me than my recently deceased grandmother, Kathleen Jordan, whose affection I appreciate enormously. My relationship with Lori Andrew was a significant part of my life during most of the years while I worked on the book, and I value her support as well as enduring friendships with Christie Launius, Ciara Healy, Heather Jobson, Beth Barr, Desirée Reitknecht, Bob Eckhart, Mollie Blackburn, and Natividad Treminio. Various cats have traipsed across my keyboard or snuggled in my lap as I've worked on the project, and more recently I treasure the dogs who have become part of my family. For Cathryn Bailey, who introduced me to the joys of canine companionship among many other things, I offer my deepest gratitude, respect, and love.

Introduction

In 1956, Toms River (New Jersey) High School senior Barbara New-man enrolled in an elective family relationships course. In carefully scripted handwriting, her homework earned her high marks and bountiful praise from teacher Elizabeth Force. "High quality work! Much appreciated," she noted on Newman's first assignment in the course workbook, *Ten Topics toward Happier Homes*. Although the historical record does not reveal why New-man took the course or whether she was especially interested in sexuality, the completed workbook nevertheless provides a window into sex education in mid-twentieth-century public schools. The ideas central to the Toms River course—"family relationships" and "happier homes"—prompted students to reflect on gender, sexuality, and social norms. In classrooms such as this one, Newman and countless other mid-century teenagers actively formu-lated ideas about who they were. They imagined, wrote about, and engaged in class discussion about their personalities, relationship preferences, and personal values. What that learning process encouraged was the develop-ment of heterosexuality—more specifically, heterosexual consciousness.

Coming of age in the mid-twentieth-century United States meant, for most adolescents, attending public school. In addition to reading, writing, and arithmetic, young people learned social norms. They gained knowledge about sex, gender, and sexuality not just from teachers but from peers. Stu-dents exchanged impressions and information about their changing bodies and sexual curiosities on playgrounds, in lavatories and hallways, and at their desks through verbal comments, written notes, gestures, touching, and other behavior. Classes and policies attempted to channel thoughts and energies into what educators deemed "respectable" conduct. Although physical education classes and recess periods could siphon off some of the young people's physical energy at school, other approaches were required for their sexual imaginations.

Public school teachers had sporadically introduced lessons on sex education since the beginning of the century, but formal instruction did not acquire popular support or become widespread until the 1940s. During the 1940s and 1950s, hundreds of school districts added sex-related curricula. These were not federally or state-mandated programs but experiments that emerged in local contexts, building from a national dialog among social hygiene and education professionals. Schools employed a variety of methods, from brief units to full courses, the latter often bearing such titles as family life education or social living. Like the Toms River family relationships class, the courses traced the events of a typical life, from puberty to parenthood; discussions of dating, engagement, and marriage were sandwiched between those of growing up and raising children of one's own. Although sex and family life education involved instruction about acquiring heterosexual maturity, the courses also invited a youth-centered discussion about adolescent behavior and forming intimate relationships.

What might have been a straightforward imposition of social norms turned out to be a more complicated process for two reasons, one related to pedagogy and the other to content. First, instruction about sex, gender, and sexuality increasingly took the form of dialog in small classes. Young people's voices dominated classroom discussions, and although teachers did not fully abdicate authority, they had to compete with peer groups for young people's attention and respect. Second, the fluctuating social norms of the 1940s and 1950s led to contradictory messages in the content of sex education. In particular, mid-century psychological perspectives on gender and sexuality challenged viewpoints based on tradition, religion, and biology.

Historical studies of sex education in the United States explore how the topic has been conceived. Scholars have primarily examined documents and instructional material that reflect educators' views about sex education. More recent research has begun to pay attention to the history of sex education pedagogy, although studies typically offer cursory impressions of the middle decades of the twentieth century.[1] My concern is with the confluence of sex and family life education—or education about sex, gender, and sexuality—in the 1940s and 1950s. My intent is to offer a deeper understanding of the dynamic process of sex education, in part by shifting the vantage point to consider adolescents' perspectives and contributions along with those of educators.

On the one hand, the history of sex education could be viewed as an exercise of social control whereby educators upheld power relations based on race, class, sex, and age. Educational scholars and historians have demonstrated that schools often inculcate middle-class values and rules of conduct and preserve the status quo of power relations.[2] Although sex education has reinforced normative heterosexuality and harnessed dialog about sexuality under the control of a teacher or another adult authority, the social control thesis risks reducing students to a submissive captive audience. It also overstates the homogeneity of educators, a problematic contention given the paucity of standardized training about sexuality, particularly in the early decades of sex education. As teachers developed lesson plans and responded extemporaneously to students' questions and comments, their messages varied in relation to specific classroom environments, students' personalities, and individual teacher's inclinations.

On the other hand, there is a temptation to interpret increased discussion of sexuality as evidence of sexual liberation, although scholarship influenced by Michel Foucault has urged scholars and activists to avoid viewing discussions about sex as inherently liberating.[3] Mid-century educators wanted adolescents to be interested—but not too interested—in sex. Classroom dialog about sexuality occurred under the teacher's surveillance, and some viewpoints received greater reinforcement than others. Many students no doubt suspected that there were consequences for articulating unpopular or unconventional ideas. Still, as Foucault's work reminds us, power is not exercised in an exclusively top-down fashion, and young people's voices and peer standards exert influence alongside teachers' authority.

Classrooms and schools, then, were arenas in which students voiced consent as well as dissent to the social expectations of mid-twentieth-century gender and sexual norms. Evidence from historical accounts of mid-century sex education programs suggests that students were more often compliant with teachers' expectations, but it is important to pay attention to defiance as well. Those who questioned or challenged their teachers or conventional norms contributed to the emergence of a liberal approach to sex, sexuality, and gender in many mid-century classrooms. The imperative to adjust to heterosexual expectations remained strong in the curricula, but a number of teachers acknowledged gray areas with respect to gender roles and sexual conduct. Most educators did not censure tomboys, married women working for wages, and young people who "petted"; rather, they acknowledged variability in accepted standards of femininity and chastity.

Like the Victorian Era that provides the historical context for Foucault's claims, the 1950s represents old-fashioned gender and sexual norms in popu-

lar memory. Revisionist historians in both periods have contested the sim-
plistic (and often self-serving) dismissal of the periods as prudish and wholly
conservative given the variety of sexual behaviors and proliferation of sexual
discourses.[4] The post–World War II mythology of socially conservative families and conformist gender roles nevertheless thrives. Accordingly, many assume that "abstinence"—today's framework for sex education that condemns
"premarital" sexual activity—reigned supreme in classrooms of the 1940s
and 1950s. Curricula and discussions in the mid-twentieth century, however,
hardly invoked sexual intercourse at all. Instead, conversations affirmed the
development of heterosexual maturity through dating, engagement, and, ultimately, marriage and parenthood. Sometimes youths wanted to talk about
sexual intimacy on dates, but that became a discussion topic rather than a
question of yes or no. Such conversations might incorporate analysis of personalities, likes and dislikes, popularity among peers, and the sexual double
standard. The multiplicity of ideas up for discussion engaged young people
in self-analysis and social critique. Sex education classes' attention to psychological dimensions of behavior and choices encouraged critical thinking
skills and acknowledged individual decision making. Such efforts held the
potential to shape young people's sexual imaginations in divergent ways.

This study of sex and family life education in the middle decades of the
twentieth century reveals the unfolding of a participatory, discussion-based
sexual pedagogy between adults and adolescents. Classrooms often featured
teenaged girls and boys learning about and discussing heterosexual relationships and a myriad of normative (as well as some nonnormative) behaviors.
A relationship-centered course was different than home economics courses
that entailed girls learning the "art" and "science" of homemaking, domesticity, and family care. By focusing on human relationships and their gender
and sexual underpinnings, relationship-centered courses attracted both boys
and girls. This new type of class, typically offered in the latter grades of high
school, reframed girls' discussions about marriage, family, and sexuality. Although a consumer-oriented society expected the girls to moon over wedding
plans and imagine domestic obligations as wives, mothers, and consumers,
in the 1940s and 1950s educators introduced new ways of analyzing sex,
sexuality, and gender. Boys, by far less socialized to ponder relationships and
marriage, gained different outlooks, too, but the new perspectives were less
effective in weakening masculine imperatives. In class, boys might participate in discussions of relationship dynamics, but they still bore the burden
of initiating dates, engagements, and marriages. Breadwinning remained a
male imperative, and "sissy" behavior was highly stigmatized.

A considerable number of young women who came of age before the sexual revolution of the 1960s attended classes in which they participated in dialog about dating, marriage, and reproduction. These topics—especially successful heterosexual partnerships—induced girls to be self-reflective, pursue self-improvement, develop sexual subjectivity, and expect fairness in relationships. Formal sex education was only one of many experiences that shaped their self-perceptions during adolescence. Other public school experiences—formal and informal curricula—occupied daily life as well in the context of compulsory schooling and rising high school completion rates.[5] Public school education—specifically, sex and family life education—thus provides a meaningful avenue for investigating the dynamic process of gender and sexual socialization. Girls' opinions and perspectives, embedded in contemporary accounts of sex education and youth cultures more generally, enable a better understanding of that process.

The idea that girls' lives merit scholarly attention is a relatively new one, especially in the field of history. The field of girls' studies has extended and modified many of the insights of women's studies through historical research, analysis of representations of girls in popular culture, and social science investigations of girls' self-esteem and development in adolescence.[6] Since the 1970s feminists both within and outside academia have called attention to sexual abuse as well as sexual empowerment, and scholarly research on sexuality has begun to historicize what Adrienne Rich labeled "compulsory heterosexuality."[7] Feminist perspectives as well as queer scholarship on sex, gender, and sexuality provide analytical frameworks for understanding sex education.[8]

Historical scholarship has captured many dimensions of formal and informal instruction about sex, with special attention to the moralizing aspects of sex education, trends in method and epistemology, and critiques of educators' agendas.[9] Underdeveloped in this largely intellectual history is a sustained critical analysis of gender and its role in shaping sex education theory and practice. To some degree, that neglect results from attempts to develop a periodization of sex education in relation to scientific ideas and social movements in the United States. At the same time, few historians have demonstrated curiosity about the gender dynamics of sex education, taking for granted that it reflected the patriarchal gender ideology of the larger culture.[10] Yet assumptions about gender were at the core of how sex education's content and methods developed. Furthermore, gender ideologies were not as predictable or stable as they might seem to those who view the period through the lens of 1950s' mythology. Glossing over gender in the history of sex education risks marginalizing or writing girls and women out of this history and underestimating the possibilities of gender as an analytical tool.

Inspired by feminist critiques of sexism in education and science, many scholars outside the historical profession have been attentive to gendered messages in sex education and have used empirical studies and textual analysis to tease out meanings and mistakes of sex and sexuality education, especially for girls.[11] The premise, which feminists widely accept, that sexuality and gender are social constructions, defined historically and culturally by society rather than fixed and determined by nature, biology, or divine forces, informs this scholarship. Feminist thought has further influenced skepticism about interpreting printed curricula as evidence of what happens in the classroom. In particular, curriculum theorist Bonnie Nelson Trudell has drawn attention to the politics, conflicts, and school cultures involved in formulating, teaching, and learning about sex education.[12] My research builds on and speaks to both historical and multidisciplinary feminist scholarship in an effort to illuminate exchanges of ideas about gender and sexuality and their significance for girls and young women.

* * *

Sex Goes to School consists of six chapters that explore how young people learned about sex in U.S. public schools during the 1940s and 1950s. The first begins by defining the scope of formal sex education and methods of implementing it in various school districts across the country. It demonstrates broad support for sex education in public schools, partially attributable to assumptions about shared belief in normative heterosexuality and the family. In spite of the social upheavals accompanying World War II, expanded liberalism in the late 1940s, and the sexually, socially, and politically conservative ethos of the cold war, sex education did not recede during the era, nor was there a backlash against it. Programs, whether ongoing or newly developed, remained remarkably consistent. One element of that consistency was antifascist and anticommunist posturing and an ideology of the superiority of "American"—that is, white, Christian, middle-class, and nuclear—families.

Chapter 2 examines the intellectual underpinnings of the practice of sex education during the 1940s and 1950s. Discussion-based, participatory pedagogy allowed students to shape the classroom experience; their viewpoints not only affected class dynamics but also informed the instructional material developed during this era. Students' experiences and professional literature prompted teachers to incorporate liberal views of psychological development, human relationships, and democratic ideals into the curricula, but without fully eliminating sexism and ethnocentrism. Authoritarian patriarchal families were rebuked in favor of cooperative marital partnerships and family units, albeit ones in which men retained masculinity and certain male prerogatives. Nevertheless, classes in sex and family life education encouraged girls to reflect on their personalities and relationships, develop their own ideals, and voice their viewpoints—including critiques.

Chapter 3 lays out the distinctions of three communities' approaches to sex education and shows how the experiments represent competing methods with shared underlying assumptions. Commentators hailed Oregon's movie *Human Growth* as groundbreaking, San Diego's curriculum was one of the most extensive and widely accepted programs ever, and Toms River's course was perhaps the best known curriculum among contemporary sex educators. Oregon, San Diego, and Toms River represent different tendencies in mid-century sex education curricula, but they each contained the common denominator of student discussion. The programs derived from a variety of sources of leadership, placing varying emphasis on health, human relations, and family life. Class, racial, and cultural differences were submerged in most accounts of sex education during this period, but these dynamics shaped the curricula and classroom composition. A closer look at these notable experiments shows the contradictions and tensions within sex education.

Chapters 4 and 5 examine the content of sex education curricula, especially their attention to biological sex and gendered personality expectations. The first of these two thematic chapters considers knowledge about sexual anatomy, masturbation and sexual arousal, menstruation, and reproduction as presented in curricula from the 1940s and 1950s. The study of the female body, more prominent than that of the male in education material oriented toward adolescents, included discussion of physical development during puberty and menstruation as well as how babies develop from the union of sperm and egg. Social and cultural assumptions about gender and maturity accompanied biological explanations for human behavior. Ultimately concerned about the psychological impact of their teaching, sex educators equivocated in what they believed to be useful information and therefore offered inconsistent views of what was natural and normal.

Chapter 5 more fully explores how ideas derived from psychology influenced sex education, and it also considers the extent to which sex education challenged traditional beliefs about femininity and heterosexual relationships. Educational material from time to time conflated biological imperatives and social norms but not without providing alternative viewpoints. Whether in coed or single-sex classrooms, girls learned that self-monitoring was an essential aspect of being feminine and attracting a date (or mate). Yet while reinforcing facets of femininity and even submissiveness to dating companions and potential husbands, sex educators also espoused liberal ideas about gender roles and relations. Teaching students to evaluate messages about love and desire in confessional magazines and the cinema, for example, helped demystify the romantic notions peddled by media and Hollywood and sharpened pupils' analytical acuity.

Finally, chapter 6 addresses the informal sex education occurring outside classrooms. Within schools as well as beyond their grounds, girls encountered information and developed impressions about sexuality and heterosexual femininity through taking cues from peers and adults. Their learning experiences included proms and other school dances; senior superlative awards, homecoming courts, and similar popularity contests; and on-campus club activities. Off-campus gathering spots and social activities for teenagers included movie theaters, dance clubs, music halls, and parks as well as organized summer camps and youth groups that ranged from religious and community organizations to fan clubs and gangs. Moreover, the more private and often surreptitious discoveries about sex—in books, magazines, darkened theaters, and parked cars—shaped girls' growing awareness and consciousness of gender and sexuality. Such influences in girls' education about sex occasionally echoed but sometimes were at odds with messages at school.

The book ends by considering mid-twentieth-century sex education in light of early-twenty-first-century controversy and confusion surrounding sex education. It examines how girls, their bodies, and their sexualities fit into policy questions as well as educational practices. Preoccupied with messages of abstinence and pregnancy- and disease-prevention, today's policymakers and educators have a lot to learn from what transpired in sex education classrooms more than fifty years ago. Students and teachers collaborated to create a kind of sex education that was innovative as instructors brought anatomical facts, psychological theories of adolescence, and the rhetoric of democracy, fairness, respect, and choice into classroom dialog with young people who sought to make sense of their lives. Even when instructors reflected the sexism, racism, classism, and homophobia of their time, young people—especially girls—stood to benefit at this crossroads of knowledge, advice, and discussion. Teachers encouraged them to conceive of preferences and possibilities, simultaneously expressing a desire to protect as well as empower maturing girls. In this way, educators' ambivalence about girls' autonomy embodied longstanding tensions within modern feminism.

Girls in mid-twentieth-century schools raised questions and sought their own agendas but stopped short of rebellion. Many, in fact, were content to adhere to the values of their parents' generation, although some were developing assertiveness and entitlement to respect and egalitarian relationships. Mid-century sex educators did not have overtly feminist goals in mind in trying to reduce ignorance and improve marital success rates, but their messages and methods contained a feminist undercurrent that flourished in the 1960s. Mid-century teachers were heavyhanded in promoting heterosexual, nuclear family living, but the democratic and gender-egalitarian principles presented in school gently stretched the limits of acceptable behavior. By the onset of the 1960s, girls formerly enrolled in sex, family life, and human relations classes—now adult women—inhabited a transformed sexual and political environment. Not everyone experienced the 1960s as a moment of sexual liberation just as not all students enrolled in sex education courses during the 1940s and 1950s acted on the curricula's more iconoclastic messages. Those who agitated for social and sexual change in the 1960s, however, responded to cultural tensions and contradictions whose roots were evident in sex education of the two preceding decades.

1

Momentum and Legitimacy

"Shall Our Schools Teach Sex?" queried *Newsweek* special projects editor Harold Isaacs in the May 19, 1947 issue.[1] For decades, numerous educators had answered that question in the affirmative, but the American public was probably unaware of this fact. The popular press before the 1940s had rarely commented on sex education in schools, but at the dawn of the 1940s, surveys began reporting significant public support for sex instruction. Increasingly, these statistics circulated in the popular media and in resources for educators.[2] By the late 1940s, when popular magazines questioned whether sex education should occur in schools, most gave the distinct impression that it should.

In fact, sex education was already underway in a number of schools, as readers of *Newsweek* and other mass-circulation magazines soon learned. Journalists often emphasized the issue as a battle, pitting church leaders, conservative teachers, and reluctant parents against progressive school administrators, social reformers, and open-minded citizens. Few writers failed to link efforts at sex education to changing social mores, juvenile delinquency, and rising divorce rates, and their commentaries encoded racial and class anxieties. White, middle-class educators and magazine contributors feared that sexual activity and loose moral standards were to be found among young people of color and whites who resided in low-income neighborhoods; they also worried that white, middle-class teenagers from suburbs, small towns, and prominent families were more and more relaxed in their sexual conduct. Especially troubling in the context of World War II were naïve girls who entertained soldiers as a contribution to building morale.

When they characterized sex education as a battleground, national media depictions tended to concede a few points to the opposition but largely presented a persuasive case for proponents. "The Battle over Sex Education Films" described in *Look* in 1949, for example, drew attention to opposition to sex education in Middletown, New York. The story revealed that "the majority of the townsfolk clearly favors the showing of the film in school. Most of the opposition comes from Catholics and a smaller number of townspeople"—those who tended to oppose sex education outside the home and church in general. A photo spread provided pictures and the opinions of seven adults, three teenagers, and one family. Among these figures, only three opposed sex education: a Catholic priest, a barber (also noted to be Catholic), and a married woman identified as a "cleaner."[3] The *Newsweek* feature two years earlier likewise identified Catholic dissent but also documented individual Catholics' support for sex education. The reservation expressed in the conclusion of the article concerned the far less charged issue of how to prepare teachers for this work.[4]

Encouraging teachers to cooperate in providing education was not the stumbling block that some perceived it to be. During the 1947–48 school year, the popular media introduced success stories based on several existing programs. *Better Homes and Gardens* publicized "Sex Goes to School in Oregon," and *Time* printed "Sex in the Schoolroom," a story on the Oregon-produced sex education film *Human Growth*. The *Ladies' Home Journal* contributed an article on the "San Diego Pioneers" of sex education, and *Parade* featured an account from Toms River, New Jersey, "They Study How to Live."[5] In no case did the teachers have elaborate training in sex education. Rather, school officials placed responsibility in the hands of reliable nurses, guidance counselors, and health, home economics, English, and social studies teachers.

Although "sex" figured prominently in much of the publicity surrounding sex education in secondary schools, journalists noted that sex education was given several other names. Explained Issacs in *Newsweek,* the term *sex education* did not capture the various classroom agendas. Therefore, "In Los Angeles the program is known as 'Family Life Education.' In Newark Valley, N.J., it is called 'Life Problems.' In Kansas City, the term is 'Human Science.' In Minnesota, as in many other places, it is simply known as 'Human Relations.' In each case, the object is the same: to provide the means through the broad school curriculum of not only teaching the 'facts of life' but also stressing the shaping of attitudes, ideals, and social responsibility."[6]

In a definition that remained relevant up to the 1960s, a leading sex educator, Lester Kirkendall, described sex education in 1944 as "much more than the sheer physical aspects of sex. It is concerned with those relationships between men and women growing out of the many differences between the sexes. The emotional, social, and ethical aspects [are] considered, and the place of sex as a constructive, up-building force in successful marriage and satisfactory family life [is] stressed."[7] Accordingly, when the feature on Toms River noted, "Sex education as such is not part of the program," the author was disavowing education about the physiology of sex but not the spectrum of sex-related emotions and relations central to most sex education curricula of the mid-twentieth century: heterosexual social adjustment, family problems, relationships, and attitudes and behavior.[8]

What in the late 1940s prompted such notice in the popular media? Not, as it turns out, the programs in Oregon, San Diego, and Toms River. All three had roots in the late 1930s (chapter 3). But 1947 was the year of the release of *Human Growth,* and attention to the first movie devoted to sex education in a classroom cast a spotlight on a number of endeavors. In addition, the 1948 publication of the first volume of Alfred Kinsey's *Sexual Behavior in the Human Male* created a media splash and prompted many to assess the status of sex education in schools.[9] Although a number of popular periodicals had presented abstract viewpoints on sex education since the 1930s, by the late 1940s more articles addressed the topic with accounts of actual programs in practice. In the short span of four months in 1948, readers encountered tales of sex and family life education in schools in *Today's Woman, Time, Newsweek,* the *Ladies' Home Journal, Parents' Magazine, Parade,* and *Life.*[10] Numerous other publications saw a flurry of articles devoted to sex instruction within homes and for adults as well.[11]

Headlines in newspapers and magazines often attracted attention by espousing controversy, but in fact the controversy was minimal in the 1940s and 1950s. Catholic leaders were typically behind the opposition to sex education, and a few publications headlined their organized objections to sex education classes and movies.[12] Attacks, battles, and warfare—words that cropped up in the headlines—however, were hardly apt metaphors for sex education at mid-century.[13] For the most part, articles alluding to controversy called attention to the ways in which sex education curricula were nonthreatening and merited while acknowledging a negligible opposition movement. A small number of dissenting opinions appeared as letters to editors, but positive responses always outnumbered negative ones.[14] Implementation of sex education inspired very little popular dissent until the 1960s, when parents and adults outside the schools organized a movement to eliminate it.[15]

This chapter provides an overview of ideas and inspirations for sex education, focusing especially on how mid-century sex educators distinguished themselves from their earlier counterparts in how they thought about sex, gender, and sexuality. Analyzing the intellectual and social currents that propelled educators to create and sustain sex education programs in the 1940s and 1950s brings the reasons behind public support for the topic into sharper focus. A secondary goal of the chapter is to reveal the continuity of sex educators' approach to sex education during the two decades even though historians usually place World War II and the 1950s (or post-1945) in separate periods. Consensus among educators was never fully achieved in matters of sex instruction and understanding sex more generally, but the patterns identified here resonate widely in instructional material and publications that detail projects in hundreds of locations around the country.

Sex Education: Meanings and Methods

Sex education has meant different things to different people over time, reflecting in part the changing meanings attributed to sex and sexuality. Although distinct connotations applied to the terms *social hygiene, sex, family living,* and *human relations* education during the twentieth century, educators and popular commentators frequently used the designations interchangeably. Sex education could refer to instruction about anatomical differences between boys and girls and men and women, human reproduction, birds-and-bees tales of reproduction among plants and animals, male-female ("boy-girl") relations, family relationships, and gender roles and conduct more generally. In some instances, sexual acts and reproduction were peripheral to the material; in others, sexual reproduction was the main point of instruction. During the mid-twentieth century, sex education was a wide-ranging concept that encompassed instruction about anatomy, conduct, personality, and relationships. What qualified the various curricula as sex education was the common thread of heterosexuality and how, educators believed, it shaped the similarities, differences, and attractions between men and women and boys and girls.

Although commonly thought of as shorthand for explaining intercourse and human reproduction, sex education has always involved other information and messages. Nearly all discussion of sex education in twentieth-century schools has encompassed a broader spectrum of gendered (and less apparently sexual) activities and behaviors. In other words, sexual activity and intercourse are components of sex education but not necessarily at the center of its curricula. Moreover, sexuality is often inseparable from gender, race, class, and age, such that analysis of sex education must involve attention to norms and ideologies not on the surface specific to sexuality.

The origins of sex education in public schools date back to the turn of the twentieth century and formation of the social hygiene movement.[16] Committed to eliminating venereal disease and such sex-related vices as prostitution, activists organized conferences, lobbied for legislative changes, supported medical research, and promoted sex education. Members of social hygiene organizations viewed themselves as enlightened by science; indeed, many activists were associated with the medical professions. Social hygienists' views on "hygiene," however, were as much about middle-class, Christian morality—and the ubiquitous racism and sexism of the era—as about scientific knowledge of disease.

Especially with reference to the origins of sex education in schools, historians and educators have characterized the topic as "negative" (emphasizing the dreadful consequences of illicit sex) or "positive" (affirming the creative potential of sex, usually within marriage). Emulating the negative/positive polarization of contemporary eugenics, which coerced those deemed "unfit" to limit procreation, on the one hand, and promoted the childbearing capabilities of "fit" parents, on the other, sex education had its own positive and negative poles. Recent historiography on the topic has examined these tendencies and has begun to problematize the relationship between so-called positive and negative sex education. Scholars have also made astute observations about the relationship between sex education and eugenics, a topic ripe for further analysis.[17]

Occasional and sporadic experiments in sex education in schools began in the early decades of the twentieth century. One set of efforts took the form of lessons orchestrated by local educators, primarily through science classes in public and private schools; such experiments were publicized in articles the major U.S. social hygiene organization, the American Social Hygiene Association (ASHA), published in its journal.[18] Another means of teaching young people was to employ a medical professional or another lecturer from outside the school to address an audience of students about "social hygiene," especially to warn about the dangers of venereal disease and the importance of remaining sexually pure.[19] An additional way in which sex education entered schools was through curricula modeled on military training material that sought to ward against venereal disease among soldiers. Some of the nation's first sex education pamphlets and movies for young people originated during World War I. Growing awareness of young soldiers' sexual contacts, which in many cases had occurred before enlistment, prompted some agencies to expand educational endeavors among civilians through youth organizations as well as some schools.[20]

When researchers commissioned by the U.S. government assessed the extent of sex education in public schools in 1922 and 1927, the published results suggested that it occurred in nearly half of the responding schools. That optimistic portrait, however, was qualified by data that revealed that many topics dealing with human sexuality were omitted, most teaching took place in larger high schools, and the rate of response to the survey diminished between the first and second studies. Nevertheless, the reports suggested government interest in sex education and that there was more of it than most people suspected.[21]

The influence of medical, social hygiene perspectives in public school sex education was waning before U.S. entry into World War II. Meanwhile, U.S. government and educational agencies were trumpeting the cause of sex education with emphasis on "normal" rather than vice- and disease-driven narratives of sexuality. No federal guidelines for sex education emerged during the first half of the century although government officials did periodically measure and show support for sex education endeavors as well as make recommendations about how it should function. Studies during the 1920s were followed by a report in 1939, published under the auspices of the U.S. Public Health Service with the title *High Schools and Sex Education*. In the foreword to the volume, the U.S. surgeon general explained that secondary schools should focus their sex education curricula on "psychological and social" rather than medical needs, a message that found many adherents in subsequent decades.[22]

By 1940, sex education was usually "integrated" into school curricula such as science and health or absorbed into new curricula about gender, sexuality, and relationships. Three frameworks emerged: the biology of physiological sexual development and reproduction; analysis of male-female and family relationships; and the study of individual personality and psychosocial development, the latter being the newest trend and an offshoot of family relations.[23] The former, the idea of offering instruction about the biology of puberty and reproduction, had the lengthiest history in public schools, with eugenics, heredity, and reproduction the best-covered subjects. Biological sex education persisted into mid-century, especially instruction about puberty, and, for girls, menstruation, while family living and human relations education opened new avenues for the consideration of gender, sex, and sexuality in schools.

Advocates for sex instruction in the mid-twentieth century—including teachers and school administrators, social science researchers, and health professionals—viewed sex as integral to understanding individual personalities as well as relationships. The focus on personalities and relationships was more than window dressing intended to divert attention from sexual behavior. Mid-century sex education proponents wanted to guide adolescents' entries into adulthood. In the long run, they forecast, these efforts would address such social problems as delinquency and divorce. Finding physiology and eugenics less malleable than the burgeoning social sciences for these purposes, numerous educators applied psychological concepts to sex education for school children and teenagers. Psychological concepts derived primarily from developmental psychologists and, to a lesser extent, from behaviorists, psychiatrists, psychoanalysts, and sexologists.[24] Many teachers, influenced by so-called Progressive curriculum reform movements, believed that education could generate social and behavioral change.[25]

By the middle of the twentieth century, social science perspectives on gender were less rigid than medical, biological, and Darwinian views of sex and sexuality. Much of the educational material from the 1940s and 1950s downplayed gender-differentiated standards of conduct and promoted complementary, if not always egalitarian, male and female roles. Male domination and female subordination, the mid-century American texts proclaimed, were vestiges of the past or features of less-developed societies.

In addition to their reconsideration of gender hierarchies, mid-century sex educators empowered students to talk about sexuality in sex and family life education classes. Just as they characterized their ideas about gender roles (really, women's roles) as forward-thinking, they also imagined themselves to be harbingers of modern viewpoints on sexuality. They largely rejected the Victorian notion of the "innocent child" and instead acknowledged children's curiosities, desires, and knowledge (including misinformation) about sex. Only infrequently did mid-century educators couch sex education in language of religion and morality, which was central in previous decades; although many educators referenced religion or God, they avoided language of contamination and sin and gravitated to more secular concepts.

By the 1940s, educators had at their disposal decades of child study and Freudian-inspired research and writing about childhood sexuality.[26] They also encountered sensationalized media focused on youthful sexual behavior ("juvenile delinquency"), especially that of girls. In the midst of this evidence, albeit much contested, mid-century educators became convinced that it was possible, desirable, and perhaps even obligatory to discuss sex with adolescents in a school setting. They had in mind not merely lectures or presenting pamphlets or books but inviting dialog and building on students' impressions and knowledge as points of departure.

With encouragement from young people who sought discussion, information, and guidance related to social and sexual behavior in adolescence, educators generated a sex education that had a new emphasis. Some lessons remained situated in biology, health, and physical education classes, but during the 1940s and 1950s these were diminishing in significance to courses devoted to social and psychological aspects of heterosexuality and other "problems" of youth. The new courses bore such titles as social relationships, senior problems, and family living. Meanwhile, the study of puberty and sex in the sciences and in health and physical education classes increasingly considered "mental hygiene" as well as physical well-being.

Educators in the 1940s and 1950s had less trepidation than had their social hygiene predecessors about extolling the positive aspects of heterosexual interests among adolescents. Whereas experts early in the century had favored a sex education program that would minimize curiosity about sex—aiming to "keep sex consciousness and sex emotions at the minimum" and "avoid everything which tends to awaken or to intensify either"—such sentiments were out of vogue, although not entirely eradicated, by the 1940s.[27] Other early-twentieth-century orthodoxies concerning how to teach sex education were falling from favor as well. An "established point" of the topic from 1924 onward was that teachers should avoid such titles as "social hygiene education" and "sex education," what the social hygiene leader Maurice Bigelow considered "convenient headings under which educators are organizing and directing research and training" but "*not* names proposed for new courses of study in schools or colleges."[28]

The term *sex* emerged, seemingly sanitized and appropriate for adolescents to discuss with adults in public schools at the end of the 1930s. Granted, students would not find "sex education" on their course schedule or transcript in the 1940s and 1950s because teaching about sex was integrated into courses with a variety of titles. But as media coverage and other sources convey, sex education was prominent on secondary schools' agendas. Mid-century leaders in the movement for sex education in schools, like the public at large, had grown less reluctant to employ the terminology of "sex," whether in writing for popular and professional audiences or when interacting with young people.[29] (The term *hygiene,* however, became less common in the sex education lexicon by the end of the 1950s other than as a reference to personal hygiene.)

The idea of "integrating" sex material into existing courses was decades old, and the integrationist position favored instruction by regular teachers rather than outside professionals such as physicians.[30] Integration had a particularly charged—and racialized—meaning in the 1940s and 1950s, as the civil rights movement, which sought to end racial segregation in public schools and other public and commercial establishments, was gaining ground. The term *integration* had the potential to arouse white people's anxieties about social change. Integrated sex education, however, did not contribute to dismantling racial segregation or race and class hierarchies in any direct way.

The term *mixed* also possessed multiple meanings and was laden with racial connotations. Mixed classrooms and mixed marriages, accordingly, had the potential to challenge racial segregation and hierarchies. In the context of sex education, however, the word *mixed* meant coed—combining boys and girls; in the case of marriage, it implied marrying across religious faiths. Thus, mixed classes and marriages disrupted the status quo, but their challenge was more to religious conservatism than white supremacy. When curricula dealt with the subject of choosing a mate, for example, educators typically had in mind marriage between a Catholic and Protestant.[31] Discussion of interracial marriages was more explicit in the sex education plan from Detroit, Michigan, yet it was more common for teachers and texts to question whether people of different faiths could form a healthy marriage.[32] Although it did not often overtly discuss racial qualifications, the discusion of how to select a mate hinted at the topic when it mentioned heredity, similar backgrounds, and similar interests as important considerations.[33]

It would be difficult to overstate the concern of educators with youths' attitudes toward sexuality, marriage, and family life. Whereas early social hygienists had been involved with monitoring sexual behavior and controlling the spread of vice and disease, mid-century sex educators concentrated on shaping the minds and imaginations of young people, more so than their bodies. In adopting language from psychology and sociology, mid-century educators resembled late-Victorian purity crusaders, emphasizing attitudes over facts.[34] Unlike moralists, however, mid-century sex educators found inspiration in the secular realm of research on child development and cross-cultural analysis of family norms. More attuned to the values of marriage counselors and Progressive Era reformers known for decades as proponents of egalitarian and companionate marriage, sex educators in the 1940s and 1950s stressed successful married life rather than sexual depravity.[35]

Family life education focused a great deal on the nuclear family and its domestic life and was in part an outgrowth of the training in homemaking that public schools offered girls. Although integrated into homemaking classes, family life education also became a distinct category of instruction that numerous schools transformed into freestanding classes. Family living courses more often than not enrolled both sexes and dealt very little with household skills. Although women taught approximately half of mixed-gender family life education courses, those in the spotlight were not usually home economics teachers.[36] The Dover Township, New Jersey, school superintendent, for example, recruited Elizabeth S. Force, who taught English, to develop and teach the Toms River High School course on family living. And while girls' enrollment in the course surpassed boys for several years (especially during the war, when girls outnumbered boys in school generally), increasingly boys signed up for the coed course.[37]

Unlike the feminized realm of home economics, mixed-sex family relations courses, usually offered in the upper grades of high school, promised guidance on how to have a successful and emotionally gratifying family life. Household accounting and consumer education might be covered, but the courses also emphasized the dynamics of family and human relationships. Family living courses considered pupils' present family situations and commonly discussed such topics as sibling relationships and unchaperoned dating. Students received guidance in the more abstract process of imagining their future marriages but little scientific knowledge of reproduction or their bodies. With units on dating, mate selection, engagement, and marital adjustments, however, human bodies and sexual relations could not be ignored in the curriculum—nor eliminated from students' thoughts and questions.

Human relations education, a close cousin of family life education, emphasized heterosexual gender roles rather than the family proper. Like family life education, human relations education appeared in schools during the mid-twentieth century and was a product of the movement toward functional education intended to have real-life implications for students outside school grounds. Recognizing that most pupils did not pursue higher education, school personnel offered practical preparation for adopting adult responsibilities; they began providing driver's education, expanding shop classes, and teaching about personal finance. Practical and vocational courses became more prevalent in mid-century high schools, as were those designed to aid in life adjustment or the process of adapting to adult society.[38] The movement for intercultural understanding also overlapped with human relations education, given its aim to improve how people related to and understood one another across differences of race, ethnicity, nationality, and culture.[39]

As they designed new curricula in the realm of human relations, educators worked toward the goal of promoting emotionally stable individuals, successful families, and thriving communities. Their view of success, highly influenced by their typically privileged racial, class, and religious backgrounds, was contingent on amiable male-female relationships, a strong work ethic, sound mental health, and elimination of prejudice. Similar to family life courses, human relations incorporated instruction in family psychology and sociology and focused on individual psychological development and adjustment in society more generally. Few writers or educators bothered to distinguish between family life and human relations education. For instance, a one-semester, required course at Brown High School in Atlanta, Georgia, reported its teacher, was formally called "personal and family living" but nicknamed "social living."[40] It and others like it dealt with personal concerns, family conflict, and community relations. Although the report leaves race unspoken, this segregated white school in the South of the Jim Crow Era institutionally if not verbally validated racial inequality.

Regardless of the intellectual trajectory and institutional dimensions for each course related to sexuality, school officials tackled similar questions about how the course would operate. Who would teach it? Would boys and girls attend the same class or meet separately? Was the course compulsory or elective and did it require parental permission? At what grade levels would students enroll? Many combinations of methods were possible. When researcher Jacob A. Goldberg surveyed 185 superintendents in the mid-1940s, he noticed the diversity of sex education experiments and provided synopses of forty distinct programs. He concluded that within his sample, "A few school systems are attempting to do some teaching in the elementary schools; about 25 percent cover human relations materials in the junior high schools; while all of those listed carry on some type of activity in the senior high schools."[41]

Even as curricula underwent modifications during the 1940s and 1950s, the continuity is striking. Health, physical education, and biology classes in junior high schools covered similar topics in both decades. At the same time, new and ongoing courses for older teens in senior high schools continued to proliferate without departing from the basic form they took in the early 1940s. Many schools implemented more than one type of sex education at different grade levels and in different departments, as exemplified by San Diego, California. Coordinated by the district's director of health education, San Diego schools offered sixth-grade students lessons on puberty and growing up. For junior and senior high school students, an innovative class called group counseling was designed to answer their questions in an informal setting.[42]

Variation among schools, even within the same district, was common. High schools in Denver, Colorado, in the 1950s, for instance, offered several different programs yet consistently separated male and female students for instruction. West High School students took senior planning, a required course that included twice-weekly sessions with physical education teachers;

North High School seniors might opt for a home and family living course, a social science elective; at East High School, the social problems class was optional for seniors; and South High School seniors could elect to take home living from the home economics department.[43]

There were no federal guidelines for sex education in the mid-twentieth century and rarely did any two schools have identical programs, because individual personalities, institutional configurations, and community dynamics created different environments for launching and teaching sex education. Yet the similarity is remarkable in an array of accounts, including, for instance, those from junior high schools in suburban Connecticut, Arlington Heights, Illinois, and Los Angeles, California. These programs, originating in the mid-1940s, resembled one another in that health and physical education teachers or nurses met with single-sex groups of adolescents to provide information about human sexual anatomy and discuss concerns and questions about puberty and adolescence.[44] Likewise, analogous programs emerged during the mid-1950s in Highland Park, Michigan; Council Grove, Kansas; Charlotte, North Carolina; and Corona, California. These high schools each offered a coed family living course to senior students, focusing a great deal of attention on dating and preparing for marriage.[45]

In all their incarnations, programs across the country emerged in the midst of a national dialog that occurred in numerous print sources. Few teachers of sex education were likely to be unfamiliar with the Oregon film *Human Growth* once it was featured in *Newsweek* and *Life* magazines. Educators who did not have direct contact with the ASHA would likely have come across some of the association's dozens of widely cited pamphlets or broadly distributed publications. Sex education textbooks, teachers' guides, and monographs found space on library shelves, earned book reviews in a variety of professional publications, and appeared on numerous references lists. Those not contacted by a graduate student interested in studying pupils' reactions to sex education would no doubt have read public opinion polls on the topic as well as letters to the editor and guest columns in national publications and local papers alike. With such apparent interest and a variety of models to emulate in health, human relations, and family life education, many school administrators and teachers joined the effort to educate about sex.

Popular Support

Public receptiveness to sex education appeared to commentators and researchers to be on the rise in the mid-twentieth century. Although support appears to have remained rather steady throughout the two decades, writers at the time presented the support as gaining ground. The expanding acclaim indicated, educators thought, adults' purported decreasing secrecy about sex; moreover, advocates explained, parents were becoming more aware of their inability to provide proper instruction and guidance at home. Although manufactured to suit the purposes of sex educators, these theories were repeated as truisms.

From the earliest appearance of national polls on the subject, a persistent majority favored sex instruction. Most remarkable about these results is the lack of explanation of what pollsters meant by "sex education"; many people, apparently, were willing to sanction it without having a clearly stated definition. Whatever sex education might be, they seemed to want it—or so they said. A 1938 poll in *Successful Farming* discovered rural adults were in favor of sex education by 64 percent.[46] In June 1943 the first national opinion poll on the topic found approval for high school sex education at 68 percent, with 16 percent in opposition and another 16 percent having no opinion (or possibly mixed opinion).[47] Concern about female juvenile delinquency inspired 79 percent of responding *Woman's Home Companion* "Reader-Reporters" to sanction sex education in high schools in 1943 as well.[48]

Polls conducted at the county or state level were likewise favorable. A 1946 poll of Los Angeles county parents reported 95 percent endorsed sex education in junior and senior high schools. Moreover, 75 percent of these Los Angeles parents favored sex education in elementary school, an unusual mandate for initiating sex instruction before puberty.[49] On the East Coast in 1950, a statewide New Jersey survey posited that 81 percent of adults approved of local schools teaching about sex, with 83 percent of parents with children in school concurring. Fewer people in New Jersey (4 percent) were undecided compared to the 1943 national poll showing 16 percent without opinion. Revealing receptiveness similar to Los Angeles, most New Jersey parents surveyed wanted sex education to be initiated in junior high school, although some preferred earlier or later grades.[50] Seventy-three percent of 515 Washington state adults, in a survey conducted by the Washington Public Opinion Laboratory in 1951, approved of sex education in schools; 19 percent did not, 7 percent didn't know, and 1 percent did not respond. Some survey responders who did not support sex education had a qualified response such as "not if taught in mixed groups," suggesting that it was the methodology and not the concept that was unfavorable.[51]

Parents and school leaders emerged as friendlier toward sex education than the general public, according to several statewide and national polls.

In Washington state, parents of school-aged children approved of sex education by 81 percent, whereas the approval rating of those without children in school was 69.3 percent.[52] The professional journal *Nation's Schools* found that 96 percent of five hundred representative public school administrators favored some form of sex education in 1944. The journal's pollsters discovered similar rates of approval among a smaller sample of parents.[53] By the end of the 1950s, a second survey in *Nation's Schools* indicated that 72 percent of administrators felt that public senior high schools were *obligated* to teach sex education; 58 percent agreed that the education should appear also in junior high schools and 31 percent in elementary schools.[54] Those most engaged in the work of raising and educating young people tended to take greatest interest in expanding sex education.

Beyond the classroom, young people made their convictions and needs for sex education known. At the national YMCA-YWCA Conference for high school students in Grinnell, Iowa, in 1947, for example, twelve hundred teenagers adopted resolutions demanding more and better education on sex and family life.[55] New York City radio station WQXR held a youth forum in 1948 about whether to include sex education in high schools: the six students' opinions prompted a *New York Times* headline, "Parents Held Lax in Sex Education."[56] The "boy governors" at the 1949 YMCA-sponsored conference in Washington, D.C., concluded that "ignorance about sex and lack of preparation for family responsibilities are the No. 1 handicaps of American youth."[57] Fifteen-year-old Donald Kaiser of Joliet, Illinois, reportedly wrote to *Look* magazine in 1951 to express the need for sex education in his school as soon as possible. Teachers, he claimed, presented more reliable information than that picked up outside class.[58] In Columbus, Ohio, where high school students met for a mock legislative session in 1952, Cleveland high school student and "Governor" Mike Lewis argued that sex education should be mandatory.[59] New York state's and New York City's Hi-Y model legislatures repeatedly adopted laws mandating sex education in public schools.[60]

Young people's enthusiasm and parental support for sex education were critical in implementing plans for sex education. Most schools gave students the option of being excused from classes where sex would be discussed, but fear of parental disapproval nonetheless hindered many schools from offering sex education. A major factor in dismantling parental reluctance was the endorsement of local, state, and national Parents and Teachers Associations (PTA). Chapters across the nation established study groups and public meetings on social hygiene topics during the 1930s and 1940s.[61] With a few exceptions, state PTAs in the 1930s, 1940s, and 1950s had social hygiene committees that led such work.[62] In May 1944, the national PTA articulated resounding support for a "well-planned program of social hygiene instruction . . . throughout public school training." Meanwhile, many state and local PTAs, earliest among them New Jersey, had already advocated and would continue to support sex education.[63]

In collaboration with teachers and professional organizations, parents helped build legitimacy and momentum in the movement for sex education. In San Antonio, Texas, a sex education teacher called on all local PTA presidents to go over every detail of the new curriculum and was met with "enthusiastic approval."[64] A state PTA convention in Florida in 1947 inspired the Hillsborough County schools' family life education program led by Martha Johnson, the county's PTA "social hygiene chair."[65] Public screenings of sex education films and invitations for parents to join panels and discussions on the topic accelerated parental approval. Groups of parents in Mamaroneck, New York, and Cranston, Rhode Island, overwhelmingly approved the use of *Human Growth* and other films, including McGraw Hill's *Human Reproduction,* for their public school students.[66] By the end of the 1940s, the National Congress of Parents and Teachers, the American Association of School Administrators, and the National Conference on Education of Teachers all favored sex education in classrooms and teacher training on that topic.[67]

Parental and community support for sex education was not, of course, unanimous, however much proponents preferred to focus on affirmation. Up to a third of those surveyed, after all, were hesitant or objected to it altogether. School authorities sometimes tried to dismiss the opposition, using a range of explanations such as the idea that parental resistance to sex education came primarily from those inadequately prepared for conducting the job at home. By downplaying the legitimacy of "ignorant" opponents, educators assured their own ascendancy to the role as guardians of how sex would be taught to children of those less educated or who came from poorer backgrounds, people often imagined as being of color and immigrants. As a high school science teacher in Collegeboro, Georgia, noted in 1941, "Parents may be problems in some instances, but more often they are only imagined as opposing any attempts at sex education in the schools."[68] Countless reports of school sex education programs relayed that no more than a handful of parents ever prevented their children from attending the classes.[69]

Some parents were relieved to have trained teachers assume responsibility for sex education, whereas others hoped to supplement domestic efforts to instill moral values. Already by the end of the 1930s, articles in popular periodicals gave voluminous quantities of advice to parents about sex education in the home. Mothers, doctors, journalists, and other experts contributed their viewpoints to a wide array of mass-readership serials and best-selling books.[70] Numerous sources geared toward parents became available in the mid-twentieth century, heightening adults' awareness of arguments in favor of sex education for children and adolescents. In addition to PTA meetings and public forums, books and pamphlets proliferated—intended for a general audience of parents and teachers—to guide those teaching children and teens about sex. Noted authorities published books with popular presses and pamphlets sponsored by the ASHA, public health and medical associations, and other social service agencies. At issue, though, was the fact that not all parents were inclined to pursue such self-education, and many—especially mothers who worked outside the home, a large proportion of whom were African Americans or immigrants—had little time to devote to their own education.[71]

Colleges had begun to offer more courses in marriage and family life, responding primarily to students' demands for such practical and functional education. As historian Beth L. Bailey has pointed out, sociologists in particular took responsibility for researching and teaching the subject as a result of changing norms for marriage during the Great Depression and World War II, providing professional endorsement to students' quest for information about love, marriage, and sex. Marriage education courses at the college level dated from the late 1920s, with significant expansion in the 1940s; more than five hundred colleges offered marriage courses by the end of the 1940s.[72] Not only were such courses a boon to future teachers, but educators also believed that those enrolled would endorse programs in their future children's schools and offer more informed instruction in their homes.[73]

School boards, state legislators, and the U.S. government gave periodic, official shows of support during the mid-twentieth century. The District of Columbia's board of education approved sex education in 1943, and the South San Francisco school board made a similar move sanctioning human relations and family life courses in 1949.[74] Two states—Oregon and Michigan—passed laws during the decade that sanctioned but did not mandate teaching sex education.[75] A failed legislative challenge to sex education in California in 1947 allowed educators in San Diego and across the state to proceed with their programs.[76] Having created the Division of Venereal Disease within the U.S. Public Health Service as early as World War I, the federal government continued to demonstrate interest in the related tasks of venereal disease prevention and sex education. Especially through its subdivisions concerned with educational policies, the Division of Venereal Disease collaborated with the ASHA to bring greater attention to the need for sex education.[77]

By the end of the 1950s, educators had acquired two decades of cumulative support and had collected data and testimony that revealed many of their ideas in practice. Numerous schools had implemented planned programs, parental and public resistance appeared negligible, and a handful of professionals had successfully carved out careers in promoting and teaching sex education. Even if the overall exposure to the topic in this generation did not reach all students across the nation, a significant number of future parents would have classroom experience to assist their efforts at educating the next generation.

As the apparent common ground among sex educators began to erode toward the end of the 1950s there was also cause for concern. An incident in a Los Angeles classroom, which garnered *New York Times* and *Newsweek* publicity along with local press coverage in 1959, led to a backlash against sex education and the dismissal of Cecil M. Cook, a social studies teacher. The instructor solicited anonymous questionnaires from his Van Nuys High School students, asking them to reveal their sexual experiences, from kissing to heterosexual and homosexual activity to other "abnormal sex practices." A public hearing ensued, prompted by a young woman and her parents' complaint, and the teacher was ultimately relieved of his job.[78] In the midst of the controversy, the *Los Angeles Examiner* featured an article, which, much like the upbeat 1947 *Newsweek* article that began this chapter, asked "Should Sex Education Be Taught in Schools?" By 1959, Los Angeles authorities were far less sanguine about sex education in schools. In fact, the district's deputy superintendent for education denied that schools taught sex education. "What we do teach is 'human reproduction,'" she claimed.[79]

Even as local support for sex education retracted in light of the Van Nuys controversy, a minority of sex educators, influenced by the work of Alfred Kinsey and adopting a more secular and permissive viewpoint, argued openly that premarital intercourse was not always harmful.[80] Such bold actions and statements revealed fault lines and foreshadowed controversies to come.

Conclusion

Sex education in the 1940s and 1950s appeared in various locations in a decentralized fashion. Building on the leadership of various organizations and interest groups, including social hygiene, home economics, progressive reform, parent-teacher associations, and government agencies, a multidimensional program of sex education emerged in various sites across the nation. The era's voluntary sex education programs did not emanate from government officials or school principals but rather from collaborations among school administrators, teachers, nurses, students, and surrounding communities.

Diverse practices and avenues for offering sex education became apparent, publicized among professional educators as well as the general public. The dominant frameworks that developed during the period were health, family living, and human relations. In all cases, participatory pedagogy invited or sometimes required young people to articulate their viewpoints and thoughts on matters of sex, gender, and sexuality. As social hygiene emphasis gave way to health, family living, and human relations education, some elements of the earlier reformers' ideas persisted, especially the acceptance of racial and class hierarchies. Yet sex education's transformation in the mid-twentieth century reveals that new concepts of the family, sexuality, and human relationships were in ascendance, ones that prioritized mental health and downplayed androcentrism in the pursuit of stable, democratic, and happy families. Positive in its outlook, integrated throughout the curricula, and mixed to the extent that it reached both boys and girls—together or separately, mid-century sex education lay the groundwork for what in the 1960s would be called comprehensive sex education.

In the 1940s and 1950s, when the nation was politically preoccupied with national security and suspicious of left-wing causes—to say nothing of sexual "perversion" and the growing movement for African American civil rights—sex education programs gained momentum without subscribing to reactionary or wholly conservative values. Ending delinquency or preserving the institution of marriage was often at the core of educators' motivation, and their understanding of the "problems" involved racist, elitist, and nationalistic assumptions, but an agenda of aiding psychological adjustment inspired their actions as well. Prominent among their hopes was that young people would gain knowledge and establish moral standards appropriate to their individual psyches and communities. Mid-twentieth-century sex education, as so many endeavors, brought with it unintended consequences. A backlash in the 1960s would forestall decades of developing sex education curricula, yet not before young people gained self-awareness and opportunities to discuss and critique relationships and gender roles, including sexual dynamics.

2

Reconstructing Classrooms
and Relationships

Moral and medical aims—encouraging sexual purity and preventing venereal disease—shaped the emergence of sex education for young people in the early twentieth century. Such concerns pervaded curricula throughout the century, articulated in different ways over time. Sex education terminology, for example, shifted from chivalry and chastity in the early 1900s to respect and abstinence at the century's end. But the fundamental idea at the core of much sex education—refraining from sexual activity during adolescence—remained the same. Young people have learned through sex education to associate sexuality with transgression and adverse outcomes such as adolescent pregnancy and sexually transmitted diseases. Sex is sinful. Sex is risky. Immoral and dangerous, sexual relationships are to be avoided outside the institution of marriage.

Or are they? During the mid-twentieth century, educators created curricula to assist young people's psychological "adjustment" and "development" during adolescence.[1] Fundamental to this project was accepting one's sex (male or female) and developing an interest in the so-called opposite sex. Heterosexual interests and relationships were critical components of healthful adolescent development, according to mid-century psychologists, experts, teachers, and laypeople. Adolescent heterosexuality, positioned precariously apart from promiscuity, homosexuality, and asexuality, was not a brand new idea. It was, however, one that received greater attention from education and mental health professionals during the 1940s and 1950s. Evidence from contemporary social science research suggested that psychological well-being did not naturally or automatically occur; rather, environmental influences—such as sex-saturated popular culture and dysfunctional families—could disrupt the process of acquiring and accepting adult responsibilities and gender roles. Even children raised in "normal" two-parent, white, middle-class families might struggle with the challenges of psychosexual development. Schools were well positioned to intervene and guide adolescents of all backgrounds in their transitions to adulthood.

Assuring adolescent heterosexual development was one component of a popular vision of sex education during the mid-twentieth century. Another component involved adult heterosexuality, more specifically, a future as a husband or wife and a parent. If an adolescent could be over- or undereager in heterosexual development, likewise an adult could be overzealous, or, less often the problem, underzealous in pursuit of family formation. Professionals deemed rushed marriages and large families undesirable; so, too, were young adults who never moved out from under their parents' roofs. To put it simply, acquiring a heterosexual identity during adolescence—and achieving marriage and having children in adulthood—constituted the pinnacle of individual adjustment. Mid-twentieth-century educators did not, for the most part, believe these outcomes were biologically driven or inevitable. Rather, to be successful, they involved introspection and thoughtful pursuit.

Ubiquitous in sex and family life education by the 1950s, interactive pedagogy allowed students to participate in shaping the curricula; teachers suggested that this means of teaching was particularly American and democratic. In various ways, adolescents took command of classroom time and discussion, albeit under the scrutiny of adults and peers. Encouraging adolescent heterosexuality and promoting marriage and parenthood, educators employed a set of tools that stressed personal satisfaction and fulfillment. Teachers used a variety of classroom activities and material to encourage young people to reflect on their personalities, likes, and dislikes—and to connect these to puberty, adolescence, and dating. With this groundwork in place, instructors then would draw attention to engagement, marriage, and parenthood. Addressing the incentives for marrying, instructors emphasized fulfillment in terms of loving family relationships, with little attention to sexuality. That sexuality was more prominent in discussions of adolescent dating than it was to adult family relationships was one of the many contradictions embedded in sex education lessons from the mid-twentieth century.

This chapter examines the assumptions and ideals that informed mid-century sex instruction. The first section outlines significant changes between the early and mid-twentieth century, showing the influence of participatory pedagogy that centered on students' needs and interests. In discussion-based classes, teachers guided young people in complying with contemporary norms of adolescent heterosexuality, and the students educated teachers and urged them to provide more explicit and relevant information about sexuality. In the chapter's second section, I explore how egalitarian ideals of marital partnerships and cooperative family units promoted the application of democratic principles in young people's current and imagined future families. Yet gender-specific and restrictive expectations remained in the curricula, undermining claims of egalitarianism and choice. In some places, teachers and instructional material questioned rigid gender and sexual roles or critiqued patriarchal and authoritarian living arrangements. At the same time, however, texts and activities sometimes reinforced male sexual prerogatives.

Sources that reveal girls' voices and perspectives suggest that the curricula had the potential to empower the girls, but not always in ways that teachers intended. The emphasis on "democratic" relationships contributed to reconsideration of gender roles and loosening conservative standards of sexual morality while reinforcing certain heterosexual norms. Moreover, the pedagogy made room for young people—especially girls—to acquire an increased sensitivity to stereotypes, misinformation, and injustice. Like mid-century college students who experienced gradual changes that led to the sexual revolution, high school students were part of a process that unfolded before the 1960s.[2]

Youth-Centered Pedagogy

The foremost innovation in sex education pedagogy in the mid-twentieth century was its emphasis on dialog. Teachers engaged young people in discussions of the trials and tribulations of puberty, dating, popularity, and home life. In Toms River, for example, the family relationships workbooks invited students to write and reflect on personal experiences and then discuss them with peers in class. Although guided by the teacher in such exercises, the point was to allow the young people to find their voices and demonstrate maturity in being able to discuss matters related to sex. Peer pressure, conflicts with parents, and confusion about how to behave socially became part of curricula across the country as new courses adopted the human relations or family relationships framework.

Although dialog was central to the courses, teachers gave classrooms structure through a variety of tools. Among the various activities were discussions following film screenings and guest speakers; role-playing, which allowed students to adopt other personas; panel discussions to present a range of perspectives on a given topic; question boxes to collect anonymous inquiries; interviews and survey tabulation that turned students into researchers; and group discussion to evaluate social, intellectual, and moral questions about dating, popular culture, parenting, love, and the future. Central High School in Charlotte, North Carolina, employed each technique in the 1950s, and other documented programs from this era incorporated at least one or more.[3] Judging by the results of a study of family life education in Illinois in 1955, the most popular was class discussion; 88 percent of ninety-two teachers reported "good" or "excellent" results in using this method.[4]

Mid-century sex educators envisioned a participatory style of learning about sexuality and gender and were often responsive to students' questions and demands in designing curricula. In 1946, teenagers in Corpus Christi, Texas, collected a hundred student signatures to convince the superintendent to begin offering a course "so that our generation may carry out its purpose in life unhampered by lack of knowledge and superstition; and that we may learn to know the opposite sex as a friend rather than a hidden secret or supposed danger."[5] In Hayward, California, a student petition with 750 signatures led the school system to inaugurate its marriage and family course in 1948.[6] A request to the superintendent from a committee of summer school students in San Antonio, Texas, helped launch their contemporaneous program as well.[7] Although social hygienists had given some attention to young people's wishes in the early twentieth century, the phenomenon of tailoring sex education lessons to specific communities and youth interests grew more commonplace during the 1940s.[8]

Whereas early-twentieth-century leaders had largely dictated lessons based on their authority as doctors, scientists, and learned men (less often were they women), mid-twentieth-century teachers arranged instruction based on observations of young people and interactions with them in everyday classroom settings. When pupils voiced interest in the parameters of acceptable—and attractive—behavior for boys and girls and achieving a satisfying life during and after high school, teachers provided forums for discussion. These teachers, many of them women with years of experience and contact with young people, did not limit themselves to instruction in managing the sex instinct as early advocates of sex education had proposed.[9]

As students struggled to define their value systems and senses of self-worth, sex education and family living teachers opened the floor for discussion from a variety of perspectives and a flexible range of topics that students chose. "If ever there were a course in which the desires of students should be cultivated, expressed, and served," wrote sociology professor John Newton Baker in his 1942 study of high school curricula in forty-six states, "sex education is such a course."[10] The use of question boxes to elicit anonymous concerns and queries was an important component in constructing a curriculum centered on student needs.

Senior high school courses could often dispense with question boxes, especially in instances where students had learned to discuss sex without embarrassment. In Toms River, juniors and seniors posed many questions about sex and boy-girl relations aloud. "What do you do when a boy gets fresh?" asked one "comely" girl in Elizabeth S. Force's family relationships course in 1953. "Do you have to make love when you go out with the boys? If we do, will they talk about us?" girls frequently asked.[11] Although the references to lovemaking did not imply intercourse, the questions did pertain to physical intimacy and sexual reputations.

Many girls at mid-century were not too shy to ask about sexuality, nor were teachers especially troubled by their interests. Force and many other teachers invited students' questions and organized their curricula to address subjects of concern. Describing how she crafted her tenth-grade science classes according to students' needs, for instance, Los Angeles science teacher Eva Kirby noted that girls' anonymous questions tended to relate to "intercourse and birth," followed by "boy-girl relations." (Boys' questions related to intercourse, masturbation, and venereal disease.)[12]

Among the information girls requested were facts about anatomy and how one becomes pregnant; many preferred teachers as sources of such knowledge. Half of those surveyed in Howard M. Bell's Maryland study of more than thirteen thousand young people in the late 1930s claimed to have obtained most sex information from peers. Three-fourths favored sex education at school.[13] Girls claimed to have received more information at home than boys acknowledged, but many remained mystified. One reported that when her peers made inquiries during Girl Scout meetings, "The leader would look prissy and say 'a Girl Scout is clean in thought, word, and deed,'" cutting off the conversation and building an association between sex and filth.[14] Such evidence compelled educators to devise curricula that would counteract girls' exposure to negative influences, especially from reticent women who led them to link sex and secrecy or repulsion.

Students wished to remove the mystery surrounding sex and the body, and a few young women from the Maryland survey indicated that they became pregnant without understanding how or why. "School never taught me anything about my body," one individual whom Bell interviewed claimed; "I can tell you how to cut up an ant or a caterpillar, but I can't tell you anything about myself." As for where babies came from, one young woman reported, "I found out when I started to have 'em."[15] Another respondent, identified as a mother of three and a "single, colored girl of twenty who left school because of pregnancy," said, "Sex education should start being taught in the elementary schools, because so many parents are ignorant on this subject, and others are so old-fashioned that they feel that such things shouldn't be talked about." Others had similar experiences: "I know I didn't know enough. I didn't believe it even when they told me my baby was coming," and "Nobody told me anything, and I had to get married because I was going to have a baby."[16]

Unsatisfied by evasive birds-and-bees approaches, girls in the 1940s and 1950s often requested information about "petting," intercourse, contraception, and abortion. Typical subjects of sex and family life education—getting along with the other sex, learning to deal with menstruation, and looking ahead to marriage and parenthood—were also of concern. In addition, there were questions about topics that some teachers preferred to omit from the formal curriculum, including sexual pleasure and male aggression. When asked by their eighth-grade homemaking teacher in California to submit unsigned questions about boy-girl relationships in 1958, about half of the girls in the class explicitly inquired about sexual behavior. Among the reports' questions were, "What do you do on your wedding night?" "How do you have intercourse?" "Does it hurt to have intercourse?" and "Is it safe for young girls to have an abortion?"[17]

Educators posited that girls of color and those from the working class were most vulnerable to misinformation about sex as well as an absence of role models. Bell's study, for instance, found that white young people were twice as likely to discuss sex at home as were African Americans.[18] In Maryland schools, 13.9 percent of black young people opposed sex education, significantly fewer than white young people (20.4 percent) who did so. Bell found this especially notable given that "85 (or 70 per cent) of the 120 youth who *admitted* they were unmarried mothers or fathers, were Negroes."[19] The original version of "Growing Up," San Diego's sixth-grade curriculum, noted that parents of students at Logan School—predominantly people of color—were "confused and embarrassed" by their children's questions about sex. Educators perceived that the parents were "poorly informed themselves," according to the guide, unaware of their children's maturity and in some instances "filled with inhibitions about sex."[20] Educators' sense of urgency in reaching girls was compounded by wartime changes in family life, and, in Logan Heights, the lack of privacy in lower-income homes.[21]

Teachers' perceptions of their students' family lives were partial and often distorted, especially given the race and class biases that prevailed among white, middle-class educators. Nevertheless, there were elements of truth in the stories and generalizations that came from surveys, observations, and the students themselves. One, described as a "rough and ready" eighteen-year-old girl of "low socio-economic status," explained her approach to dating in an essay reprinted in an adolescent psychology textbook. Because "you meet some very bad boys, and never know whether or not to go out with a fellow who asks for a date," she maintained, it was only possible to learn from experience and then attempt to be tough. "If you think he is trying to get fresh with you. Well that is the time to tell him off. Slap him in the face. But sometimes a fellow is very persistent. The saying is that a fellow will go as far as a girl will let him. But the way I see it is for the girl to go and find out for herself."[22]

The story exemplified one end of the spectrum of girls' experiences with dating—and was apparently not unusual. The author of the textbook in which it appeared, Ruth Strang, used student writing she collected from teachers across the country as data for her work on girls' personalities. The section of the text that contained this anecdote included another similar story of dating gone awry; the chapter excerpted only one composition that depicted the kind of dating behavior displayed in prescriptive pamphlets and movies. Apparently, these stories were less common in Strang's sample, because she commented after the positive story, "We should have more accounts of parties and other social experiences that have proved so thoroughly enjoyable and desirable for adolescents of different ages."[23]

As students raised instructors' awareness of the problems and worries of young people, some teachers adapted their curricula and pedagogy to appeal to the students' sensibilities. As Geneva Gordon, a San Diego sex educator explained, "If you preach to the students, they yawn in your face. If you show shock or embarrassment of any kind, they spot it instantly and you've lost them."[24] Among the questions that girls raised in her class on a typical day were, "Why won't parents let their daughters go out—not even with girls?" and "Why do boys have so much more freedom than girls, in their families?" Other questions alluded to restrictions: "What is wrong with going on a hayride? My father will *not* let me go." Girls also sought advice about dating and petting: "What is a French Kiss? Will you discuss this with us, please?"[25] The students included a pregnant fifteen-year-old (presumably white because race or ethnicity is only mentioned for people of color), and Gordon also counseled one seventeen-year-old who had problems at home and another, a Filipina engaged to a Filipino sailor, who requested information about contraception.[26]

Seemingly not scandalized, teachers in San Diego's group-counseling program made sure that discussion was oriented toward students' needs. On the first of five meetings of the ninth-grade girls' group during the mid-1950s, the teacher would have them submit questions following a screening of *Name Unknown*. Scenarios in the film included sex crimes involving babysitting for a "strange man," parking, and accepting "pick-ups." According to Catherine Marsman Jones, a counselor in the San Diego School District in the 1950s, teachers used these questions to design course discussions to fit students' expressed needs. The questions were read to students in subsequent group meetings and informed the teacher about the pupils "since they indicate the levels of social and sexual maturity."[27] In a similar fashion, questions posed by Pennsylvania teenagers in the early 1950s also revealed some degree of personal experience. One of many reported in *The Science Teacher* was, "Is it perfectly normal for a girl to secrete a substance when she kisses a lot? Is it produced by getting a thrill and getting excited inside?"[28]

Teenagers had many unanswered questions that exposed their curiosity and confusion about sexuality, including matters of desire and consent. Recorded by a teacher in Kansas, questions of tenth-grade biology students in the early 1950s alluded to specifics of sexual behavior and indicated their exposure to sexual ideas and experiences:

> Where is the male organ placed during intercourse?
> How is a diaphragm inserted?
> What are "homos"?
> Can a woman be made pregnant if she wasn't willing?
> What causes rapists?
> Is a homosexual case over-loaded with hormones of the opposite sex?
> Do homosexual cases desire to be around the opposite sex?
> What are crabs?
> How do you get crabs?
> What is Spanish Fly?
> What is the cause of a broken "cherry" in the female?
> Can a woman have intercourse during menstruation?
> What is the name of the fluid that the woman secretes before intercourse?
> Why is it necessary to pet a woman before sexual intercourse?[29]

As these questions suggest, young people wanted to know why people had intercourse as well as how they did it. Questions about rape, homosexuality, and aphrodisiacs took the focus away from normative heterosexual reproductive sexuality and on to topics more deeply shrouded in mystery.

For many young people the information provided in school was too elementary and not relevant to their present concerns. Teachers invited not only students' questions but also their feedback through surveys and questionnaires following sex education units and speakers.[30] A number of students in western Michigan regreted that their lessons had not encompassed or adequately dealt with "sex vices and crimes," "venereal disease," "sex cravings," "birth control," "wedding night," and "place of sex in marriage."[31] High school girls in Geauga County, Ohio, similarly suggested improving sex education by discussing "how to improve personality," "accidental pregnancy," "effects of kissing, sexual feelings," "dirty jokes and actions," "prostitution," "how to say 'no' without hurting feelings," "sex conduct and self-control," "venereal disease," and "birth control."[32] One of the more common concerns among girls was that society expected them to stop sexual activity before it went too far. A girl in San Diego wanted practical advice: "What is a good way to stop when he gets ideas?"[33] Likewise, Charlotte, North Carolina, teacher Fannie B. Masten continually heard the question, "How do you keep a boy from going the whole way?"[34]

Teachers thus learned a lot from young people through class discussions, anonymous questions, and individual consultations. As San Diego City Schools' health education director G. Gage Wetherill reported, educators "see so many of the sex-social problems of high school students and counsel them day after day," making teachers ideal sex educators.[35] He also noted that "some of these youngsters come up with pretty perplexing and involved sex problems that are appalling to the naive and uninitiated."[36] Yet printed curricula and demonstrations in the community or with parents tended to downplay controversial and risqué topics. In part, that was because such topics usually arose when students—not always predictably—volunteered them.

High school teachers in the 1940s and 1950s embraced discussion as an important classroom tool, employing small groups, panels, "socio-dramas," and role-playing. Such learning activities were more amenable to classes in which it was less important to retain information than explore ideas and issues, such as current events.[37] The National Defense Act of 1958, however, placed emphasis on science, foreign languages (including Russian), and mathematics—subjects not well suited to open discussion but ones that rewarded teachers who provided rigorous instruction.[38] Many political leaders, and people in general, seemed to think that educators attached too much value to personality growth and not enough to academic skills. Discussion, however, remained an essential component of sex and family living courses at the end of the 1950s.

Particularly popular in garnering community support for sex education and related classes, the panel or roundtable discussion allowed various opinions and approaches to sex-related topics to be expressed and were sometimes used when promoting sex education to the public. Whether as in San Diego, where panels convened at high schools in evening open forums to solicit support for beginning a sex education curriculum, or as in Portland, Oregon, where student panelists conveyed the needs for sex education to community leaders, the demonstrations offered a range of viewpoints.[39] Participants usually conveyed similar attitudes, however, and thus created the appearance of consensus about instituting sex education. Although individuals and groups of ordinary citizens and young people genuinely promoted and encouraged it, panel coordinators handpicked participants to express the ideas that suited them. Thus, major objections would have had to come from the audience, a position with less influence. In addition to managing public opinion, popularizing sex education in this way was a means of staging contemporary, progressive pedagogy.

Instructors often gave up some of their authority to impress students with the principles of democratic cooperation. As students placed their chairs in circles for classroom discussions, their communication with one another was not always mediated through an adult leader. Panels, sociodramas, circle discussions, and small buzz groups put their expressions at the center of attention, bolstering the importance of peer communication.[40] Just as boys and girls learned to get along with and speak respectfully to one another in classrooms, teachers emphasized the benefits of camaraderie between husbands and wives and among siblings.

In classrooms, group and panel discussions usually involved peers who expressed differences of opinion about matters related to sex.[41] Although teachers often guided students to focus on particular topics, they did not exercise control over the content of pupils' comments. In Fair Lawn, New Jersey, for example, Elliott E. Kigner's ninth-grade science class—all girls—submitted anonymous lists of "their five most vital personal problems." After the collected lists were read to the class, "Students then voted for a committee of five girls who would plan what could be done and organize the agenda, after considering the views of the class," Kigner explained. Following the third period of discussion, girls indicated on evaluations "that they felt good (a) at being able to express their problems and (b) in realizing that other people have similar difficulties."[42] The exercise apparently delighted the girls, and the school subsequently instituted a group guidance program. In sum, the experiment raised girls' awareness that other girls encountered similar problems, lowered their inhibitions in group discussions, increased willingness to pursue individual consultations outside the class as needed, and fostered overall improved self-understanding and maturity.[43]

Even more so than in the public forum, classroom discussion and group guidance allowed for an array of opinions and perspectives with little more than peer consciousness and self-censorship prohibiting dissent. In classroom discussions and course evaluations, students revealed opinions and experiences sometimes contrary to adult standards. Virginia Milling's 1944 senior English class in New Jersey, for example, explained to their teacher that the protagonist from William Allen White's story "Mary White" "wouldn't be popular in West Side Newark." "I liked Mary White," Milling wrote in the journal *Clearing House*, "but I warned myself quickly that that was no reason why my pupils should."[44] In the process of listening, some teachers revised their assumptions as well as their lesson plans. Milling, for example, had pupils devise lists of what made boys and girls popular at their school, with each sex laying out the features they found attractive in the other.

Prompted by students and their questions, numerous schools established sex and family life education courses in the 1940s and 1950s. These courses empowered young people to request information and guidance and urged them to make decisions for themselves. As Masten put it, "Of course, there are no cut-and-dried, magic-wand answers to such poignant and delicate matters."[45] Although teachers coordinated the classes and shared their personal ideas and interpretations of gender and sexual norms, and thereby never fully relinquished authority, students nevertheless provided and shaped much course content, especially when discussing personal problems and boy-girl relationships.

The Framework of Human Relations

Whereas the early-twentieth-century sex education movement was closely linked to the medical profession, mid-century school officials centered their efforts on what they called "human relations," the province of psychology. "The purpose of these classes is to help our boys and girls develop more robust personalities so that they may face up to emotional problems later in life without breaking down," explained H. Edmond Bullis and Emily E. O'Malley in their guide for coed human relations classes.[46] Initiated in Delaware in 1941, the courses encouraged junior high school students to identify and solve personal problems. "For children adrift on the tides of puberty a constant worry is the boy-girl relationship," Bullis and O'Malley wrote.

Orienting their discussions "to four inner human drives: self-preservation, adventure, interest in the opposite sex, and recognition," the teachers found it "refreshing to hear boys and girls speak openly, somewhat nobly, in fact, of 'interest in the opposite sex' as a powerful driving force of human beings. It was reassuring too to hear this inner drive tied to the emotion of love rather than shame or vulgarity."[47]

Sex educators' concern with human relations occurred as social sciences gained authority in American culture and the study of marriage and the family—as well as adolescent behavior—became more prominent.[48] Social and sexual relations became an arena for personal introspection as well as professional intervention, fueled by the rise of the helping professions and steeped in psychological and psychoanalytic language. Sexuality, as presented in classrooms and within society in general, was less often relegated to the medical and scientific community and was viewed instead as an issue of social concern.[49] Nothing indicated this better than the popular attention given publication of Alfred Kinsey's data on sexual behavior.[50]

As Oregon educator Lester A. Kirkendall entitled his influential 1950 book, "sex education as human relations" was the ascendant understanding of sexuality among mid-century sex educators.[51] Teachers conducted sex and family relationships courses in which relationships and emotions occupied a prominent place. Minimal training or expertise on sexuality were needed; some college training, along with common sense and community respect, sufficed as preparation for teaching about sex through a human relations framework. Toms River's Elizabeth Force was a case in point. A graduate of Toms River High School, she first taught English at her alma mater and was recruited for family relationships in the early 1940s. It was only later that she began graduate study in psychology at New York University. After earning a master's degree in 1947, Force continued her education about sexuality and family relationships, eventually studying with well-known experts Paul Popenoe and Frances Bruce Strain.[52] Her original qualifications for teaching family relationships were based on character and esteem rather than factual knowledge or advanced training.

Analysis of heterosexual attractions and interactions, a common focus of mid-century sex education discussions, was intended to promote maturity and signal preparation for marriage. Not only did teachers explain the meaning and significance of growing up and becoming sexual beings but they also encouraged students to be attentive to gender and heterosexuality. That boys and girls had unique contributions to make to discussions about dating, sex, marriage, and the family was especially apparent in classroom activities that compared their opinions. In sex and family life education classes, teachers often had students create lists of responses to a particular question such as, What traits do you seek in a mate? Then the answers could be examined collectively.[53] The exercise emphasized gender differences as well as the supposed desire of young people to attract a suitable dating partner and future mate. San Antonio family life educator Payton Kennedy stated hyperbolically that such a classroom activity "makes it possible for boys and girls to develop insight into the feelings of each sex that would be utterly impossible elsewhere."[54]

Kennedy was not unique in thinking that many young people—especially girls—were underprepared for intimate heterosexual relationships because of their ignorance about the "opposite" sex and heterosexuality. As graduate student Lloyd S. Van Winkle wrote, educators and administrators were bothered by counselors' wartime reports of "pure ignorance on the part of the very young high school girls who were marrying with seemingly no preparation from home or 'abroad' for such an undertaking." Among the complaints of young brides was that "they had found sex life revolting, which was one of the many things creating a state of unhappiness in this relationship toward their husbands."[55] Counselors held mothers responsible for conveying "a negative attitude toward boys in general, thus creating in the minds of the girls themselves, an almost insurmountable feeling of fear and misunderstanding toward the whole matter."[56]

Nor were girls were alone in needing guidance. Boys, too, had much to learn about human and sexual relationships, which is why such courses as family relationships were coed and fostered cross-gender dialog. The focus on building relationships—especially in the domestic sphere—highlighted the traditionally female realm of caring and nurturing, but teachers sought to interrupt gender conventions by involving boys in contemplating relationships as well. Recognizing that girls were more prone to analyze relationships and imagine and plan for marriage than boys, *Ten Topics toward Happier Homes* drew both sexes into the discussion: "Boys, what specific preparation for marriage can you make during the dating period? . . . Girls[?]" queried the workbook.[57] The workbook required both male and female students to engage in the activity of planning for marriage.

The family relationships workbook suggested that boys and girls had distinct and complementary roles in preparing for marriage. *Ten Topics toward Happier Homes*, like other curricula, gave students concrete scenarios to analyze as points of departure for discussing values. The responses of student Barbara Newman in 1956 reveal a more egalitarian impulse than that suggested by the book. The instructions for itemizing marriage preparation tasks gave as examples one common point—"Read some books on marriage preparation"—along with two unique and stereotypically gendered points each for boys and girls. Young men should "save money" and "take out additional insurance," whereas young women should "collect items for your home" and "practice cooking."[58] Newman filled in the blanks of her workbook with identical answers for boys' and girls' necessary preparations, minus the gender stereotypes. "Talk to minister, parents & friends" and "observe other married couples" were the items she inserted.[59]

In designing the workbook and teachers' guide, Force and her colleagues sometimes endorsed and other times critiqued gender stereotypes. The text consistently highlighted gender consciousness—students' awareness of being male or female. In one discussion prompt, for instance, the following anecdote prefaced the question: "'This is my wedding,' declared the bride-to-be firmly. 'I shall have it as I like; not as Aunt Tilly likes, or as Grandma likes, or my in-laws like.' Is she right? In error? Discuss your attitude toward her statement." In conjunction with this question, the teachers' guide stated that "boys' answers and girls' answers will probably differ considerably."[60] The guide recommended comparing boys' and girls' responses in classrooms—accenting and reinforcing gender consciousness while making gender differences a topic for class discussion.

Alongside the view that heterosexuality is a "drive" were cultural understandings of different-sex attractions and gendered interests as learned behaviors. Some texts even disputed gendered sexual stereotypes in a forthright way. Taking great care to avoid overgeneralization about gender and sexual stimulation, *Life and Growth* (1937) stated, "It is thought that boys need less stimulation than girls, that their sex organs respond more quickly under emotional excitement. For many this is true. There are, however, great differences." *Life and Growth* encouraged each boy and girl to take responsibility for setting personal limits. Without prescribing a proper course of action, the author assumed that variation was inevitable but not necessarily based on gender: "Both the boy and girl involved in a petting situation where there is love-making, kissing, and caressing must realize the point at which such stimulation may lead them further than they want to go."[61]

Other classroom material reiterated stereotypes of uncontrollable, more easily aroused boys and placed the burden on girls to be circumspect and chaste. With uncommon explicitness, the authors of the 1953 American Social Hygiene Association (ASHA) curriculum developed in conjunction with "preinduction" classes for future soldiers held girls responsible for boys' behavior. According to the text, which was used in a variety of high schools, "Since boys are more easily stimulated than girls it is wise to avoid sexually stimulating situations (parked cars, darkened living-rooms, etc.) and to dress and act decorously."[62] Rather than teach boys to respect girls, the curriculum conveyed that girls should monitor their dress and behavior to accommodate boys and that sexual risks were greater for girls than for boys.

In general, a single rather than a double standard of sexual behavior prevailed in most sex education lessons. Yet students still learned that girls and boys had separate roles in upholding the standard. Some courses emphasized the common goal and others paid greater attention to the different gendered responsibilities. In mixed-gender classes, teachers were more likely to point out uniform obligations for boys and girls, even as they perpetuated the gendered roles concerning who asked and paid for dates. An account of the coed home and family living course for seniors in Highland Park, Michigan, in the early 1950s indicated that they discussed "the responsibility of each partner in the area of lovemaking" during the engagement period.[63] That cryptic allusion to sexual roles may have meant gender-specific responsibilities akin to those mentioned in the ASHA curriculum, although it could have involved general responsibilities for both boys and girls, similar to *Life and Growth*.

Gender-specific advice was to some degree warranted, given the experiences and consequences of sexual aggression that some girls encountered while dating.[64] One sixteen-year-old who hoped to place limits on her boyfriend's intentions to "do it" was pleased when a class at her northern Ohio school addressed the subject in the mid-1940s. Her sex education course "helped her to find an answer," explained Elva Horner Evans of Cleveland's Family Health Association, remedying a situation in which none of the books available at her school "could give her the help she needed to limit Tom's lovemaking."[65] And given the types of questions eighth-grade girls posed for a visiting sex education lecturer in the late 1950s, knowing how to deal with boys' aggressiveness or coercive behavior concerned many: "What happens when you are seduced?" "How does a boy rape or fuck you?"[66] "What should you do if a boy tries or does rape you?" and "Why are men so eager?"[67]

At times, curricula appear to have granted girls power, suggesting that they were not potential victims of male aggression but had equal influence or greater responsibility than boys for preventing sexual coercion. In some cases, teachers even implied that girls possessed control over their dating partners, naming "weakness" to sexual temptation as a problem for girls and boys alike. Although susceptibility to sexual arousal could occur for girls or boys, no evidence suggested that girls used coercion to satisfy their desires whereas much suggested that boys (and men) did. In a distorted view of power relations in dating, the "emotionally mature" girl, the ASHA curriculum guide maintained, "refuses to subject any male to undue sexual stimulation and protects him from his weakness or poor judgment and against her own weakness. She knows that she can always say 'no' and wisely uses her control over him."[68] In another instance, an eighth-grade girl who attended talks in her California homemaking class responded in a survey two weeks later that the talks had been informative. Among the answers she claimed to have received at the lecture was "that a boy couldn't rape you against your will unless you were too afraid to help yourself."[69] The source does not reveal whether that was actually the lecturer's message, but an alleged local incident of rape, highly publicized in the media, may have led the instructor to perceive girls' questions and fears as expressions of paranoia rather than based on reality or personal experience.[70]

Some educators and students seem to have believed that control was not always gendered in traditional ways. Both boys' and girls' lessons in the ASHA preinduction curriculum called attention to how people could exploit each other in relationships, without assuming the propensity of one sex more than another.[71] Kirkendall and Curtis E. Avery's 1955 framework with which to evaluate successful heterosexual relationships made no allusion to gender roles and held each partner accountable to the same standards of honesty, trust, values, empathy, and affection.[72] They as well as students suggested that gender did not determine sexual exploitation or assertiveness. A high school student anticipating medical doctor Bert Y. Glassberg's sex education lectures in St. Louis, Missouri, submitted an anonymous question, for example, that implied that girls sometimes pressured boys to have sex. "What," the student asked, "can a boy do if the girl starts thinking of inercourse [sic] and marriage?"[73]

Lessons did not rule out the possibility of girls taking things too far, but teaching material tended to emphasize emotional disturbance and social stigma as results of doing so. Posing an example of a girl whose heterosexual interests were greater than the norm, the Delaware curriculum warned, "Suppose we let this INTEREST IN THE OTHER SEX become too important? What may happen to a girl who is too 'boy crazy'? What might happen to her school work? What might happen at home to her family relations?"[74] The solution was to keep human drives—those that affected all humans—in balance. To do so, the lesson implicitly suggested, without directly addressing the risk of pregnancy, that the problem was greater for girls than boys.

Balanced interests appeared to have gendered dimensions. In the Delaware lessons, boy-crazy girls came under scrutiny along with sissy boys (but not tomboys). The chapter on emotional conflicts focused on a boy who was a "sissy," close to his mother, disinterested in sports, shy, and a daydreamer.[75] In this instance, the authors advocated a balance of interests, holding up effeminacy in boys as a measure of emotional instability. Girls who were boy-obsessed and boys who seemed feminine tested the limits of gender flexibility in the curriculum.

Curricula generally held both men and women, as well as male and female teenagers, to similar expectations of emotional maturity in heterosexual relationships. Such maturity would engender "democratic" family relations, writers and course material maintained. To instruct about mature and democratic relationships, a common lesson taught students to be empathetic. Encouraging activities "which develop an ability to put oneself in someone else's shoes," Detroit's curriculum guide recommended "role-playing, dramatization, case studies, and discussions of scenes from plays and current fiction."[76] The students learned to avoid or minimize girl-boy, parent-child, and sibling friction through imagining and learning about other perspectives. "Actual contact with infants and small children helps the adolescent to think about the adjustments that must be made in the home by young parents," wrote Denver, Colorado, educators Kenneth E. Oberholtzer and Myrtle F. Sugarman. In addition to contact with children, they recommended using novels and short stories to foster discussion of what students would do in various situations.[77]

Understanding someone else's perspective enabled responsible and mature participation in groups. Suggested role-plays for Detroit's unit on family living patterns included acting out decision-making in one family that applied what they termed democratic principles and another that did not.[78] Democratic family councils worked only when participants were able to be empathetic toward others in the group, or, as Glassberg explained, when children and their parents "come to recognize one another as human beings."[79] Thought by many to indicate immaturity, selfishness was considered an impediment to group decision-making (not to mention a precursor to developing exploitative relationships); role-playing and peer cooperation, therefore, would help boys as well as girls be less selfish.

White students and those of color learned to develop problem-solving skills while viewing and discussing *Palmour Street*, a movie made by and for African Americans. The film featured a southern black family with two working parents; it explored the family's emotional ties and hardships. A mental hygiene film, it was concerned with children's emotional growth and development.[80] *Palmour Street* proved effective among all groups, according to family living expert Thomas Poffenberger. Among non-black groups, he advised, it was "helpful to prepare the audience by saying that the film was made for Negroes, but because of its excellence is now used with all groups."[81] Based on screening the film for predominantly white adult groups in Oregon, he commented that the value of *Palmour Street* lay in how it dealt with universal problems, including sex education, as well as its potential to improve cross-racial understanding.[82]

Apparently sharing that perspective, Force asked students in her study guide for viewing the film, "What makes this a good home?" On Newman's corrected worksheet, Force added the positive comments "patience & interest, physical care" to Newman's response: "There was love, security, and recognition within this family. There was also the understanding present to overcome the difficulties which inevitably arose."[83] At the end of the film, the husband and father suffers an injury, imposing a strain on other members of the household, especially the wife and mother. In closing, the film's narrator asks the audience what the woman might do.[84] The film thus prompted viewers to identify universal values and human needs through the perspective of a black woman. Such values and needs, the film indicated, could be satisfied in families outside the white, middle-class norm.

Most teaching material centered on white and middle-class families, but the information was not usually male-centered and, in fact, often offered critiques of male dominance. The rhetoric of mature, democratic human relations rejected overtly patriarchal families. Reflecting the increasing presence of married women, including mothers, in the workforce during the 1940s and 1950s, family living and human relations classes acknowledged that men were not their families' sole breadwinners. Educators appear to have made a concerted effort to show men's roles as being fluid; household tasks were demonstrated as both women's and men's work. In textbooks, benevolent fathers appeared not as authoritarian figures but as active participants in household affairs, engaged in such activities as washing dishes, cooking, and spending time with children.[85]

The creators of textbooks and other classroom material called attention to expanded men's roles within the family and the erosion of their roles as patriarchs; they also commonly accepted women's roles as workers outside the home and decision-makers within it. In financial matters, women could be both earners and spenders, and they were active participants if not "experts" on budgeting, consumerism, and home finance. As the authors of *Personal*

Adjustment, Marriage, and Family Living: A High School Text explained, "We are growing away from the patriarchal type of family, and in not so many American families is the husband the absolute authority on all matters. Most modern young people think of marriage and family living as a democratic way of life. They expect to make all important decisions jointly."[86]

Expanding conventional gender roles and challenging the usual power discrepancies, however, did not mean upsetting distinctions of masculinity and femininity. San Antonio's curriculum guide posited as an objective of its marriage unit "to look upon wifehood and motherhood as a career demanding not only command of a variety of homemaking skills but also the best in personal growth and adjustment for success; to recognize the real greatness of achievement of a man who is a good husband and father, not just a good provider for his family."[87]

In contrast to patriarchal households of the past, modern democratic marriages and families supposedly recognized that both men and women contributed to negotiating relationship dynamics and household decisions, which suggested a significant change in domestic life. Textbooks encouraged students to compare contemporary marriages to those of the past as a way of recognizing and appreciating freedoms that were once unknown. The author of one 1948 high school textbook signaled this perspective with the subheading "You Should Make Good Use of Your Freedom of Choice" in a chapter on "Finding the Suitable Lifemate."[88] Whereas patriarchs ruled preindustrial European American families, contemporary marriage was "approaching the ideal of equality between husband and wife," read a caption to two illustrations demonstrating that point in *Your Marriage and Family Living*, a high school textbook.[89] These images indicated progress for women, no longer relegated to the subordinate role of "obedient helpmate who confined her interests to home and children."[90]

Images of modern democratic families and modern women were inevitably depicted as being white. White women, textbooks suggested, were newly confronted with options not generalizable to women of color. Force's *Your Family, Today and Tomorrow* presented this change with an illustration entitled the "Modern Girl's Dilemma." A modern (white) woman might choose to marry and have a family combined with education and paid employment, or she might choose to enter a career, with or without a spouse or children. During the Victorian Era, by contrast, a white woman was expected to construct her life around motherhood and domesticity.[91]

Even though roles were less rigid, student material illustrated persistent gender divisions and ignored the lack of improvement in the lives of people of color. In one workbook question, *Ten Topics toward Happier Homes* noted, "At one time the man's duties and the woman's duties were rigidly divided and clearly defined." Assuming this assertion was not debatable, the author inquired, "Why is this no longer true?"[92] In her reply, Barbara Newman accepted that change had occurred and contended forthrightly and perhaps optimistically, without expressing her feelings about the change, that working women had created households in which men contributed to household chores. Sharing, along with empathy, captured the relationships that made marriages and families modern and democratic. Observed Newman, "In our modern era, a great many women work including many mothers. This alone has created a great change in married life. Very often, the man shares in the household duties."[93]

The notion that men and women shared household responsibilities struck a chord with some students, appealing in particular to the idealism of youth rather than reflecting the realities of most contemporary households. On the following page of the workbook, an exercise involved listing in separate columns for husbands and wives tips that might minimize exhaustion and nervous tension in a marriage—a striking supposition that men might suffer from traditionally "female" ailments. In response, Newman wrote a single list rather than two lists differentiated by gender. Her advice was seemingly applicable to both men and women: budget, do not worry about minor things, be healthy, maintain a positive attitude toward chores, vacation and go out periodically, listen to music, enjoy occasional indulgences, and develop a work philosophy.[94] Men and women should not only share the burdens of housekeeping and remain cheerful but also enjoy the pleasures of recreation—at least in the abstract.

Teachers touted democratic and complementary male-female roles, but they tended to reinforce a division of labor that left women responsible for most care work. In Highland Park's senior family life education course, during which both boys and girls visited a nursery school laboratory, students gained "practical experience in preparation for parenthood."[95] The teacher emphasized that the nursery exercise enabled future parents to study children's behavior and emotional needs. The activity did not train young people to change diapers or juggle tasks because coed family life education promoted equal interest in the family, but not restructuring the division of labor between mothers and fathers.

Gender differences persisted in families that educational material depicted, but gendered hierarchies often were absent, subtle, or disavowed. The family in *Human Growth*'s opening scene, for instance, showed the father and mother engaged in gendered recreational activities—him reading the newspaper, her doing needlepoint—but both parents display interest in their children's school work and appear to be equal partners in parenting. Evening activities as well as household duties continued to be based on gendered assumptions, and teaching material ignored how privileges were built into the division of household labor. In single-sex classes, San Diego school nurse Viola I. Lampe and others who followed her lesson plans emphasized the household contributions that girls and boys could make during wartime. Girls could help by "washing dishes, making beds, and helping to care for the baby and younger brothers and sisters," and boys should act as "the man of the house" when fathers were absent.[96] Such recommendations presumed that tasks for boys and girls were separate but equally important to households.

Pleasing one's marriage partner took various forms according to gender, judging by the attention to marital relationships and roles in sex and family living curricula. Husbands and wives had different roles to perform, and society also tended to use different scales to measure their success. *Ten Topics toward Happier Homes* asked students to observe married couples and list men's and women's attitudes and behaviors that contributed to marital strife, presupposing that each gender had different standards and guiding students to articulate them in gendered terms. Newman entered three criticisms of husbands into her workbook: "(1) Not being appreciative of what their wives do for them (2) Forgetting everyday courtesies (rudeness) (3) Arguing in public with wife." Wives, she suggested, displayed objectionable behavior and attitudes on two counts: "(1) Being bossy or nagging" and "(2) Not caring about appearance."[97] When stating in positive terms what traits made for "harmonious relationships between married couples," Newman listed three behaviors and attitudes for each partner. For men, she noted performing courtesies, remaining interested, and complimenting wives; for women, she indicated taking interest in "husband's work and welfare," maintaining an attractive appearance, and exercising courtesy.[98] It is probably not accidental that these suggestions mirrored advice in contemporary magazines and popular media.

The family relationships workbook probed the causes of gender differences as a way of addressing the delegation of tasks in the home. "Even very young girls are interested in dolls and babies. Were you? Boys usually reveal less interest in children. Is this because girls have a 'maternal instinct,' and boys lack a 'paternal instinct'?" Force queried. "How would you explain this apparent difference?" Newman responded with allusions to both nature and nurture: "This is a many-sided question. Most believe that this is natural in-stinct, which tends to make a girl more interested in motherhood and boys interested in manly things. There is also the theory that this is not instinct, but instead a cultural tendency. That is, one does what is expected of him in a given society."[99] Even had Newman not made up her own mind, she was aware of different approaches to the question and perhaps confused about her relationship to a maternal instinct, given her lack of response to the opening query. If, as the workbook argued, it was true that gender roles had changed in the past hundred years of U.S. history, Newman may have been inclined to accept the cultural-tendency point of view.

Students also learned to challenge and critique the stereotypical and exag-gerated claims of advertisers and the cinema when asked to examine depic-tions of love, romance, and beauty. In the ASHA curriculum guide, educa-tors alerted them to the potential confusion that media fostered in girls and women who were "living in a world in which normal interest in sex is highly exploited for profit and frequently misrepresented or overemphasized (in advertisements, plays, magazines and newspapers, on the radio and in bur-lesque shows, etc.)."[100] Risks for boys were quite different. Apparently, boys were less vulnerable to the mixed messages in popular media and more at-tracted by the pull of an underworld of commercialized prostitution. Teachers provided boys' classes with a list of myths and facts about male continence and prophylaxis.[101] Lessons for both boys and girls included exposing myths and fallacies about love and sex.

Some teachers went so far as to have students select and critique represen-tations of romance and sexiness in popular culture, an exercise that would reduce the types of risk that, according to the ASHA curriculum, dispro-portionately affected girls. One teaching guide, published by the Teachers College at Columbia University, suggested having students "analyze adver-tisements to find which make an appeal to interest in the opposite sex and what relation this has to the advertised product" as one of several devices for evaluating what students had learned in the course. This same teaching guide also mentioned that students might "analyze advertisements relating to 'feminine hygiene' to discover the facts presented or implied in them; errors; omissions. Same for advertisements of 'doctors' or 'institutions' claiming to restore 'virility' or to combat 'loss of manly vigor.' Summarize your conclu-sions as to the trustworthiness of the advertisements."[102] *Ten Topics toward Happier Homes* instructed students to clip advertisements and point out the false claims they contained: "Copy below from these advertisements about love and marriage that you consider misleading, untrue, or inaccurate."[103] The workbook also had students, in two places, evaluate the realistic content of family life in recent motion pictures.[104] The teachers' guide, however, warned against "sounding cynical or bitter about marriage" in exploding the myths. "A good laugh at the 'romantic nonsense' woven about love and marriage will establish reasonable attitudes more clearly than will cold analysis. Have fun with this unit," the manual advised.[105]

Discussion and essay questions that involved evaluating the popular media were fun, and the activity gave students tools they could use to examine messages about love and romance from other sources, including parents, teachers, and peers. Explaining her preference for this type of exercise, Force remarked that it generated "immediate interest," showed how broad the scope of family living was, and made pupils "'Family Relationships' conscious."[106] Classroom and workbook activities also made students more gender conscious and aware of how sex could be manipulated for commercial purposes. And if the authority of books, movies, and other media was subject to critique, so, too, were other supposed authorities on any number of questions, including nature/nurture debates, dating and sexual standards for men and women, and household obligations.

Depictions of nonauthoritarian households nevertheless hinted that gender equality was still elusive in democratic families and in sex and family living classrooms. Expectations for women and men had changed but continued to restrict women in significant ways. Although forward-thinking teachers such as Force suggested that girls could chose from several paths for their futures, the overwhelming message to them was that they would discover fulfillment in heterosexual marriage and raising a family. Boys, too, might anticipate such satisfactions but in different degrees. In the 1940s and 1950s, a woman's pursuit of marriage and family meant being overworked or compromising one's wage-earning work, struggling with rare access to reliable and affordable childcare, coming under scrutiny for child neglect or maternal overinvolvement—and, for women of color, dealing with racism.[107] Even though family living courses often discussed the "working wife," the abstract terms of textbooks did not convey what feminists have called double duty—combined responsibility for going to work and performing most of the household labor, notwithstanding husbands' "help."

Girls in sex and family living courses did not learn to view all aspects of heterosexuality and family life through a critical lens, but they nevertheless obtained analytical tools that could be broadly applied. Classes gave them a degree of expertise about male-female and family relationships. As explained by veteran sex educator Helen Manley of University City Schools in

Missouri, the young person entering adulthood, work, or military service "needs a fortification stronger than mere facts and physical prowess—He needs an understanding of human relationships, the values of which will insure his emotional maturity and his ability to come through any experience unscathed."[108] He, and she, needed insight into human behavior, including individual preferences and personalities, empathy, sharing, and cooperation. Such education assisted young people in acquiring maturity and building strong marriages and offered practical, and potentially liberating, applications for the near future.

Conclusion

Sex education material between the early 1940s and the late 1950s embodied the contradictory messages about gender, sexuality, maturity, and relationships that were prevalent in society more broadly. The 1940s marked the onset of numerous sex and family living programs in schools, but the ideas that fueled new curricula had been percolating for at least a decade. As early as 1932, the National Education Association's organization of school administrators, for example, identified cultural reasons to institute sex education that were little different from concerns of the World War II era: women's increasing autonomy, urban features of mobility and anonymity, the availability of birth control and prophylaxis, Sigmund Freud's insights into behavior, the sex stimuli available through popular culture, and a fluctuation of common sex standards.[109] Moreover, families had been changing since the nineteenth century; urban dwellers outnumbered rural residents, and the ranks of wage-earning women grew by comparison to those never employed. Further development of these trends after World War II revealed that the war years were not so much an aberration as a continuation of ongoing social and demographic change.[110]

Educators identified the family as less patriarchal and more democratic during the 1940s and 1950s, but the shift toward democratic families was not complete if children needed to be taught, via sex and family living education, that families were democratic institutions. Many families, no doubt, had not adopted family councils and still harbored authoritarian adults and coercive disciplinary procedures. Capitalizing on youthful idealism, however, teachers applied the rhetoric of fairness and consideration to family and human relations in the hope that young people would grow up to be less exploitative and domineering—and more open-minded—than their parents. Young people might obtain values at school that their parents neglected to offer, especially those from the working class and families of color—or so the white, middle-class sex and family life education leaders thought.

Although the family was allegedly the fundamental building block of democracy, teachers and other commentators judged its ability to socialize children into model boys and girls as inadequate. Critics endlessly lamented the rise in juvenile delinquency and the increasing frequency of "broken" homes. Some believed that mothers who worked outside the home and the absence of male role models during World War II each contributed to young people's independence and rebellion against social norms and laws. As home life underwent change, schools were in a position to offer guidance and stability. Girls whose mothers had paid employment could rely on female teachers to help in developing femininity; boys whose fathers were absent could turn to male coaches who often gave informal advice and sex education lessons. Coed classes modeled "normal" male-female relations, something expert observers found lacking in many mid-century homes.

Educators were concerned about both boys and girls during this period, but worries about girls were prominent in rationales for sex education at mid-century. Female teachers, nurses, and reporters provided evidence of girls' changing behavior and lack of guidance. In the first network radio show that dramatized the issue of sex education for youth, the *Doorway to Life* presented in 1947 "the story of Trudy, an eleven-year-old girl who was sheltered from the facts of life by her well-meaning if misguided parents." Advised by social workers and psychologists, script authors William S. Alland and Virginia Mullen "used the example of the specific girl by way of filling in the larger pattern of evils which can come from what is basically parental deceit." Trudy's quest for answers led her to "look for hidden meanings in almost every aspect of her life, with a consequent deterioration in her attitudes and values."[111] Her story revealed the heightened vulnerability of girls who did not receive sex education at home as well as the potential benefits of sex education in schools.

Some aspects of sex and family life education increased girls' skills of analysis regarding changing marital relations. Explaining the "big" reason that students should study marriage and family living, Barbara Newman wrote in her workbook a response that highlighted social change: "Time changes many things, and this one field, that of marriage and parenthood, has altered tremendously within recent past generations. This difference lies in a higher standard of living, education, and social growth. The latter, especially, has pulled family unity farther apart, making happy marriages and family life sometimes difficult to create."[112] History was not a narrative of progress, but neither was there a blissful past to return to, as Newman realized. After viewing the film *Family Circles,* she noted that "the problems facing today's families were faced by families in the past century as well, disproving the theory of the good old days."[113]

In spite of all its democratic rhetoric, the human relations model included unacknowledged hierarchies and invoked gender stereotypes. Even though popular culture and classroom material conveyed to girls ideas of how they ought conform, prescriptive messages about gender and femininity were not seamless nor entirely restrictive. As sociologist Wini Breines has shown in her investigation of white American girls in the 1950s, "tensions and paradoxes" were inherent in mid-century popular culture's prescriptions of feminine behavior, visible in countercultural and Beat dissent, such music forms as rhythm and blues, and working-class images and conduct. These seeds of rebellion worked to undermine monolithic gender norms in an era associated with conformity.[114] In a similar way, school messages about sex and family life occasionally acknowledged realities that defied norms: teenaged marriage, single motherhood, homosexuality, male-female antagonisms, and sexual violence. That permitted girls to adapt educators' messages to their own curiosities, desires, and experiences, which were shaped by forces beyond classrooms.

While prompting young people to formulate their ideals and wishes, teachers met students on their terms and enabled the development of peer standards of conduct. In the process of scrutinizing heterosexual practices as part of their schoolwork, young people learned to value the prerogative of personal decision-making, question the depiction of love and romance in popular media, and pay attention to standards and expectations based on gender. A movement in schools that began as a means to prepare young people for stable marital relationships ultimately handed them tools with which to challenge adult hypocrisy and silences as well as the limitations of the domestic ideal.

3

Experiments in
Sex Education

By the mid-1930s, teachers were beginning to introduce sexuality in classrooms from a human behavior and relationships standpoint. Professional journals between 1935 and 1939 publicized that schools in Michigan, Oklahoma, Colorado, Illinois, and the District of Columbia were newly conducting programs in sex education.[1] Most, however, faded from the professional literature as quickly as they appeared, and none came to the attention of the broader public. In the late 1930s, newspapers and magazines publicized a debate in New York City concerning a board of education member's unsuccessful campaign for sex education in the city's high schools.[2] Accounts in subsequent years would reveal that some schools taught sex education without controversy in the 1930s, but many indicated that their success was in proportion to their discretion.[3]

Although publicized sex education was rare, quiet efforts around the country were not. Some were far enough under the radar of state authorities and researchers that a major survey of sex education in high schools that sociologist John Newton Baker undertook in the early 1940s overlooked them.[4] Baker's survey found negligible attention to sex education in twenty-seven states. He located courses in school districts that lacked statewide support in nine states. Finally, he identified ten states that offered institutional support for sex education programs. All regions of the country were represented in each category except the South, which, Baker claimed, lacked state government support for school programs in sex education in the early 1940s.[5] However helpful such data may be in identifying regional and national trends, they neglected to account for existing programs in Illinois, Michigan, Minnesota, and Missouri, and probably elsewhere.[6]

In the late 1930s, those who initiated new programs in sex education included the western state of Oregon, the small East Coast community of Toms River, New Jersey, and an urban city on the U.S.-Mexico border, San Diego, California. Founders of these programs were proud of their work and eager to spread the word. Prompted by local events and promoted by local leaders, each of the three initiatives was several years in the making. Although not the only programs with national recognition, Oregon, Toms River, and San Diego graced the pages of local newspapers, mass-circulation magazines, and scholarly publications, making them the most publicized and familiar nationwide in the 1940s and 1950s.

Meanwhile, many of the nation's educators engaged in what might be considered auxiliary activities, some of which were first steps toward offering sex education in schools. Community forums, institutes, workshops, and teacher training classes sponsored by social hygiene societies, parent and teacher groups, universities and colleges, and state departments of health and education proliferated in the 1930s and after.[7] The programs in Oregon, Toms River, and San Diego had roots in local community forums and social hygiene groups, but they emphasized educating young people rather than adults.

Accounts of Oregon, Toms River, and San Diego demonstrate the various ways in which educators approached sex education in schools and prioritized their goals; they represent a range of strategies replicated in schools across the nation. Although they did not exhaust the possibilities, they encompass the most influential models. Numerous programs across the nation and a few outside the United States contained elements of the Oregon, Toms River, and San Diego models.[8]

In the tradition of sex education developed earlier in the century, Oregon educators began introducing the topic in health and science classes in the 1940s, positioning information about sexual organs and functions within a biological narrative of human reproduction and personal hygiene. In this model, designed for older elementary and junior high students, the "facts of life"—a common euphemism for information about sex—were the focus but not to the neglect of questions about personality and conduct. Educators and administrators employing the "Oregon method" followed the example of the Oregon-produced classroom movie *Human Growth* (1947), which encouraged boys and girls to discuss puberty, human development, and reproduction with their usual teacher in their ordinary classroom, without fanfare or an outside specialist.[9]

The high school family relationships course in Toms River exemplified school personnel's growing interest in human relations within families, and it took a second approach to sex education: family-centered with little to no attention to the physiology of sex. Toms River High School juniors and seniors discussed dating, choosing a mate, and childcare, subjects of concern to young people who contemplated heterosexual teenaged roles as well as adult responsibilities. Despite the framework of family and relationships, or because of the presumed heterosexual bond of married couples, contemporaries understood family relationships, first taught in 1941, as a form of sex education.

The program in San Diego embodied a third approach, combining education about procreation and guidance for personal adjustment with the physical aspects of sex and dynamics of interpersonal relationships. Beginning their preparation in the late 1930s, San Diego educators in 1942 attempted the broadest curriculum experiment of the time by examining multiple manifestations of sex and gender in several courses between the sixth and twelfth grades and pairing older methods with more novel techniques such as one called "group counseling." By 1947 teachers had developed and conducted what San Diego educators publicized as the first districtwide public school social hygiene program in the United States.[10]

Sex education lessons of the 1940s and 1950s reflected educators' conservative aims. They wanted to strengthen nuclear families and channel young people's sexual thoughts and energies into the institution of marriage. What strengthening the family meant to educators was defending it against divorce and other dysfunction such as male domination, overprotective mothering, or the absence of moral guidance. In other words, middle-class educators wished to ensure the continuation and emulation of the types of families they were expected to maintain.

Yet this vision of a strong and healthy family was not a mere continuation of the status quo. Educators sought elements of empowerment for adolescent girls and boys. They encouraged young people to discard verbal inhibitions, ask whatever questions they had, and discuss their diverse viewpoints on matters related to sex, gender, and sexuality. Curricula occasionally reduced sexuality to a biological given, omitted important details, and reinforced heterosexual gender conformity and middle-class standards of morality, but the experiments broke new ground as they invited frank discussion of dating, marriage, and sexuality in public school classrooms. Teachers broached subjects that many still felt were adult or impolite. Especially significant for adolescent girls, who for decades had been expected to remain aloof about sexual matters, sex and family life education classes encouraged pupils' entitlement to sexual information and showcased a range of knowledge and opinions about gender and sexuality.

Oregon

Mid-century sex education in Portland, Oregon, was rooted in the city's longstanding interest in social welfare causes. Hoping to eliminate venereal disease and sexual vice in the early twentieth century, Oregon social hygiene activists had actively promoted sex education in addition to implementing campaigns against disease and prostitution. Established in 1911, the Oregon Social Hygiene Society (OSHS)—like its counterparts in cities across the United States—increasingly focused on educating young people.[11] The society's leaders initiated an elementary school–based program, with help from the American Social Hygiene Association (ASHA) and federal funding, in three Oregon communities in 1920.[12] Early efforts were bolstered in 1929 by the financial assistance of Ellis C. Brown, a local medical doctor and OSHS member. After he died, Brown's will provided continued monetary support for reducing sexual ignorance, particularly among young people.[13]

Although OSHS leaders fought to maintain funding for their projects from Brown's half-million dollar estate, the will stipulated that the University of Oregon's president would administer the Brown endowment, and lawyers found no support in the document for continuing to fund the OSHS.[14] Multnomah County Medical Society members, moreover, maintained that the "education of school-children with respect to sex, as with other phases of health education which involve the judicious interpretation of medical knowledge, should be carried on by or under the direction of graduates in medicine, rather than lay persons."[15] The social hygiene society lacked medical credentials. "In the course of our conference with representatives of the Oregon Social Hygiene Society," claimed the medical society's committee on school health, "it was evident that one of the difficulties arises from the fact that the Society has no established relationship with the organized medical profession."[16] Medical professionals thus pulled rank on the reformers affiliated with the OSHS.

Resolving the dispute, officials established the E. C. Brown Trust, attaching university clout and resources to the project of sex education. Trust leaders quickly built a formal relationship with the medical profession, distinguishing it from the OSHS. Distancing their organization from the social hygiene reform movement, trust directors shared the county medical society's opposition to having laypersons give "emergency" or occasional talks to young people in schools and clubs or at individual conferences. Ultimately, however, the trust moved toward working with teachers and training them to integrate sex education into the regular curriculum. As explained in a 1928 summary of the Oregon biology innovation, "It was hoped, indeed, that a course in biology, under the leadership of competent teachers, and infused with the spirit of science, would prove to be an effective way of providing for sex education in the school curriculum."[17] In the 1940s, it would succeed under the direction of a new set of leaders who shared many of their predecessors' goals.

University of Oregon president Donald M. Erb took charge in 1939 and launched the trust's activities in 1941 as the nation was entering World War II. Unfamiliar with the social hygiene agenda, Erb, an economist, undertook a study of the literature on social hygiene and discerned that the point of sex education was to educate young people about reproduction. He was, however, skeptical about the "emotionalism" he attributed to social hygiene efforts to combat vice. Considering social hygiene approaches outdated and undesirable, Erb wanted the trust to devote itself to a more "scientific atmosphere and setting."[18] Thus, he selected as trust director a medical doctor, Adolph Weinzirl, Portland's city health officer and the leading opponent of OSHS's sex education efforts.

Under Erb and Weinzirl's leadership, the trust instituted training programs and provided appropriate literature to teachers and administrators interested in sex education. This medical and public health approach to sex education had lasting implications even though the trust endorsed the national trend of enlisting regular teachers to give the instruction. Trust leaders sought new methods of conveying sex education in classrooms, but they still understood the proper classroom focus to be founded on science and objectivity. The outcome of their quest was the production of the movie *Human Growth,* which offered a solution for reticent and reluctant teachers and administrators who lacked scientific expertise.

Financial and legal incentives prompted the creation of the film. Trust officials learned in April 1944 that Brown's estate was generating large revenues for the trust, exceeding their expenditures and thus making it imperative that they undertake a larger project to retain nonprofit status.[19] Meanwhile, the Oregon state legislature passed a law mandating physical and health education statewide, further enabling the work of the trust and paving the way for *Human Growth*'s success.[20] Social hygiene or sex education was not made compulsory by this law, contrary to the assumptions of numerous writers who contacted the state superintendent of public instruction.[21] But sex education advocates were nevertheless inspired. After the law's passage, the Brown Trust published in bulk a manual for health education in secondary grades, which implicitly endorsed sex education by recommending units on social hygiene.[22] Secondary teachers throughout the state received the manual as evidence of how teachers could comply with the new statute.

In 1946, Erb's successor, Harry K. Newburn, continued the development of a sex education motion picture, altering plans midway for pedagogical reasons.[23] When a New York film studio produced a movie script that emphasized animal reproduction, trust officials rejected that version and commissioned a local psychologist to start anew.[24] Known for his filmmaking for the U.S. Navy during World War II, University of Oregon psychologist Lester F. Beck used his experience and expertise to create a movie that focused on human reproduction.[25] By 1947 Beck had written the script for *Human Growth,* and the trust had commissioned Hollywood actor Eddie Albert to produce the movie. Professional actors portrayed the adults, and seventh-grade students from a Los Angeles classroom served as the cast. Completed in fall 1947, the movie circulated widely in Oregon, and by early 1948 it enjoyed national publicity and demand.

Popular magazines and local newspapers gave favorable coverage of *Human Growth.*[26] "The film, 'Human Growth,' candidly presents the long-touchy subject, sex education, as educators and social hygiene supporters have long sought—objectively, with a simple scientific vocabulary for replacement of gutter terminology, and for the first time, from the human point of view rather than in the terms of other animal life," an Oregon journalist wrote.[27] Calling it an "epoch-making movie," a writer for *Life* maintained that young viewers "by their serious interest and response, had proved the film successful," while *Time* indicated that the movie's content was "casual" and "decent."[28] Adding to its acclaim, revisions of the state health education manual for teachers recommended use of *Human Growth,* and spokespersons for the state board of education boasted about the innovative movie in response to inquiries from across the nation.[29]

Human Growth became a vehicle and model for sex education in classrooms in Oregon and across the country. Attempting to present an objective portrait of sex, educators touched on mental health and social development as well as physical well-being.[30] As was the case with the social hygiene movement, the Oregon method of the late 1940s rested on Protestant ideals, depicting small families and middle-class domesticity.[31] Religion and other controversial topics, however, were largely sidestepped. Helping ensure the film's popularity were the trust's considerable financial and institutional resources and an absence of competing sex education films.[32]

Human Growth typically was screened in seventh-grade health classes. The explicit goal of the film, according to the teachers' guide, was to "develop wholesome feelings concerning the subject matter" of reproduction and growth. As documented in promotional material, the trust sold 1,353 prints of the film, and more than two million school children viewed the first edition between 1948 and 1962. Twenty minutes in length, the movie features four scenes. First, it displays a white, middle-class pupil's home on the evening before a classroom screening of *Human Growth*. The second scene shows the teacher and classroom, with students from a preview committee (who screened the movie in advance) highlighting key points in the film. In the lengthiest portion, the pupils learn about reproduction from an animated "film within a film," and then the final scene returns to the classroom, where the teacher fields questions from the students, based on the movie they had just watched.[33] Integral to the use of the film in classrooms was a question-and-answer period following the screening led by a health or science teacher.

Its creators intended *Human Growth* as a tool for teaching sixth- to ninth-grade students, with parental permission, about sexual development and reproduction in mixed-gender classrooms. Equally important to hesitant school administrators, teachers, and parents, the movie demonstrated how such subjects could be discussed among adolescents. Thousands of parents viewed the film at Parent-Teacher Association (PTA) meetings and screenings organized by the trust, and surveys repeatedly demonstrated near unanimous consent for showing the movie to adolescents.[34] The widespread acceptance resulted in part from the producers' conviction that objective facts could be presented without being explicit or threatening.

Sex education through *Human Growth* was only the most visible and nationally broadcast part of a larger, integrated curriculum of health education. Sex instruction as well as information about venereal diseases (in a unit on communicable disease) and such topics as mental health appeared at other grade levels in various Oregon schools.[35] A senior girls' class in Bend, Oregon, for example, in 1947 discussed "questions on premarital sex relations, premarital physical examinations, petting, necking (the girls call it 'snuzzing'), how to get the boy friend to meet a girl's parents, the value of a kiss, and a few questions about engagement behavior from girls who were planning to get married when school was out."[36] Although the Oregon method was not reducible to a single movie, *Human Growth* was what made the state curriculum unique. Other aspects of the curriculum, including questions and discussions about boy-girl relations and mental health during adolescence, were remarkably similar to lessons at other schools.

During the tenure of Curtis Avery as trust director, beginning in 1948, Oregon sex education efforts became more closely linked with family life education and made further inroads into smaller communities.[37] Avery and his colleague Lester A. Kirkendall, an Oregon State University family living expert, argued that there was more to sex education than teaching about human anatomy and reproduction. It included "information and attitudinal development with respect to sex roles, and their psychological, social, and economic implications."[38]

From the beginning, Oregon social hygiene advocates and educators had embedded their values into sex education, and although there was a "facts of life" emphasis in the material, especially in *Human Growth*, morals and emotions were never absent. "Genital education" with a strict focus on anatomy might have been an easier approach claimed health curriculum author Howard S. Hoyman, but he and other proponents of sex education in Oregon maintained that such "short cuts in providing sex education for modern youth" were inadequate.[39] As discussion of family and relationships took precedence in sex education, sexuality remained relevant if understated in publicity about the Oregon method.

Meanwhile, ASHA leaders in the movement for sex education had grown skeptical of a medical approach to the topic during the 1940s. Maurice A. Bigelow, chair of the ASHA committee on education, wrote to former OSHS executive secretary Fred B. Messing that physicians, especially Weinzirl (whom he had heard speak), were "not very successful in lecturing to lay audiences, such as parents and teachers." Simultaneously inquiring and advising, Bigelow wrote, "I want to know what is actually being done by schools under the direction of their own officials. That is the only kind of social hygiene work which is permanent."[40] Ultimately, trust leaders had arrived at the same conclusion about sustaining sex education. Although *Human Growth* facilitated the entry of sex education into the curricula, it was Oregon educators—no longer beholden to the medical profession or the social hygiene movement—who adapted and institutionalized curricula across the state. And it was Oregon students' questions and concerns that provided the content of the question-and-answer sections of the film and accompanying book, modeling for other schools and youth groups how to initiate discussions of sex with adolescents.

Toms River

Toms River, New Jersey, grew rapidly during the mid-twentieth century as industry and highways developed along the Jersey shore.[41] No longer a community of chicken farmers and small business owners, Toms River confronted new populations and new challenges to the status quo. Educators felt that young people were especially affected by such changes because they received little or no training for making adult decisions about money, jobs, love, and their futures. Concerned about juvenile delinquency and the growing incidence of divorce, community leaders attempted to intervene by targeting the young people through schools. In the late 1930s, Edgar M. Finck, superintendent between 1919 and 1948, convinced the Dover Township Board of Education to support an experiment in family life education.

Although popular in the predominantly white community of Toms River, Finck aroused consternation in the surrounding African American population in the 1920s when he oversaw creation of a separate and decidedly unequal "opportunity school" for black students from Berkeley Township and Seaside Park Borough—"tuition pupils" who were temporarily attending Toms River schools.[42] Black families boycotted the one-room school, which had no indoor plumbing, and embarked on a legal challenge and an appeal to the governor. They were assisted by the National Association for the Advancement of Colored People.[43] In 1927, the state commissioner of education ruled that the segregated school for black pupils was unlawful. The Dover school board responded by refusing to admit Berkeley Township elementary pupils, and in 1927 South Toms River became a separate borough and school district, effectively ensuring de facto racial segregation.[44] The failure to integrate probably came as no surprise for the African Americans involved, given that Klansmen in neighboring Lakewood used the high school facilities for changing into their robes. The Ku Klux Klan initiation ceremonies in August 1923 attracted thousands to the town.[45] As a graduate student sympathetic to Finck wrote in his 1957 study of the school, racial segregation was "the most unfortunate incident" of the superintendent's first ten years but not one that tarnished his overall reputation.[46]

Following this public relations debacle, Finck's efforts to transform public school education to meet students' vocational and personal needs attracted virtually no controversy. He worked with Elizabeth S. Force, a young, widowed English teacher and graduate of Toms River High School, to institute a course that at first glance seemed similar to home economics.[47] Based on an examination of subjects promoting healthy family life and sound interpersonal relations, the coed course of study responded to teenagers' concerns about popularity and social acceptance and emphasized adult responsibilities. Although they did not conceptualize the discussions as about sexuality per se, boy-girl relations during youth were prominent in the lesson plans and course workbook.

Relying on peer and community standards—rather than scientific re-search—as the measure of appropriate behavior, Force and her colleagues formulated a method of sex education somewhat different than social hygiene efforts to impart knowledge, shape attitudes, and control vice. Whereas Oregon's film concentrated on teaching younger adolescents the facts of growing up, Toms River's curriculum included few "facts of life" and instead encouraged older adolescents' examination of gender roles and sexual norms. When Toms River classes viewed *Human Growth* in the 1950s, it was discussed in the context of parenting and educating children.[48]

Family relationships, designed in 1939 and first taught in 1941, placed Toms River in a position of national prominence for what was called "family life education."[49] A semirural area along the East Coast, Toms River and Dover Township were home to a single high school until the early 1950s.[50] The 1942 graduating class included the first set of Toms River students to enroll in Force's one-semester elective course. A group of approximately twenty to twenty-five junior- and senior-year students—"representing a variety of social, religious, economic and cultural backgrounds," according to Force—gathered in a space decorated to resemble a living room in the high school's vocational building.[51] There they discussed gender roles, dating, necking, petting, engagement, and marriage. Their discussions were prompted by a workbook, *Ten Topics toward Happier Homes,* that each student completed for the course.[52] Because of enrollment patterns during the war years (when fewer boys attended high school), three times as many girls as boys took Force's class. Although the numbers had evened out by 1946, the experiment had its start in a predominantly female classroom environment.[53] As was typical of much coed instruction in sex and family life, the teacher was a woman.[54]

Similar to Oregon efforts, Toms River educators initially pursued community support. To the project's credit, Force was well known in the area, and the community trusted her leadership. Furthermore, family relationships joined social behavior, economic competence, and consumer education as courses that would make school more relevant, especially given a student body of which only 3 percent pursued postsecondary education.[55] The course was intended to serve the students and the community as well as the broader society. Not only knowledge but also "the values of strong homes and families in the American way of life" were essential to "fortifying American Democracy," as the promotional brochure for family relationships student workbooks indicated.[56]

Toms River educators, like Oregon educational leaders, grew to understand their curriculum as a method of ensuring adolescent mental health. But whereas *Human Growth*'s producers mainly intended to ease adolescents' concerns about the physical aspects of puberty and teach them that sex was not a taboo subject for classrooms, the Toms River class reflected educators' assumptions about older teenagers. Teachers hoped to enlighten juniors and seniors about how to overcome social problems and prepare them to face adult futures. Significant factors influencing mental health, according to a New Jersey health education guide, included the socioeconomic background of the student, whether the family was "broken," siblings and birth order, and the family's connection to "local culture."[57] Furthermore, the state guidebook advised teachers that "the importance of television, radio, movies, comic books, magazines, and the like, must not be overlooked," given that such sources "color the adolescent's thinking, influence his behavior, and contribute to the formation and development of his sense of values."[58] Family relationships offered guidance in making sense of all these issues.

Joining other commentators, Toms River educators denounced the changes that took place in family structures during the 1940s and 1950s. A local increase in divorce rates and a belief that two parents were essential to meeting children's needs motivated the course's focus on creating stable families, as Force and Finck pointed out in their manual for teachers and administrators. "Our course in Family Relationships is, then, a frank attack on the divorce evil. Concurrently, it is an attack on juvenile delinquency, much of which originates in broken homes."[59] Temptations for teenagers—associated with the allure of motion picture romance and the newly opened local drive-in theater—made such guidance timely.[60]

Although a medical model originally guided educators in Oregon, Toms River's inspiration was much more situated in a sociological and psychological framework. Arguing that there was no single way to handle the topic of sex, Force and Finck suggested that successful programs should include an examination of community needs. They likewise called for personnel with an ability to convey "proper attitudes and ideals."[61] The word *proper*, with its Victorian connotations, no doubt referred to middle-class values, those appropriate to such professionals as Force and Finck. In addition to the middle-class etiquette and values offered such in companion classes as social behavior and consumer education, family relationships clarified how to apply democratic ideals to marriage and the family and remain conscious of status.

Educators in Oregon never suggested that teachers defer to the students' standards, but the Toms River program more or less did. When the topic of dating arose, the teachers' guide advised, "Do more listening than talking! Keep ears and mind and heart open! Guidance and standards are more likely to be accepted if they come from the group than if you pronounce them." Young people, Force continued, more readily accepted standards of peers than adults.[62] To understand why Toms River teachers exhibited such open acceptance, consider Force's impeccable reputation, the town's relative homogeneity, the curriculum's lesser emphasis on facts, and the older age of the students being addressed.[63]

In spite of broad parental support statewide for sex education, estimated at 81 percent in 1951, Toms River school authorities were reluctant to go into depth about sexual behavior, at least in the written curriculum.[64] Force claimed that she handled information about sex on an individual and as-needed basis, and the family relationships course did not include a unit on human reproduction. A journalist writing in 1948 maintained that "sex instruction is not given in the course, even though the students would like to have it." Suggesting a contrast between conservative parents and permissive educators, the author explained that the absence of lessons on sexual reproduction was "because the parents of the community aren't ready yet for such an 'advanced' classroom attitude. But individual advice on sexual and all other problems can be had, on request, in special consultations."[65] Most newspaper and magazine articles at the end of the 1940s clarified that parental permission was required for personal conferences or referrals to further information or community resources related to sex.[66]

Like the Brown Trust, which had abandoned the social hygiene method of personal counseling for young people in the late 1930s, Toms River educators downplayed personal consultations. Such individualized services could be obtained elsewhere through guidance departments in schools, churches and synagogues, or various social service agencies. Instead, Force and other teachers emphasized problem-solving skills in a variety of areas, including preparation and requirements for marriage, myths and realities of married life, self-evaluation of marriage potential, rights and responsibilities of family members, economic matters in marriage, dating, engagement, marriage ceremonies and vows, living together, and parental responsibilities.

The use of *Human Growth* in the 1950s illustrates that facts about human sexuality were not entirely omitted from Toms River classrooms; students discussed how to teach children about puberty and reproduction. Screening a film in high school designed for sixth-grade students, however, was unlikely to raise eyebrows. Opportunities for discussions about sex in the Toms River model arose in several other places, especially because of teachers' views about the meaning of "sex." According to Force, sex was "a thread running through all life and therefore essential for our consideration. Physical aspects of sex," the course planning committee had concurred, "could not be isolated from the emotional, social and spiritual life of an individual. We did not devote special blocks of time to this but took up issues related to sex as they naturally arose. Our consideration of these matters was thoughtful and frank. We used films, pamphlets and books to meet various maturity levels."[67]

Although Toms River educators lacked associations with social hygienists, they deferred to medical professionals only on occasion, such as for the unit on engagement. This unit posed a single question about physical preparation for marriage, advising a visit to the family doctor to assess individuals' health. The teachers' guide indicated that physicians could become a source of sex information, and if one were invited to make a class presentation, teachers should advise the doctor to be sure "he" did not undermine other messages in the curriculum.[68] Perhaps such briefings ensured minimal attention to sex. Force mentioned that doctors who visited the class usually responded to students' questions on such subjects as "obesity, acne, diet, use of alcohol and tobacco, nervousness, [and] the effect of radiation on the next generation."[69]

Toms River curricula therefore focused on the concerns young people had about getting along with their families and peers, emphasizing middle-class norms of adulthood, marriage, and family. Unit 4 of the course, for example, aimed "to guide the individual in the selection of a proper mate, . . . teach individuals . . . to adjust themselves [so] that neither one's personality is dwarfed, . . . help individuals find an agreeable method of courtship, [and] give them the knowledge necessary in the legal preparation for marriage." Other units offered teaching about "necessary influences for happiness in marriage" and brief coverage of "the family's biological aspects," which included heredity and development.[70] The topic of venereal disease was likely to arise only incidentally during discussion of legal requirements for marriage.

Despite the fact that Force later wrote a textbook based on Toms River, family relationships was not conceived as a "textbook" course but one built around the course workbook, popular periodicals, movies, and guest speakers.[71] Force encouraged students to conduct mini-surveys of community opinion and interview older friends, neighbors, and family members. She provided access to copies of newspapers (the *New York Times* and *New York Herald Tribune*) and periodicals (*Harper's, Atlantic Monthly, Saturday Review,* and the *Annals of the American Academy of Political and Social Science*), as well as items from popular magazines to serve as "readers" wherein students might find articles on divorce trends or youth problems and pertinent advertisements.[72] Conscious that the study of family relationships was not an exact science, the teachers' guide to the course workbook advised flexibility. Most questions posed had no right or wrong answers, and Force evaluated students' work in terms of the thoughtfulness of the response.[73]

Toms River advocates of family life education attempted to estimate the course's effectiveness, measuring specifically their goal of reducing divorce rates as well as evaluating the mental health implications of the course.[74] In September 1947, they conducted a survey of all pupils who had completed the course. Among the replies were those of seventy-five former students who had married during the first few years after graduation. "Exactly none" was divorced, although "at the national rate of one divorce for every three marriages, we might have expected twenty-four divorces."[75] Such knowledge emboldened Force and Finck to credit family relationships for "tangible results."[76] Notwithstanding the likelihood of divorces in the future, they felt that "it is hardly likely" that those among former students "will ever approach the national rate."[77] With such optimism, Force left for New York City in 1957 to work for the ASHA committee on education, and Toms River High School continued to offer family relationships as an elective.

After a decade of instruction, Force commented that a "mental health emphasis" prevailed in teaching the course, and popular ideas about mental health were changing. Initially, the class emphasized "the importance of mutual interest, of common social, economic, cultural, and religious background to happy marriage," but students discovered contradictions through observing actual marriages and thus determined that similarities were not the most important factors.[78] As Toms River educators responded to the needs of students and attempted to shape their attitudes and personalities, they remained flexible about how one might increase the potential for family success.

San Diego

Evolving from a vacation and retirement area to an urban industrial and war production center, San Diego experienced major growth during the 1940s and 1950s and faced dramatic social change.[79] As elsewhere, new faces and large crowds added to the temptations, and popular amusements seemed to lure young people down the wrong track. The numbers of single military men and blue-collar workers exacerbated fears about the safety of girls and young women. As was the case in other West Coast cities, the police perpetrated racial violence against young Mexican Americans and African Americans in 1943 in what were called "'zoot suit' incidents."[80] As the city's

African American population grew and concern about protecting national borders preoccupied some city leaders, racial tensions abounded alongside concerns about gender and sexual norms.[81]

In a letter to parents, Logan School principal Martha Farnum premised sex education lessons, beginning in 1943, on the dramatic demographic transformations that occurred in San Diego as the United States entered the war. It was no longer a small town, and, Farnum noted, "training and protecting children is complicated by the presence of so many strangers (war workers and service men), by over-crowded housing conditions, by inadequate recreational facilities, [and] by decreased parental supervision due to war work."[82] Within communities of color, these structural problems were compounded by pervasive racial discrimination within the police force and in recreational facilities as well as a postwar employment decline that affected as many as three thousand African American families whose breadwinners had worked for the government or the war industries.[83]

Describing the unprecedented work being done in San Diego's new sex education program, a *Ladies' Home Journal* article conveyed how young people's stories inspired the curriculum. "Maria," who exemplified administrators and teachers' concerns, was "from a district of very poor Mexican immigrant families, where both parents are often forced to work, and where barriers of language and superstition—not to mention the extremely early age of maturity of Mexican girls, sometimes as early as eight years—make the illegitimacy rate among grade-school girls a serious problem." Labeled "boy crazy," twelve-year-old Maria wished she had a steady boyfriend, and, according to school authorities, was "out of hand" and "headed for plenty of trouble."[84] Experts believed that Maria misbehaved not because of sexual desire but rather a lack of knowledge that might help her "to avoid the situation."[85] In their view, education could brace girls like Maria with information to help minimize teenage pregnancy; nothing was said about changing men's and boys' behavior.

De facto residential segregation of African Americans and Mexican Americans in the city seemingly influenced how administrators confronted social problems in different neighborhoods and schools. Educators devised curricula to aid pupils in their transition from elementary to junior high school and from junior to senior high school, important markers in adolescent development and passage into adulthood. Working in committees and in close collaboration with nurses, teachers, PTA members, and civic organization leaders as well as national leaders in sex education, the director of health education for San Diego City Schools launched an impressive curriculum. Although principles behind the Oregon method and the Toms River experiment in family life education appeared in San Diego's curriculum plans, school officials there paid attention to various aspects of growing up in a number of different ways.

After educators and other professionals in the late 1930s established a public dialog among adults about sex education—they proceeded toward educating pupils about sex. The district's health committee announced that during the 1937–38 school year, doctors would be available to give talks on sex education to parents; the committee sent letters to each local PTA, and a copy of the letter appeared in the district magazine. Urging PTA members to "let your president know of your interest in sex education," Evelyn L. Dowdy averred that readers "should be especially interested in this timely subject," which would be added to the "modern school curriculum in the near future." The parents' responsibility was to "be progressive" and enlightened about their children's education.[86] Several months later, the magazine published high school sociology teacher William J. Lyons's entreaty in favor of school sex education: "Very little is being done to teach the social phases of sex in general"—a situation Lyons lamented—"which would include the development of proper mental attitudes."[87]

Fueled by positive reception at community forums, G. Gage Wetherill, a medical doctor and the director of health education for the San Diego City School District, worried little about opposition to sex education. Local educators adopted strategies similar to Toms River's promotional scheme, and they also strategically used the medical profession's influence. Working in favor of the forums, Wetherill argued, was the fact that doctors and nurses who commanded the community's respect conducted public discussions. Perhaps realizing its potential for failure elsewhere, or that times had changed in the intervening decades, Wetherill stated that he did not recommend San Diego's public forum approach to launching sex education.[88] Yet in his experience, he claimed, the school only encountered dissent from the unenlightened, and they were eventually won over.[89]

San Diego educators chose to integrate sex and family life education— what they termed "human relations education"—across the general school curricula in the mid-twentieth century. Wetherill's evaluation of the Stephen Kearney Junior-Senior High School curriculum in the 1940s revealed that human relations education was already part of biology, home economics, general science, physiology, hygiene, social problems, physical education, mathematics of personal bookkeeping, social studies, and English.[90] Further steps were taken in the school district in the 1950s, and without major fanfare or requests for permission from parents courses integrated material related to sex, emphasizing personal growth and human relationships. Some tenth-grade English courses adopted the title "personal and social adjustment to living" in the early 1950s, catering class discussion to "problems which students are facing, and which therefore interest them." Such concerns included self-understanding, getting along with others, and establishing social relations.[91] In home economics courses—offered over six consecutive years of junior and senior high school—girls focused "primarily on the improvement of the individual as a member of a family and of the society in which she lives."[92]

School personnel devised the curriculum guide for the sixth-grade social hygiene course. "Growing Up," as the lessons were called, helped students deal with the onset of puberty. As Wetherill explained, school officials chose to begin sex education with an introduction to the "biology of reproduction, plus only a few of the more basic concepts of family life education, because we found these to be the areas of greatest interest at this level." It might seem ironic that sex education, without overbearing emphasis on the family, was deemed appropriate for San Diego youths in the early stages of puberty, yet educators felt that basic tenets of reproductive knowledge should precede the more practical family life education. "It was useless," Wetherill argued, "to try to teach the total broad concept of family life education before satisfying the curiosities concerning reproduction and the usual sex interests and misconceptions so common in the thinking and discussions of children at this stage in development."[93] Clearing up misinformation—or substituting reliable sources of knowledge for peer or street education—motivated San Diego educators. The context was different from Oregon's movie, but allusions to the family were likewise common in the curricula.

San Diego schools first implemented social hygiene education to classes of sixth-grade girls in May 1942 at Logan Elementary School. Fifteen additional elementary schools offered the lessons in the following year.[94] Logan was located in an interracial neighborhood, a predominantly African American and lower-income section of the urban school district, and the community's girls seemed to school officials in special need of education—as Maria's story, among others, had suggested. Logan Heights was one of few places in the city where youths of color could participate in activities, visit recreational facilities, and walk the streets with little fear of discrimination or discomfort.[95]

Coordinated by the school's female principal and nurse, the social hygiene program sought to alleviate female pupils' alleged ignorance about their bodies, especially regarding menstruation and physical hygiene.[96] School personnel initiated classes for boys the following summer, apparently prompted by parents' eagerness to have personal hygiene instruction for them as well, and an adult leader from the San Diego Boys' Club took charge of instruction.[97] Teachers and community leaders' fears of urban transformation shaped their view of what was best in terms of children's welfare and possibly made white educators consider it urgent to educate children of color. Prominent among their assumptions was that communities of color lacked appropriate adult role models.

The original "Growing Up" lessons began with acknowledgment of wartime social change in gender roles. Many fathers were away at war and mothers were working outside the home, destabilizing the ideal family of a breadwinning father and a homemaking mother. The lesson plans conveyed a need for greater protection of girls in the midst of such upheaval.[98] Given the growing proportion of mothers who did work away from home, Viola I. Lampe, the school nurse and curriculum author, began the first lesson with emphasis on new adolescent responsibilities. Addressed to students, the narrative instructed them to respect the limits their parents placed on their freedom. Lampe provided an example of a twelve-year-old named Jane whose mother would not let her attend a military show on a school night because of the late hour and her concern about potential danger. Jane's mother feared her friendly daughter would "pick up an acquaintance with some stranger" and ultimately encounter "difficulties, even real trouble."[99] Allusions to dangers euphemistically suggested, in contemporary language, molestation, rape, or pregnancy. The guide thus reiterated concern about protecting girls and the importance of selecting friends carefully and avoiding strangers—using girls' behavior as a starting point for their sex education.[100] And unlike Maria's prototypical Hispanic mother, who apparently had no control over her daughter, this anecdote suggests that Jane's mother—ostensibly white and middle class—was "good" and worthy of respect.

As explained in the letter requesting parental permission, the original three-lesson plan for girls instructed pupils in the names and functions of anatomical parts; "the story of the baby"; and how girls' bodies change during puberty, including menstruation and personal hygiene.[101] Unlike the Oregon experiment, which placed young adolescent boys and girls in the same classroom, San Diego's curriculum involved instruction in single-sex classrooms. Wetherill noted that San Diego schools had attempted mixed-gender instruction but found students less than willing to discuss such subjects as menstruation and nocturnal emissions under those circumstances.[102] San Diego teachers were prepared to discuss intimate sexual issues and separated boys and girls to facilitate their inquiries and personal disclosures, but their approach alternated between straightforwardness and evasion.

In the first lesson of "Growing Up," not only did the teacher share advice about girls' social adjustments but she also called attention to various organs of male and female anatomy. Teachers did not ordinarily mention external female genitalia in lessons for school children during the mid-twentieth century; San Diego's guide for teachers, however, took care to identify the labia, demonstrating the curriculum planners' sense that girls should know the appropriate names for body parts. (The clitoris was apparently not considered important, given that discussion of it was omitted.) The guide directed instructors to explain the location of the labia "in front of the anus and between the legs" and describe them as "two folds of skin" that "we have." The narration continued with an anecdote meant to be shared with the class: "The other day a girl came to my office; her face was red and she was embarrassed. She said she had a sore down there, and pointed between her legs. If she had known the right name to use she would have told me she had a sore on her labia. She wouldn't have been embarrassed and I would have known just where the sore was."[103] The suggestion that vocabulary was the source of embarrassment evaded the possibility that the sore may have resulted from poor hygiene, masturbation, consensual sexual contact, incest, or rape—situations likely embarrassing to share with an adult regardless of the terms available.

In contrast with this specific naming of female genitalia, San Diego educators also employed the birds-and-bees approach with sixth-graders. In the second lesson pupils read Karl de Schweinitz's *Growing Up: The Story of How We Become Alive, Are Born and Grow Up*, which discusses plants and animals before turning to the topic of "mating" in humans.[104] What kinds of information they derived can only be imagined. The chapter on mating includes pictures of a crowing rooster, a male peacock with open feathers, and works of art that supposedly show human interest in love and beauty. De Schweinitz approached information about human intercourse indirectly: "With animals, the male usually tries to place the sperm in the body of the first female he meets after the time for mating is come"; and "Like the animals a man and a woman may feel like sending the sperm to join the egg but they do not do this unless they love each other. Each man and each woman waits to marry the one whom he or she can love."[105]

Teachers in San Diego thus presented lyrical and metaphorical materials to explain sex. The reading of de Schweinitz's *Growing Up* was called an "appreciation lesson," indicating the goal was not to convey facts but inspire awe. According to the first edition of the San Diego curriculum guide, "Since the purpose of this lesson is appreciation, no oral questions or discussions will be included." Lampe advised teachers to complete the de Schweinitz story then "say to the children, 'If there are parts of this story you have not understood, or if you have questions you wish to ask, you may write them on a piece of paper, sign your name, and put them in the question box.'"[106] In subsequent years the appreciation lesson began with the same justification for the lesson plan but a greater openness to questioning. "Since the purpose of this lesson is appreciation," the new wording asserted, "oral questions or discussions will be included during the reading."[107] The teachers eventually consented to answering anonymous questions from twelve- and thirteen-year-olds—the same sixth-grade students with whom they discussed labia and wet dreams—but continued to use a reader that euphemistically discussed reproductive intercourse in humans. It seems likely that the educators' assessment of young people's needs led to more honesty, openness, and explicitness, yet they retained contradictory presumptions about childhood innocence and obliviousness.

Writing for national publications, Wetherill asserted that the interests of children and young people had determined the subjects that teachers addressed. San Diego teachers adopted what he referred to as a "factual or scientific approach" but one mediated through plant and animal biology. Wetherill also posited that parents were generally better able to give information to their children "pertaining to romance, growing up and marriage . . . than reproduction."[108] As in the other schools, San Diego educators did not assume they were the only source of information about sex but considered themselves working in conjunction with sex education in homes, churches or synagogues, and community agencies.[109]

Over time, San Diego educators expanded the number of class sessions in the "Growing Up" curriculum, and by 1951 the guide was reconfigured into five lessons. In lesson two, during which pupils watched four films on plant and animal reproduction, boys and girls began attending the lessons together—a departure from the former three-lesson plan where classes were sex-segregated.[110] But the guide continued to have boys and girls separated for the other lessons, with separate screenings of *Human Growth* for boys and girls featured in lesson five.[111]

The new lessons, moreover, included greater differentiation of the content for the two groups. Boys' classes covered units on glandular changes, growth of sex organs, formation of sperm, seminal emissions, masturbation, menstruation, reason for body change, sex relations, and self-control.[112] Girls' classes covered sex organs, menstruation (at length), masturbation, reason for change, sex relations, and self-control."[113]

Shortly following the "Growing Up" pilot project, San Diego City Schools implemented a second experiment for junior high school girls, "Know Yourself and Others." Beginning at Roosevelt Junior High in the 1943–44 school year, the sessions involved a similar program for boys in subsequent years. Explaining the original mission of the course, Sue Ernest, the dean of girls, commented that "young people have never lived in a more chaotic world, nor in one wherein so frequently adolescents assume duties of adults."[114] The course followed a series of informal talks to girls in the school gym. Pupils requested more information at the conclusion of such talks and eventually received a six-week course of study during physical education.[115]

Evolving out of the "Know Yourself and Others" experiment, San Diego administrators encouraged a program they named group counseling in the high school years, most commonly in the last year of junior and senior high school.[116] At each grade level, students were to determine the issues of greatest concern for group discussion. Group counseling attempted to provide education and guidance for young women and young men. Recounting "some of her own problems and experiences as a girl [and including] both serious and humorous situations that she had encountered," Ernest would ease into the subject with female students. This approach reduced their reticence; pupils "realized that they, for once, could discuss freely the problems about which they were curious but could never mention except in isolated circumstances." The teacher began by establishing the purpose of the lessons: "to consider friendship, boy-girl, parent-child and family relationships, and to establish wholesome attitudes and practices in personal and family relations." On the first day of group counseling, students were asked to submit unsigned written questions that would determine the plan for the class.[117]

With consultation from the dean of girls and the school nurse, the ninth-grade science teacher in charge of the original group counseling course, Margaret Olsen (formerly a school principal in the Midwest), then assembled the girls' questions according to how frequently they appeared. She conducted the sessions in reverse order of interest, allowing "time to get acquainted and build up wholesome attitudes before discussing the more difficult problems."[118] Most commonly asked, and apparently most "difficult," were questions regarding social and sexual behavior: "how to be attractive to boys, how to act and what to talk about when with boys, social etiquette, petting, how long to go with the same boy, and emotional controls." The next category dealt with physical development, reproduction, and "sex relations in marriage." Additional questions pertained to family relations and personal attractiveness, with the latter category encompassing cosmetics, poise, and "health for attractiveness."[119] Of three "home relations" issues of discussion, one was "more acute problems such as a mother's jealousy of the father's affection for the daughter," revealing how teachers may have interpreted girls' comments as variations on the so-called oedipal complex.[120]

Slight modifications were made to group counseling methods in its first five years. The purpose of the lessons enlarged, adding "social problems in this changing world, personal conduct and personality growth" to the topics of discussion. The 1951 account of group counseling no longer mentioned unsigned questions, although that method undoubtedly persisted in some schools.[121] Unlike sixth-grade teachers who could rely on the recommendations of "Growing Up," counselors did not work from detailed guidelines; rather, they were expected to adapt the lessons to students' needs at each school.

Group counseling was much less predictable than "Growing Up." Schools invested authority in high school counselors based on an assumption that they were capable of countering the negative influences of pupils' home environments once they were aware of the students' particular challenges. Wetherill advised, "It is important that social-hygiene counselors understand the backgrounds from which some students come. Teachers protected by the environment of the better social circles may be unaware of these backgrounds," which included "excessive drinking, bickering, and vulgarity."[122] He also noted that "some students come to school from families where there is marital unhappiness, perversion, and prostitution." More explicitly, he commented that "teachers are often shocked when they learn that certain of their students are confronted with problems of incest in their homes, sexual perversion among friends or seductive sex attractions in their immediate environments."[123] Although he refrained from identifying particular perversions, it is probable that they included exchanging sexual favors for money and sexual activity with persons of the same sex. San Diego counselors were cognizant of the problems that students faced in their daily lives, and Wetherill suggested that sex researcher Kinsey's findings provided statistical support for what he learned anecdotally from teachers and counselors. Teenagers were not innocent and unaware of sexuality; either they had personal experience or had witnessed sexual incidents accidentally or deliberately.

Unlike educators in Toms River and Oregon who avoided discussion about sexual variation, education leaders in San Diego found the Kinsey reports pertinent to their work.[124] San Diego guidance counselor and sex education advocate Richmond Barbour reluctantly commented on the female report in his column in the *California Parent-Teacher*, indicating that not only educators but also teenaged girls were talking about Kinsey's alleged claim that young women were too inhibited. Barbour had received numerous letters from parents, concerned that the 1953 report was influencing their daughters. In his interpretation of Kinsey, Barbour contended that the book advocated petting and suggested that "girls who experiment with sex before marriage are apt to become happier wives than those who don't." Barbour shared his advice to his daughters: Kinsey's conclusions are only theories, and Kinsey—a biologist—was inadequately trained to speak to questions of sociology and psychology. Young women should, in his opinion, ignore Kinsey's opinions and know that his theories were subject to criticism.[125]

Similar to the Toms River curriculum, San Diego sex education did not necessarily assume that the ideal American family was the reality for students. Wetherill and others had a sense of the diverse family situations from which their pupils came. Yet San Diego educators acknowledged that family problems seemed more varied than divorce and delinquency, in part due to a greater disparity of wealth and different cultural environments in the city. More concerned with immediate goals than with preparing students for future marital success, the instructors taught them about their bodies, reproductive capabilities, and social challenges. Compared to Oregon and Toms River, teachers were far more vocal about students' personal and family struggles related to sex as well as race, culture, and class.

Conclusion

Enjoying periodic public attention and largely uninterrupted local support, the programs in Oregon, Toms River, and San Diego sustained themselves in their respective communities during the 1940s and 1950s. In their longevity, they were somewhat of an aberration from contemporary efforts to educate about sex through schools. Nevertheless, they were exemplary of the possibilities for sex and family life education at different grade levels, with various pedagogical strategies and curriculum content.

Each of the three cases demonstrates how sex education could be at once progressive and conservative, challenging some elements of the status quo but fortifying others. Oregon's promotion of classes in which boys and girls learned about puberty and reproduction together was unconventional at the time. But with the exception of a few lone voices that considered any discussion of sex in mixed company promiscuous, most parents and communities were won over by the absence of titillation in *Human Growth*. The opening scene depicting an upper-middle-class white family of husband, wife, and two siblings quickly put to rest any objections about transgression; family values legitimized Oregon's method. The lack of objectionable material on-screen, however, provided no guarantee that students would express their questions and concerns in proper speech or uphold conventional mores. Their comments and queries exposed young people's sexual curiosities and varying viewpoints, including those not depicted in the movie.

Toms River's course likewise fulfilled people's expectations about instilling respect for the family through schools. Yet an examination of the topics for discussion shows that family relationships treated traditional values as subject to question. Discussion and debate about dating etiquette and sexual conduct among teenagers were less about "family" and more about heterosexual norms and sexual desire in adolescence. Given Force's disavowal of heavy-handed moralizing, students in her classes could vocalize unpopular ideas; whereas literature classes might involve students in abstract discussions of a character's sexual behavior, the purpose of discussions in family relationships was to look inward. A public school course devoted to self-examination through the lenses of gender and sexuality was indeed a new development.

San Diego educators adopted greater explicitness, and their curricula seemed least steeped in emphasis on the family. Local schools delegated time in the sixth grade for the topic of masturbation and invited open-ended, small group discussions of gender and sexuality for high school students. In defiance of the move away from birds-and-bees metaphors, however, San Diego kept them as part of sixth-grade lessons and into the 1950s adopted books and films that dealt circuitously with human sexuality. Applying the broadest range of strategies for sex education, San Diego educators nevertheless reinforced gender dichotomies. They seem to have been particularly invested in preserving girls' reputations—imposing ethnocentric, middle-class ideals on those from poorer communities of color.

Media publicity about the programs in San Diego, Oregon, and Toms River was only cursory, emphasizing aspects most palatable to white, middle-class sensibilities. Young people played more active roles in shaping their experiences with sex education during the 1940s and 1950s, in these cities and elsewhere, and expressed a range of beliefs and attitudes. A closer investigation of the content and pedagogy of sex and family life education across the nation reveals that multiple perspectives and approaches to gender and sexuality flourished in mid-twentieth-century schools.

4

The Facts of Life

Physical changes occur constantly as individuals develop from infancy into adulthood, and mid-twentieth-century sex educators singled out the accelerated growth process known as puberty as a special moment in life. "It is the biological changes that set the adolescent period apart for special consideration," explained education professor Ruth Strang in her text on the psychology of adolescence, adding that sexual maturity was "of central importance."[1] Puberty referred to the acquisition of physical, sexual maturity during the early teenaged years, a period of rapid growth thought to bring emotional adjustments supposedly unique to adolescence. Educators understood adolescence as the phase accompanying puberty and encompassing psychological adaptation to the changing physical body as well as social norms. School officials paid great attention to puberty and adolescence during the twentieth century, inaugurating separate "junior" high schools beginning in the 1920s to attend to the specific needs of pubescent youth.[2]

Not only did educators find it useful to separate younger adolescents from their older and younger peers, but they also began to develop curricula that directly confronted questions and problems of adolescents. In San Diego, for example, instructors began teaching about puberty just before students entered junior high school. They prepared the pupils with the knowledge that puberty brought the ability to procreate, and they acknowledged adolescence as "the time at which boys and girls start to become young men and women."[3] As a period between childhood and adulthood, adolescence brought new physical capacities, increasingly differentiated norms of conduct for boys and girls, and increasingly expected attraction for the other sex. Sex instruction aimed to help young people adjust to the physiology of their changing bodies; it also reinforced awareness and appreciation of heterosexuality that conformed to social norms.

Educators faced a conundrum in formulating sex education, given the sexual capabilities of adolescent bodies and the social proscriptions against sexual behavior. Teachers and other professionals wanted young people to gain knowledge and appreciation of sex, but they did not want them, especially girls, to flaunt their bodies or engage in intercourse. Thus, sex education curricula relied heavily on gender socialization to blunt the suggestion that adolescent bodies were ready to engage in sex. Because physical sexual maturity preceded the age at which it was acceptable to marry and engage in intercourse, according to the norms of the day, sex education pedagogy explained physical changes while guiding young people to develop a heterosexual orientation. Adolescent heterosexuality promised to bring emotional fulfillment and social rewards but not sexual consummation before the engagement and marriage that all young people were encouraged to envision.

Girls' bodies mature earlier than boys', and educators were concerned with the implications of physical maturity for girls' safety as well as psychological and heterosexual adjustment. Mid-century pubescent girls typically experienced menarche, or the onset of menstruation, around age twelve.[4] If menarche is a relatively concealed event, the development of breasts is more visible. Popular and professional messages about managing girls' breasts reveal the contradictory quality of education and socialization meant to help with adjustment. "A girl of six years may run around in a sun-suit with practically no bra," observed psychologist Helen Kitchen Branson in 1953, but one of thirteen who had begun to menstruate should not. Breast development implied sexual readiness, and it was girls' responsibility to keep their breasts inconspicuous, she argued.[5]

Entrepreneurs and health professionals promoted brassieres for developing girls, but concern with physical and moral support competed with messages in mid-century popular culture such as the youthful "sweater girl," her breasts proudly protruding from a tight sweater.[6] Goodrich C. Schauffler, a medical doctor, reported to colleagues at a 1954 professional meeting in Chicago that adolescent girls' psychological stability was at stake. He attributed a "bosom inferiority complex" to padded bras as well as the extreme cases of "attempted suicide and total derangements contingent upon real or fancied breast irregularities."[7]

As their figures developed, girls were prone to attract male attention, which, on the one hand, might awaken girls' heterosexual consciousness—

a result educators believed normal and desirable. On the other hand, girls' visible development could attract danger, leading to precocious consensual sexual activity or what is now termed sexual assault. In the absence of a feminist critique of blaming victims and a lack of awareness of the frequency of incest and acquaintance rape, professionals and educators placed the burden on girls not to tempt sexually aggressive men and boys, usually imagined as strangers to their victims. The mid-century decades were a time of panic about sex crimes, and particular concern was directed at "child molesters" who preyed on young girls.[8] Sex education offered the hope that, given better education, fewer sex offenses would result. Equally as important was that girls learn to monitor their bodies and desires and cultivate heterosexual awareness, interests, and restraint.

Educators by the 1940s expressed the belief that students—female and male alike—needed knowledge. This was a shift from the early twentieth century, when, according to historian Kathleen W. Jones, girls' sexual knowledge was equated with "sophistication" and likely precocious sexual experimentation.[9] By the mid-twentieth century, educators believed that sex education would produce wholesome regard for sexuality and gender rather than untoward sophistication. Although educators in mid-twentieth-century public schools limited the amount of knowledge to offer girls and boys, they did not subscribe to the view that sexual knowledge led to sexual behavior. For them, misinformation was the cause of misconduct. Drawing on commonsense observations and popular literature by parents and psychologists such as Strang and Branson, public school sex educators employed varying degrees of straightforwardness and euphemism to offer education on selected topics.

The physical aspects of sexual development and reproduction, as discussed in the classroom, were not taught as unqualified biological facts. Intertwined with facts were beliefs about psychology, gender roles, and society. This chapter examines the ways in which sex education curricula presented human bodies and their functions, in particular the depiction of girls' and women's bodies. Composed of sections on sexual anatomy, masturbation and sexual arousal, menstruation, and reproduction, the chapter corresponds to narratives of growth and maturity that predominated in the curricula. Because sex education material did not always distinguish among biological processes, learned behaviors, and social norms, it is impossible to discuss their "scientific" content without analyzing the presentation of gendered norms. Although occasionally laden with male bias and lacking "objectivity" (albeit a fraught concept), information about the body and sexuality was more often contradictory than male-centered.[10] These contradictions are reminders of the effort expended to teach about sexuality in the service of constructing and reinforcing adolescent heterosexuality and gender norms.

Sexual Anatomy

Mid-twentieth-century sex education lessons pointed to the physiological changes that enabled human reproduction. Educators made choices about which body parts to discuss and what to call them. Further, they made decisions about the relevance of organs to individuals and society. Although discussion of sexual anatomy fed into a larger narrative about reproduction, instruction about puberty paid attention to young people's bodies and gender norms, treating both as facts of life.

Teachers aimed to convey respect for sexual anatomy and spoke in uninflected tones. Science classes were especially conducive to introducing vocabulary and facts, given their presumption of scientific neutrality. In Winnetka, Illinois, Russell B. Babcock, who taught sex education at a junior high school, took great care in the first few weeks of class to establish respect for scientific facts, repeating without embarrassment or emotion such terms as "'excretion,' 'reproduction,' 'sperm cells,' [and] 'ova.'"[11] Similarly, Eva Kirby, a Los Angeles biology teacher, recommended that science classes launch sex education lessons with a study of the urinary system—"an excellent place for the introduction of much of the vocabulary needed in the study of reproduction." The merit of this approach, she contended, was that it provided "understanding and objectification of the pelvic anatomy and physiology" from the outset.[12] Educators wanted to convey an impression of these body parts as worthy of discussion and thus discourage lewd or fearful associations (not to mention juvenile terms) that students may have acquired.

Through such matter-of-fact instruction, educators sought to shape young people's attitudes toward sexuality and gender during adolescence. Students could attain a positive and healthful relationship with their bodies through instruction by well-adjusted teachers and carefully selected teaching devices. Images as well as words could contribute to desirable—or undesirable— attitudes. Visual devices grew popular in mid-twentieth-century classrooms, and sex educators selected images, usually drawings and diagrams of human anatomy, from books.[13] They also screened animated films.

Anatomical drawings of external and internal reproductive organs provided a graphic component to sex education, but one that was abstract and generally truncated around the genital organs and therefore not graphic in a sexual sense. For the most part, drawings of pelvic anatomy objectified body parts and extracted them from a holistic view, thus providing little context for their location on the adult body. A rare exception was the Progressive Education Association's textbook *Life and Growth* (1937), which gave an unusual view of male and female bodies and their reproductive organs. Rather than depicting the organs in isolation, the drawings situated forms of bodies next to detailed sketches of organs.[14] It required great imagination, however, to make the vast majority of drawings correspond to human flesh.

Most illustrations drew inspiration from, if they did not directly replicate, the drawings and models of Robert Latou Dickinson, a gynecologist, sexologist, and sex reformer.[15] Although Dickinson's technically correct images were not produced for young audiences, they apparently satisfied San Diego educators' wish to instill "wholesome attitudes."[16] Enlarged versions produced by the American Social Hygiene Association were part of the teaching kit for San Diego teachers.[17] Whereas Dickinson's medical practice and research had sought to promote female sexual pleasure, that goal was no doubt lost on young pupils and their teachers; the drawings had other meaning in the context of a sixth-grade classroom.

As with other sex education endeavors, displaying visual representations of reproductive anatomy warranted consideration of their psychological impact. "As desirable as movies are for certain purposes," San Diego's G. Gage Wetherill maintained, "they do not lend themselves readily to discussion. They move so fast that it is difficult to discuss important points. When the movie is over, psychologically the children are often ready to do something else. Slides or drawings in our experience stimulate better discussion than have movies."[18] Perhaps sensitive to this concern, filmmakers loaned and sold copies of the Oregon movie *Human Growth* with accompanying slides.

According to many sex educators, the abrupt introduction of a discussion of sex organs and their functions could be psychologically damaging or potentially undermine efforts to instill wholesome attitudes. To avoid such results, Babcock first displayed charts of the nervous, circulatory, and digestive systems to his Winnetka students and then drew blackboard diagrams of reproductive organs, showing "their approximate locations." Aiding students' appreciation of these drawings was the fact that "already in a discussion of the excretory system the penis and vagina have been met," he explained.[19] Even in *Life and Growth,* when organs were shown in relationship to adult bodies, images were not prematurely introduced. Students had to wait until chapter 8 to see the illustrations.[20]

Sex education instructors selectively chose which anatomical parts to introduce, taking into consideration what they perceived as the psychological implications for adjustment to gender and heterosexuality. Individual schools sometimes developed their own visual material, but many teachers used existing diagrams and films.[21] Dickinson's diagrams of female anatomy labeled sixteen parts: sacrum, cervix, coccyx, vagina, rectum, anus, fallopian tube, ovary, fundus (upper end) of uterus, bladder, urethra, symphysis (bone), clitoris, labium minor, labium major, and hymen—a level of depth and technicality unnecessary for introducing sexual anatomy to sixth-graders.[22] Although accompanied by this illustration, the first edition of San Diego's "Growing Up" curriculum instructed those who taught sixth-grade girls to reference a smaller set of terms (vagina, rectum, uterus, bladder, and labia) as well as others not depicted or labeled on Dickinson's pelvic diagrams (breast, nipple, navel, buttocks, and bowel). For the male body, girls simply learned about the term penis.[23]

As a rule, both female and male students learned a more extensive vocabulary related to female bodies than to male ones. That is not surprising, given that the female anatomy would reappear in discussions of fetal development whereas male anatomy would not. Male and female bodies were, however, presented in a number of parallel fashions. Depictions of both were truncated above the navel and below the upper thighs; they were drawn to the same scale; and they both indicated a complex internal anatomy—contrary to the idea that women and men are opposite and that women's genitals are internal and men's external. That the two figures faced each other in perspective also vaguely suggested sexual union, but the flaccid penis and pelvic tilt in the diagrams would have made it difficult to envision intercourse even had the drawings appeared side by side.

The female anatomy that San Diego students studied in "Growing Up" was linked from the very first lesson with the production of babies, whereas the brief instruction about male anatomy did not mention reproductive roles. The difference reflected the limits of parallelism: Women's sexuality was necessarily linked to procreation in ways men's sexuality was not. Students learned about female sex organs, both internal (ovaries, tubes, uterus, and vagina) and external ("between her legs . . . two thick folds of skin known as the labia," which protected the urethra and vagina).[24] The lesson on male anatomy noted that the "testes are in a pouch of loose skin called the scrotum, which hangs behind the penis," and mentioned the function of the penis in urination.[25] Thus, the genitals of both sexes were, at first mention in the curriculum, linked with urinary function—as was the case in Winnetka and Los Angeles science classes. Initial instruction on female sex organs in San Diego also included reference to the uterus as "the part of the body in which the baby grows." Neither sperm nor eggs received mention in the first lesson of "Growing Up," but the text linked female sex organs to carrying a fetus, while the reproductive and sexual function of the penis went unnamed.[26]

"Growing Up" gave instruction on a small number of anatomical terms, unlike the large number shown in the Dickenson drawings. A widely cited volume on sex education from Minnesota recommended something in between. Developed by the state Department of Health and the College of Education at the University of Minnesota, the lessons were tested in local schools and adopted in a variety of places nationwide.[27] Although the San Diego lessons left out the vulva and clitoris in describing the female anatomy, the Minnesota book *Units in Personal Health and Human Relations* labeled them on diagrams and also offered lessons plans on how to discuss them.[28] With fewer labels, their drawings of male and female anatomy seemed less technical and therefore more suited for an adolescent audience than Dickinson's charts.[29]

Scholars have noted that sex education material and discussions have tended to omit information about the clitoris and female sexual desire, whereas discussion of boys' nocturnal emissions and masturbation described physical manifestations of sexual arousal.[30] Yet the authors of *Units in Personal Health and Human Relations* included the clitoris among the external and internal sex organs. Moreover, it was attributed no biological function other than being "equipped with very sensitive nerve endings" and "located just inside the upper junction of the inner lips of the vulva [defined in the preceding section of the lesson] . . . covered by a thin fold of skin . . . about an inch long and all but the head is hidden in the tissue."[31] The Minnesota plan is exceptional for its attention to the clitoris, especially because it is depicted as a sexual—although not reproductive—organ. There was no such parallel for male anatomy.

Acknowledgment of the clitoris did not entail suggestions about conduct; instruction on growing breasts did. Social responses—in the form of physical support and psychological appreciation—seemed to matter more than physiology in teaching about this aspect of female bodies. San Diego's lessons for girls noted visible changes in the female pubescent body (hair growth, voice changes, and breast enlargement, tenderness, and sensitivity), and the teacher advised that girls would need a brassiere to "support" their breasts at puberty—advice certainly not necessary for all or even most.[32] Yet buying and wearing brassieres became a ritual for adolescent girls and shaped their consumer practices and views of their bodies as much as developing breasts did.

For the most part, formal curricula did not teach boys about breast development in any detail. A simple acknowledgment, along the lines of ninth-grade boys' lessons in St. Louis, conveyed that it was nature's early preparation of future mothers for childbearing and breastfeeding. That piece of information sufficed for some, but St. Louis medical doctor Bert Y. Glassberg went further, commenting to male students that boys would sometimes "take a peculiar malicious kind of delight in making nasty, dirty, insulting, slanderous, disturbing remarks about the breasts of a girl who passes them in the corridor or on the street." Glassberg's lecture explained, however, that girls did not enjoy this attention, and well-informed boys "would find nothing about the breasts to make derisive, or unkind, or cutting, or slurring, or slanderous, or just plain dirty remarks that causes a girl to be uncomfortable and embarrassed."[33] The message was more about heterosexual gender norms than sexual function and was a rare intervention that called attention to, and critiqued, the objectification of girls' bodies.

While a few print materials and lectures ventured into the realm of sexual flirtation and harassment, the movie *Human Growth* kept its discussion of reproduction in stricter bounds of respectability. *Human Growth*'s animated film-within-a-film exhibits facts about sexual organs along with messages about conventional gender roles. The animated sequence is sandwiched between scenes from a classroom in which a female teacher displays appropriate sex education classroom etiquette; the entire movie is prefaced by a scene from a respectable home.

Echoing the perspective of San Diego's curriculum, the teachers' guide for *Human Growth* noted, "an approach which emphasizes interest in the GROWTH of human beings rather than the bald facts of reproduction is psychologically sound." To discuss "bald facts of reproduction" (a phrase that conjures images of naked bodies and intercourse) would potentially "incite curiosity and experimentation," something filmmakers hoped to avoid. Instead, the film provided "essential information" and promised to "satisf[y] in a wholesome way the child's need for an understanding of how life begins and continues."[34] Although information about the clitoris and breast support and appreciation was extraneous to the "essential information," prescriptive messages about gender and race were not.

Concern about the film's psychological impact is not surprising; Lester F. Beck, a psychologist, wrote the script, teachers' guide, and accompanying book. He was also no doubt instrumental in framing the movie around the family and the allegedly more wholesome aspects of growing up and reproduction. "Follow the lead in the picture," he advised in the teachers' guide; "emphasize the family life implications of the material." Facts alone were not enough to instill respect for sex, and teachers using the film needed to model appropriate behavior, much as did the actors who depicted the parents and the teacher.

The film's implicit messages, justifying and legitimating the exhibition of reproductive anatomy, occurred in the initial scenes. *Human Growth* opens with a scene from a white, middle-class home in which father, mother, and their two children, George and Josie, are enjoying an evening together in the living room. George reads a book about American Indians for school and shares aloud with his family the fact that "only the grown people have clothes on." He continues without hesitation or embarrassment, "It says here that until they were twelve or thirteen years old the children in this tribe wore no clothes at all. (*Reading*) 'The wearing of loin cloths and skirts was considered a sign of sexual maturity.'"[35]

The family setting reassures viewers of the film's respectability, but it does so by contrasting a "normal" and "civilized" white American family with the partially exposed bodies of Native Americans. Sexualized Native American bodies in the film hint at cultural variation in sexual norms but do so without calling special attention to white children's sexual anatomy.[36] In the tradition of *National Geographic* and other middlebrow magazines that show nudity in so-called primitive societies, middle-class parents were not likely to object to the exposure of unclothed Native Americans.[37] An instructional film for children, *Human Growth* has no resemblance to nudity featured in such contemporary magazines as *Playboy* and even the quasi-educational *Sexology*, but instead belongs to a Western, middle-class tradition of viewing classical artwork and images that inscribed a colonialist gaze.

Beyond this scene, depictions of bodies appear in simple drawings. According to a newspaper account of *Human Growth*, "The stylized drawings, screened in carefully chosen colors, do not have the detail of medical drawings and are warmly praised by parents who have viewed the film."[38] Male and female bodies are silhouetted and shown in cartoons, at first differentiating the sexes by gendered hairstyles and contrasting body frames rather than genitalia. Beginning with "two average babies, a little boy and a little girl," the male narrator describes how these infants would mature at different rates, indicating the moments when girls grow more rapidly than boys and appear more mature. A sequence of still images pairing the silhouettes provides imagery for the narrative, which describes the visible bodily changes from childhood to adulthood. "When they reach their late teens or early twenties they are fully mature people," the narrator maintains, "with the boy being appreciably larger than the girl."

Observations about growth, although articulated in a seemingly neutral and authoritative male voice, are subjective and influenced by culture as much as scientific facts. In discussion of the form of the body changing, growing up is not only about becoming larger but also about developing a new body shape. "The boy's shoulders are broader and his body more muscular, while the girl's body is more curved and feminine," observes the narrator. Although broad and curved are features that can be quantified and measured—and therefore possess some degree of objectivity—the references to "muscular" and "feminine" conflate biology and socialization. Muscular may be a trait boys ordinarily develop in growing up, but it is premised on physical activity. More revealing is the reference to girls' bodies becoming "feminine," a term meaning little more than "like a woman," implying, perhaps, soft and weak. Boys became muscular, girls became feminine—observations that stressed male activity and female passivity, learned gender characteristics.

The companion book to *Human Growth,* written for adolescents and published two years later in 1949, approached sexuality more openly and in greater detail—in part because it followed up on unanswered questions following screenings of the film.[39] The book also was more forthcoming in its discussion of bodies, sexual anatomy, and feelings because it had more space to elaborate and was intended to be used as a reference book for young people. Like the movie, it, too, reiterated gender conventions as facts of life.

The book's explicitness contrasted sharply with the film's oblique references to the ovaries, tubes, and vagina as well as to the "pubic region" that both male bodies and female bodies possessed. The book was, however, similar to the text of San Diego's "Growing Up" and Minnesota's recommended curriculum—both of which were available by the time *Human Growth* went to press. The decidedly unsexy and less familiar terms spoken in the film (ovaries, tubes, vagina, and pubic region) contrasted with the more interesting, familiar, and even sensuous terms in the book (legs, skin, lips, and groove), reflecting conversations with young viewers and, perhaps, filmmakers' boosted confidence in the film's success.[40]

When dealing with the female body in print, the book *Human Growth* was more specific about nonreproductive sexual anatomy and how one might identify female genitalia externally. The text defined the vulva as the "outside portion of the girl's sex organs, between her legs . . . consist[ing] of thick folds of skin known as the outer lips, with tissue underneath. A groove runs between these folds. Inside the outer lips there are thinner folds of tissue called the inner lips." Beck and graduate student assistant Margie Robinson acknowledged the existence of female sexual organs separate from discussing their role in procreation. They located the vaginal opening further back from the "opening for urination" and offered a tactile description of the vagina: a "canal four inches long, composed of stretchy muscle fiber with a rough texture."[41]

Providing youths with a vocabulary for human sexual anatomy usually involved more than learning to label body parts as though they were countries or continents on a map. Educators, in their perpetual efforts to instill wholesome attitudes and replace crude concepts with refined knowledge, did more than offer vocabulary terms in the various teaching devices. They taught about the location of sexual organs in female and male bodies, in some cases offering discussion of physical sensation and, in the case of the female, reinforcing associations between sexual anatomy and future procreation. The curricula were uninflected with negative associations such as sin and disease, but they also by and large omitted mention of sexual pleasure. Rather than celebrate the sexed adolescent body, instructional material educated young people to gain an abstract respect for their sexual organs and their supposedly natural correspondence with gender and normative heterosexuality.

Masturbation and Sexual Arousal

Educators explained the bodily changes that occurred in boys and girls during puberty as precursors to reproduction. Although only rarely did teachers indicate that physical changes produced sensations of sexual desire, they often linked puberty with interest in being around persons of the other sex—in other words, attending more closely to the heterosocial rather than the sexual aspect of heterosexuality. When masturbation was discussed, whether upon student prompting or as part of a planned curriculum, teachers tended to focus on the fact that the practice caused no physical harm (as had been believed in the past) but had potential psychological side effects that might impair marital happiness. Occasionally, classroom discussions and reading material illuminated the physical aspects of masturbating, but most attention was on its mental or emotional implications.

Only a slight percentage of schools offering sex education had written curricula that discussed masturbation, but it was an inevitable question of many young people, especially when anonymous questions were permitted. None of the questions in the movie *Human Growth* dealt with masturbation, for example, but that was not because Oregon youths differed from those in other places.[42] The film's creators hoped to evade controversy by avoiding topics that were sexually stimulating. They later explained that they deliberately chose to omit discussion of erection and masturbation in the first edition of the film for "reasons of expediency in accomplishing the over-all purpose of enlisting public acceptance of the very idea of sex education."[43]

When teaching material from the 1940s and 1950s did refer to or explain masturbation, there were a few orthodox ways of handling the discussion. The common point in all articles, curriculum guides, and resources for educators was the fact that the practice did not result in physical illness or deformity.[44] A related observation was that adolescents should not become obsessed with masturbating and be aware of social sanctions against it.[45] Mental and social— rather than physical—consequences were the risk.

In the course of discussions about masturbation, implicit assumptions about male and female differences sometimes emerged. Comparing boys' and girls' lessons reveals a gender-differentiated understanding of sexual arousal. Teachers were apparently more reluctant to discuss masturbation with girls. At Plainfield High School in New Jersey in the early 1940s, for example, plans for boys' classes paid more attention to the subject than did plans for girls' classes. Lessons for male pupils followed an outline that consisted of "Masturbation in Boy" ("definition," "effects," "treatment," and "comparison with girl") as well as "Masturbation in Girl" ("effects" and "treatment"). Meeting separately and studying a different curriculum, Plainfield girls learned about masturbation as a subset of a lesson on "The Male Organs of Generation." The teacher stressed that the practice was a habit rather than a disease and apparently said nothing about its relevance for girls.[46]

By the end of the 1950s, several sources indicate less discrepancy between boys' and girls' educations about masturbation. Plainfield's sex education lessons, offered through the physical education department and probably designed separately by a male and a female instructor in the late 1930s, seemed premised on the idea that girls and boys required different amounts and kinds of education; so, too, did the original version of San Diego's "Growing Up" lessons for sixth-graders. By the 1950s, instruction had become more equivalent. Whereas the original San Diego lesson plans from 1946 discussed masturbation only with groups of boys, lessons for both boys and girls included a discussion of it in the revised edition in 1951.[47] Mirroring the text for boys, the girls' lesson observed, "Some girls form the habit of rubbing their genitals to produce a pleasant feeling. This habit is known as masturbation."[48] The boys' lesson insisted that masturbation did not make a boy "'dirty' minded"; it also mentioned that the practice might cause lack of self-respect and prevent marital sexual adjustments.[49] The lessons were not identical; the narrative for girls omitted the allusion to dirtiness and conveyed ideas about loss of self-respect and risks for marital success in a fashion more concise than lessons for boys.

Lectures for ninth-grade boys in St. Louis distinguished between male and female propensity for sexual arousal. Glassberg explained to boys that "necking becomes a sexually stimulating experience to the young man [but not] to the young woman because there is a very considerable difference in the manner in which men and women are sexually aroused." Men would delight in touching the woman's body above the waist, he contended. "Most girls do not care for the experience," according to Glassberg, "but some of them are willing to submit to it because they believe it's part of the price they have to pay for the privilege of being taken out by such a wonderful hunk of a man as you happen to be."[50] Calling ninth-grade boys "hunks" stroked their egos, added humor (and, for some, embarrassment) to the lesson, and reinforced the concept of male privilege in dating. The lesson does not indicate the source of Glassberg's assertion that girls did not experience touching above the waist as pleasurable.

Glassberg maintained that eventually "petting arouses sexual feeling in the girl," without explaining how or why the process was less rapid.[51] Both boys and girls could eventually succumb to "the very powerful emotions which they have allowed to be set off within them," and Glassberg reminded pupils, as did other sex educators, that intercourse could lead to feelings of guilt and other unwanted repercussions, including pregnancy and disease.[52] Unlike most others who left records of their sex education work in schools, Glassberg took a firm and moralistic position against steady dating in addition to premarital intercourse.

Steady dating was more dangerous than masturbation in Glassberg's estimation, and yet he attempted to convince girls to be less uptight about the idea of sexual activity. Beginning a lecture for ninth-grade girls with a discussion of nonsexual drives such as learning and athletics, he moved to explain the sex drive, which involved "within the individual a feeling that he would like to express in some manner or other, certain things having to do with sex. But when we use the term drive," he noted, using male pronouns but probably intending both genders, "we must understand that there is nothing within the individual which is forcing him to engage in a sexual activity." He pointed out to the girls that humans have a variety of sexual drives, suggesting that individuals (not men and women) are different—and contradicting his lecture for boys in which he discussed differences in male and female arousal.[53] He ultimately conveyed that girls should set personal standards with regard to sex rather than mimic other girls, a nod to peer pressure's role in young people's sexual activity.[54]

Using motherhood as a point of entry, Glassberg went into greater depth about sexual matters with his audience of ninth-grade girls. He explained that mothers sometimes become disturbed by the ways in which their children fondle themselves but the process of discovery is natural and no cause for alarm. In fact, he maintained, mothers are likely to harm a child by calling attention to his or her self-stimulation. Innocent childhood sexual exploration in which boys and girls exhibit their genitals to one another is another opportunity for mothers to exercise restraint so children are not embarrassed or emotionally scarred by natural curiosity. A wise parent, he claimed, would simply let these interactions proceed, allowing the children's curiosities to be satisfied without interruption or self-consciousness. Even when discussing puberty with his audience of female adolescents, Glassberg advised them as future mothers. They were to inform their daughters about puberty before the onset of menstruation, using facts rather than myths and without hesitation or embarrassment.[55]

When he finally approached the subject of masturbation during adolescence with the girls, Glassberg spoke in great detail and claimed to be indifferent to whether a girl masturbated. He noted that some—but not all—"discover . . . that if they play with the sexual area of their body they arouse a pleasurable sensation within themselves." He explained that masturbation may be a temporary habit or practiced over "a very considerable period of time" but that in any case, no harm or injury would result that would detract from her ability to become a wife or mother. Moreover, a girl who did not masturbate should "know that the reason she does not engage in this practice is simply because she has no need to engage in it and she is not missing an experience which she ought to be having." Variation in girls' masturbation practices is wide, and there is no norm to which girls should aspire, he explained. Nevertheless, as a "highly individual matter," he noted, "masturbation becomes a tension relieving experience" and is sometimes used "to lessen some of the anxiety which we feel in the ordinary course of living." Whether girls masturbate, according to Glassberg, was "a matter of no consequence," although in his sole, brief caveat about masturbation's negative potential he mentioned that "sometimes it leads to worry about the practice itself."[56]

Similar to Glassberg's lectures, and yet unusual among printed sex education curricula of this era, San Diego's description of masturbation—"rubbing [the] genitals to produce a pleasant feeling"—amounted to an explanation of how to do it. Unlike Glassberg, San Diego educators took the position that young people ought to abstain from the practice. Although the pleasant feeling was not physically harmful, "Growing Up" lessons averred, it nevertheless "should be avoided," given the potential for such outcomes as guilt. Suggesting that girls would feel shame or lack self-respect if they masturbated, the curriculum's author, a school nurse, advised how to quit: choose the right friends, develop "high ideals about boys and marriage," eliminate irritation of genitals ("as may be caused by lack of cleanliness or uncomfortable clothing"), and keep busy with a variety of hobbies.[57] San Diego lessons also emphasized emotional changes and sexual sensations that accompanied adolescence, such as a girl feeling "stirred or thrilled when a boy she admires is with her." Rather than addressing methods of dealing with the feelings, San Diego teachers were to advise students to control such urges as they would anger or fear.[58]

Taking a different approach, the Minnesota unit for sex education in grades six, seven, or eight included detail about sexual arousal in conjunction with physiology. Following a description of the development of reproductive organs, the text provided answers to the question of what problems might arise for young people as they mature physically. The unit noted a number of emotional and physical reactions, including interest in the other sex and the advent of "sex tensions." Among the "various ways of reacting to sex tensions" were "daydreaming about romantic situations," erotic dreams during sleep, and masturbation.[59]

Daydreams, sexual dreams, and masturbation were nothing for young people to trouble themselves about according to the Minnesota curriculum. Daydreaming, the authors pointed out, is alright as long as it does not become a substitute for participating in social and recreational activities. Dreams with sexual content are involuntary and occasional, they explained; for boys, the dreams might include nocturnal emissions and for girls they may involve "being embraced or kissed by boys" and "sexual sensations." Young people should remember, the text continued, that the dreams are "a normal part of the growth process, and no one should feel ashamed or guilty because of them." Masturbation is "practiced by both boys and girls," the authors noted without judgment.[60]

The authors of Minnesota's curriculum described masturbation in neutral and fairly explicit terms. Masturbation, or "self-stimulation of the sex organs by manipulation," they elaborated, usually proceeds to a point at which "in the male the penis becomes erect and the seminal fluid is expelled, and in the female until the sensations reach the climax known as orgasm." The somewhat vague reference to manipulation omitted methods of self-stimulation, and there was no mention of women's genitals becoming lubricated. Yet their use of the term *orgasm*—a word rarely encountered in literature on sex education during this period—was noteworthy because it applied to female sexual satisfaction. Such an explanation may have been commonplace in sex advice books for married adults, but it was extremely uncommon in books for pubescent girls and boys.

Despite the use of neutral terms to explain masturbation, clues indicate that the authors did not intend to promote the practice to students. A multiple-choice question at the end of the unit asked them to identify masturbation with one of the following phrases: "A. sometimes causes insanity; B. is a good way of taking care of sex tension; C. is not physically harmful." The key indicated that C was the correct answer. Of the incorrect answers, A was definitely discredited by the curriculum, but B was a choice that had not been contradicted by the lessons.[61] In fact, the only "objection to masturbation" expressed in the unit "is that the individual who practices it may become satisfied with this method of responding to sex impulses and never establish normal heterosexual relationships." Creators of the Minnesota curriculum may have believed this to be an adequate deterrent for young people—or perhaps they felt there was no legitimate reason to dissuade them from the practice as long as it did not interfere with normal heterosocial relations. The Minnesota text advised recourse to hobbies and alternate activities in desisting masturbation, as had the San Diego curriculum. Not quite as nonjudgmental as Glassberg's lectures in St. Louis that gave girls license to masturbate if they felt like doing so, the Minnesota authors neither mentioned losing self-respect nor insisted on exercising self-control. The recommendations for alternative activities were there "*if* a young person who masturbates wishes to discontinue the practice."[62]

Arousal and desire, as discussed in a small number of sex education texts and lessons for use in schools, involved a significant amount of variation and choice. In that context, some material suggested the existence of gendered differences in what triggered sexual feelings and physiological differences in sexual organs as well as differences in social behavior between girls and boys. Yet discussions of masturbation tended to offer a common theory of the practice to both boys and girls. In keeping with the mental and psychological focus of the era, the "sex tensions" discussed in that material had little to do with anatomy and procreative potential and much more to do with individual inclination. Masturbation and sexual arousal, although infrequently part of the planned curriculum in the 1940s and 1950s, contrasted with anatomical knowledge that was essentially tied—especially for girls—to reproductive ability. In these lessons, students acquired a glimpse of a sexual realm pertinent to their adolescent bodies and, to some extent, independent of procreation and marriage.

Menstruation

If masturbation brought attention to adolescent sexual feelings, menarche was a reminder of how girls' bodies were preparing them for procreation. In addition, menstrual education attended to the hygiene and emotions surrounding menstruation and promoted heterosexual self-consciousness and femininity. Menarche signified growing up and leaving childhood, typically occurring at a time when bonds among girls were expected to weaken and heterosexual interest to develop. Educators approached the topic of menstruation with as much attention to girls' psychology and heterosexual orientation as to their comprehension of physiology. In modeling femininity and teaching discretion about menstruation, they failed to distinguish their undertakings from commercialized and sexist perpetuation of menstrual taboos and stigmas.

Schools that taught human reproduction in biology classes would briefly touch on menstruation, in many cases through screening *Human Growth*. The biology or life science instructor, however, was not a key figure in menstrual education. Instead, schools placed lessons in physical education and health courses and in some instances in home economics courses—situations in which girls were ordinarily separated from boys and where the subject was likely to arise. Teachers in those classes hoped to promote modern, hygienic methods of regulating girls' bodies internally and externally. They taught the importance of proper diet, regular bowel movements, rest, and exercise as well as the use of commercial products to guard against stains and odors.[63] Of all teaching about the body, menstrual education most warranted a female teacher—someone who understood menstruation firsthand and whom girls would trust to listen to their fears about their "secret," a euphemism promoted by Kotex advertisements in the 1940s.[64]

Although the Victorian taboo against discussing menstruation had partly subsided, the topic remained secretive in many ways. The commercialized, "American way" of menstruating in the twentieth century necessitated discretion.[65] Print advertisements and drugstore displays of disposable hygiene products, beginning in the 1920s, brought menstruation to the public's attention and initially served as a means for raising girls' awareness. While educators pointed fingers at neglectful and ignorant mothers, they, in conjunction with product manufacturers and advertisers, did their part to perpetuate silences about menstruation. By the 1940s, education departments of menstrual hygiene product manufacturers took more assertive measures to reach girls and offered free pamphlets in the hope of building consumer loyalty.[66]

At the forefront of education about menstruation was an unlikely duo—cartoon designer Walt Disney and Kimberly-Clark, the manufacturer of Kotex menstrual hygiene products. Disney and Kimberly-Clark's collaboration on the 1946 film *The Story of Menstruation* had a tremendous impact on menstrual education in schools. Distributed free of charge, *The Story of Menstruation* found its way into classrooms across the country. Ideas from the movie—and promotion of Kotex products—circulated even further via the pamphlet *Very Personally Yours*.[67]

Employing animation to describe the biological process known as the menstrual cycle, *The Story of Menstruation* was for menstrual education what *Human Growth* was for teaching about physical growth and reproduction. Viewed by 105 million girls and young women, the movie was in use for more than thirty-five years.[68] It was unusual in its use of a woman narrator, and among its other "feminine" features was an appeal to Mother Nature and an abundance of pink imagery. Menstruation was apparently a delicate subject best discussed in the company of women. A comparatively small number of boys viewed *The Story of Menstruation* in sex-segregated or coed classrooms, but the film was intended to reach the likely consumers of Kotex products.[69]

When Kotex manufacturers accelerated their educational agenda with *The Story of Menstruation* in 1946 they launched not only a more aggressive advertising campaign but also an intervention into the perceived maternal inadequacies of women who had come of age in the 1920s. Filmmakers explicitly intended the movie to supplant old-fashioned views and practices related to menstruation, particularly the use of homemade protection. Conveying how to use purchased products became a regular part of menstrual education in schools around the country. By the early 1950s, lessons for San Diego girls, for example, included demonstration of how to use a sanitary napkin and belt, how long to wear a pad, how to purchase them at school from a stock in the teachers' toilet room, how to carry them around, and how to dispose of them at school and at home.[70]

As much as trying to inform girls about the physiology of menstruation, the movie and other material attempted to shape attitudes about menstruation. Citing students' favorable reactions to the film, advertising copy from 1947 proclaimed that "fear and superstition are banished in the light of scientific fact. And common-sense rules for physical and mental health take the place of rumors and taboos."[71] The company recommended to teachers that above all they "clarify to the girls that menstruation is a normal function, one to be accepted as a matter of course."[72] Yet educational material presented contradictory messages about menstruation being natural and simultaneously cause for secrecy and special conduct.

Although educators were committed to scientific edification, they highlighted the importance of discretion when advising about menstrual cycles. Although boys and men should be informed about menstruation in the abstract, they need not know specifically when a girl or woman was menstruating—and teachers helped girls strategize on how to keep their cycles private. By avoiding the topic in heterosocial peer culture and at the dinner table they could avoid offending boys or men or embarrassing themselves. In the company of girls and women, such as in a girls' physical education or health class, privacy and circumspection was apparently unnecessary.

Kotex manufacturers offered etiquette advice as well. One example was a response to a sample student question about boys peeking into purses and finding pads. The teachers' guide for *The Story of Menstruation* recommended that the product should be "either wrapped in a tissue or protected by an envelope partly" for hygiene purposes and to avoid potential embarrassment. In another example, they counseled girls on how discretely to opt out of swimming or dancing (supposing they did not feel up to it) during their periods. The guide insisted that learning to decline an offer politely was a skill "we all have to learn." The answer did not mention honesty about one's feelings, nor did it recommend using a tampon for swimming, but instead validated menstruation as an excuse for sitting out of activities.[73] In an ideal scenario, they suggested, boys would intuit that the excuse was about the girl's period and not press the issue.

Ninth-grade boys in St. Louis heard similar advice in Glassberg's sex education lectures. The talk with boys explained that "girls frequently ask me how I can let my boy friend know that I'm menstruating." Glassberg shared that he had "assured the girls that you would come to know without being told, because I agree with the girls, this is a private, personal matter."[74] Acting as a mediator between boys and girls on this "private, personal matter," Glassberg further suggested that boys should be understanding, respecting a girl's wishes to decline invitations "not because she's ill but simply because she feels less well during these few days of the month than she ordinarily feels."[75]

Glassberg and other educators gave inconsistent messages to young people: Menstruation was ordinary and yet it required special conduct. Noting in his lectures to male audiences that their mothers also had menstrual cycles, Glassberg recommended that a boy be agreeable to take care of chores and demonstrate thoughtfulness at that time of the month, which would make a mother "extremely glad that she had a son like you." He continued that future wives would appreciate their spouses' extra consideration during menstruation. With that advice, boys stood to "make these women, your girl friend, your mothers, or your wives far more appreciative of you as a man than they could possibly be if you were ignorant of, or oblivious to, these profound changes taking place in the body of the woman."[76] This commentary conveyed a sense of women's emotional fragility while bleeding; moreover, it gave the impression that men's and boys' consideration for women could lapse during the rest of the cycle.

The view that girls and women needed special treatment during their periods thrived in spite of teachers' insistence, as in San Diego, that periods were no big deal. "I don't want to hear one of you girls say you are sick or having your sick period. It is not a sick period. It is a perfectly normal part of living and growing up."[77] If so, why did menstruation warrant secrecy and discretion? Why did boys and girls did not ordinarily learn about the topic together? Why should girls refrain from activities or need extra consideration during "that time of the month"? The idea that periods were disabling and disgusting persisted into the mid-twentieth century even as teachers claimed otherwise.

Advice on remaining cheerful, staying fresh, maintaining good posture, and minimizing frustrations during menstruation were all part of *The Story of Menstruation*. They were illustrated by animation featuring a pretty little white girl demonstrating ideal ways to conduct oneself during menstruation—as well as what to avoid. Don't slouch, don't sob in front of the mirror because your hair is full of tangles, but do stand tall, admire your reflection in the mirror, and go about your day. Such attractive, feminine behavior as communicated in the movie brings approval in the form of a wink and smile from the sun. In offering advice about grooming, behavior, and social norms, menstrual education, like sex education in general, combined messages about gender conduct with information about puberty and sexuality.

When they discussed menstrual hygiene and appropriate gender conduct, educators were attuned to psychological adjustment—and that concern for psychology played a role in presenting biological facts about menstruation as well. Just as *Human Growth* avoided a "bald" presentation of facts, *The Story of Menstruation* placed its facts in a package intended to comfort girls. In the process, educators sometimes misrepresented the truth in a seemingly squeamish way. In anatomical drawings of female sex organs, which explained the cycle of ovulation and menstruation, filmmakers presented menstrual blood as white. The teachers' guide for *The Story of Menstruation* explained a "definite purpose" in the filmmakers' decision to do so: "Pretesting, using the normal color, red, to demonstrate the discharge, revealed that the audience reacted unfavorably to the red. So, for psychological reasons, white was used."[78]

Perhaps they felt the association of red blood with injury and pain was too graphic for young audiences. To their credit, the makers of *The Story of Menstruation* instructed teachers to point out that the discharge is actually red. Yet without real explanation, certain facts were withheld as though they were too vulgar for an audience of young girls. Such "common sense" seems to have been shared by the creators of *Human Growth,* who also avoided red in depicting menstruation. Both movies were color productions in which the filmmakers selected white to represent menstrual flow. Although *Human Growth*'s narrator indicated that a little blood is lost while the uterine lining is shed, the film did not acknowledge its misleading imagery.

In other instances of abandoned realism in *The Story of Menstruation,* filmmakers coddled girls with simplicity, apparently in the interest of their psychological adjustment. As a reviewer explained, the "ghastly effect of a re-alistic rendering [of female bodies] was avoided" and neat diagrams adopted instead.[79] Whether this was a pedagogical concern or a marketing decision, the attempt to insert pretty imagery rather than scientific realism reflected and reinforced gender prescriptions.

Not surprisingly, the film employs metaphors to convey a "story" about how and why menstruation occurs. Recalling the impetus to eliminate su-perstition and instill faith in a scientific understanding of the menstrual cycle, the choice of cartoons and stories is interesting. Although the birds and bees are not invoked per se, a number of metaphors are taken from na-ture as well as modern imagery of a rationalized society. Mixing metaphors and allusions shows creators' concerns for young people's imaginations and psyches as greater than their quest for scientific accuracy.

Changes in San Diego's sixth-grade curriculum suggest that teachers sought to present bodily processes related to menstruation with greater objectivity. They may have second-guessed the need for metaphor and personification in telling the facts. In the 1946 edition of "Growing Up," the pituitary gland's "control-center" delivers "messages through the blood stream to the ova-ries." The second edition simply stated that upon puberty girls' bodies begin to produce mature ova.[80] Other language changes indicate a move toward straightforward terminology and away from imaginative phrasing. Originally, students learned that eggs "ripen"; by 1951 the message was that eggs "mature." Initially, they learned that the eggs "die"; by 1951 *disappear* was the preferred term.[81] In the revised version, the word *maturity* is more fitting for human tissue than *ripening,* a term more commonly associated with fruit. Rather than invoke the death of eggs—which might suggest abortion, miscarriage, or being rotten—eggs' disappearance is less troubling.

With such changes, San Diego curricula departed from *The Story of Menstruation* and its dramatic, storytelling approach. In the movie, the pituitary gland is likened to a message control center, the ultimate authority being Mother Nature. According to the female narrator, Mother Nature commands bodily functions "through automatic control centers called glands."[82] Taking metaphor and personification to an extreme, *The Story of Menstruation* portrays Mother Nature as giving "orders," hormones as "busy little messengers," and the pituitary gland and ovaries obedient participants in a passive female body.[83]

If one compares the narrative frames for menstruation in girls with erections and ejaculation in boys, it becomes clear how significant gender was in conveying these facts about sexed bodies. Although it is problematic to assume that menstruation and seminal emissions are parallel events (only one is associated with orgasm and pleasure), they do share the characteristics of beginning during puberty and eliminating sex cells from the body. San Diego lessons treated menstruation and seminal emissions as parallel processes to a certain extent, given that both involve discharging bodily fluids through reproductive organs. They are also alike in that any major instruction on the topic occurred in sex-segregated classrooms, based on an assumption that most adolescents experienced them with some level of confusion, shame, and embarrassment.

Both menstruation and nocturnal emissions were called "natural" in the San Diego lessons, but rather than sperm cells dying or disappearing—language used for eggs—emissions were described as "a natural way by which the body disposes of the excess fluid."[84] In the same lesson for boys, teachers explained menstruation in conjunction with its larger implications. Teachers were guided to say that "since the girl is *too young* to have married and mated, there is no sperm to meet the egg and start it growing to be a baby, so it stays in the uterus for a little while and then passes out through the vagina."[85]

The language "Growing Up" used to describe menstruation suggested that somehow it is more problematic than seminal emissions. Menstruation as a loss or injury appeared in the original San Diego lesson plans, working at cross-purposes with the effort to persuade students that it is perfectly normal. Teachers were to explain that the uterine lining would gradually heal in preparation for the next month's menstrual period.[86] The revised curriculum did not mention healing but referred to a rebuilding of the lining, a mechanical rather than organic metaphor but nevertheless suggestive of a problem to be fixed.[87] Such language was absent in discussions of seminal emissions and wet dreams.

Menstruation education was, in many ways, an extension of providing children with proper bathroom etiquette, but it possessed greater implications for heterosexual adjustment. Advice about hygiene predominated, indicating how girls could remain in good taste, avoid offending others—especially the other sex—and be feminine during what teachers insisted is a natural process. In spite of their commitment to removing the superstition surrounding it, educators perpetuated silences and euphemisms about menstruation, perhaps because they personally retained the belief that it is repulsive.

Among the contradictions of menstrual education was an attempt to supplant ignorance with objectivity—an agenda undermined by lessons that focused on secrecy on the one hand and Mother Nature on the other. Menarche and participation in heterosexual activity may not have coincided in many girls' lives, but menstrual education linked starting one's period to femininity and attraction to boys. Educators associated the advent of menstruation with girls' increased attention to their appearance and acceptance by boys, and, in *The Story of Menstruation,* linked menarche to a fun-loving and active heterosocial lifestyle. The film and other educational material acknowledged procreative capability but put the capacity for it into the future, after marriage. Meanwhile, the material encouraged girls to be self-conscious and self-regulating in their pursuit of hygiene and heterosexual attention. As mid-century menstrual education trained them to comply with heterosexual gender norms upon menarche, knowledge about the menstrual cycle receded to the margins of a narrative primarily about gender and sexual conformity.

Reproduction

Whether educators designed the instruction for mixed-sex audiences or for sex-segregated classes, boys and girls learned about reproduction in much the same terms—how a sperm cell meets an egg cell and begins the process of creating human life. "Sperm are deposited close to the mouth of the uterus," the San Antonio, Texas, teachers' guide for senior high school classes explained in response to the question, "How is the egg fertilized?"[88] The school's unit on "Reproduction: The Story of the Beginning" initially pointed out that parents are involved in reproduction and claimed that fathers are responsible for the child's sex. Yet the discussion of how pregnancy occurs left out any mention of humans, bringing the mother back into the picture only when the fetus had begun to grow in her womb.[89]

Reproduction narratives in mid-twentieth-century sex education were generally heroic and full of normative prescriptions, metaphors, and euphemisms. Also replete with metaphors, women's failure to conceive resulted in menstruation, which was discussed in much less glorified terms. Teachers described successful conception and prenatal development as a triumph of human biological capacity. San Antonio's lessons went so far as to proclaim reproduction as the "closest thing to divinity that man [sic] possesses."[90]

Vagueness about men and women's roles in procreation detracted attention from the people—more specifically, the sexual activity and potential pleasure—involved in intercourse. The emphasis, after all, was on reproduction rather than sexual stimulation or climax, which must have left students very confused about taboos surrounding reproduction and sex education. The narrative of reproduction focused on the union of egg and sperm cell, anthropomorphizing sex cells as though characters in a fairy tale. Similar to what feminist anthropologist Emily Martin discovered in her examination of college textbooks of the 1980s, the "romance" preceding the union privileged male sperm as active and female eggs as passive, mirroring stereotypical gender roles and heterosexual courtship norms.[91]

Young viewers may have blinked and missed it, but *Human Growth* did imply that married adults who participate in the act of "mating" instigate the birth process. Without defining the term or explaining the act of mating, the film left students to read between the lines, or make connections to previous lessons in animal biology, if they wanted to understand this all-important sex act. The film, however, continued apace with its story of "how life begins," moving directly to the drama of sperm and egg. In the question-and-answer portion, the teacher praises Alan, a student, for correctly answering the question of when human life begins with "when a sperm cell enters an egg cell." The cursory mention that the father's sperm cells "pass from the penis into the vagina of the mother" was, by the end of the film, an insignificant detail in the process of human reproduction—no doubt a move intended to desexualize the film.

Educators chose metaphorical language and avoided the topic of intercourse—and sometimes conveyed inaccuracies—in teaching adolescents at various stages of primary and secondary education. Classes for primary and junior high schools from Illinois to California relied, for instance, on de Schweinitz's children's book *Growing Up*. Before 1947, this book, in obvious defiance of truth, claimed that intercourse only occurs in the context of love between married women and men. The author deployed the sperm-and-egg story but alluded to human agency.[92] Avoidance of discussing the "sex act itself" worked best with older adolescents who surely had gathered some knowledge of the subject, as an account of a twelfth-grade family living course at an Indianapolis, Indiana, technical high school indicated.[93]

The Story of Menstruation's narrative was especially evasive about intercourse, although it drew attention to the "story of the egg."[94] In fact, the movie never mentions sperm cells in describing conception. Pregnancy occurs, the narrator explained, "when a woman is going to have a child." It is the egg that is impregnated—not the woman—making the woman an invisible participant in her own pregnancy. In the teachers' guide to the movie, sample questions pertained exclusively to menstrual hygiene and conduct, including such concerns as the "normal" amount of flow and length of the period, whether girls should use tampons, and what activities are permissible during menstruation.[95] Altogether left out of the teachers' guide were questions and answers explaining what human behaviors caused pregnancy.

Omission of information, however, did not preclude students from pursuing answers to questions about sex. Most mid-twentieth-century sex education classes included a question-and-answer session, often through anonymous question boxes. Students had an opportunity, then, to obtain information left out of the film and question the content of class presentations and movies. A report from Hillsborough County, Florida, for instance, indicated that most queries following a screening of *Human Growth* were about the baby, but students also insisted on learning about intercourse. Teachers were regularly asked, "How do the male cells get into the female?"[96] Those who followed the suggested responses from the book *Human Growth* explained, "The sperm cells pass from the penis into the upper part of the vagina. This happens during mating, or intercourse. In mating, the penis becomes stiff and hard, so that it can fit naturally into the vagina."[97]

The questions and answers in *Human Growth* explained that intercourse does not always result in pregnancy and that some children are born to unmarried mothers. To convey moral standards, the authors pointed out social norms and encouraged young people to identify with the infant and child born out of wedlock rather than the adults engaging in nonmarital sex. Offering an adult perspective, the book noted, "From time to time all human beings who have reached sexual maturity feel the urge to mate with the opposite sex. This urge can lead a young man and woman to mate before they are ready to marry and establish a home. As the result of such a union, a baby may be born." The response then shifted focus from the adults to society and unwanted children: "Since our society disapproves of unmarried parents, not only must these parents face the disapproval of society, their child must also face it. Moreover, because these unmarried parents are not prepared for the responsibilities of a home and family, they are not able to give their child the care and love all children need."[98]

The queries dropped into school question boxes in San Diego likewise acknowledged students' ongoing pursuit of answers about sexual acts or perhaps their amusement at forcing adults to address such topics. They also reveal that San Diego educators were willing to provide some information about intercourse and sexual pleasure. Given that the "Growing Up" curriculum—especially in its revised edition—circulated as a model of how to teach sex education, it is noteworthy that San Diego included questions about sex and answers to them. "How do sperm cells get out?" the students wanted to know, and, "How long does the penis have to stay in the vagina for the sperm to enter the mother's body?" (indicating they already understood that the penis had to be inside the vagina for mating to occur). "Do men and women," they also inquired, "mate just when they want to have babies?" and "What is another word meaning mating?"[99]

San Diego sex education leaders adopted a relatively straightforward approach to responding to questions about sexual activity, although they, too, sometimes lapsed into moralizing. Two examples illustrate the straightforward, factual approach. Before sperm cells exit the penis, they explained, the organ becomes erect; "muscular contractions squeeze the sperms and semen into the tubes and out of the penis."[100] "Not very long. Perhaps only a few minutes. The time varies" was the suggested answer to the question about how long the penis remains inside the vagina during intercourse.[101] These answers attended to biology in matter-of-fact ways but steered clear of sexual feelings.

Inserting reverence for marital heterosexuality—and therefore morality—into the discussion, the answer to the question of why adults have intercourse echoed de Schweinitz's emphasis on love and marriage. The text finessed the issue of nonmarital sexual activity in a manner more evasive than the *Human Growth* book. "Growing Up" guided teachers to answer questions about when intercourse occurs with, "A father and mother may love each other very much, and mating is one way of showing their love."[102] Regarding synonyms for mating, the guide first answered "sexual intercourse" but followed with the explanation, "There is also the common four-letter word which we often see written on the walls of toilets. It means to mate, but it is a cheap and ugly word." The text further pointed out that children who did not know proper terms for sex used the four-letter word because they lacked "the right information" and knowledge of "how wonderful" the birth process is. "Any boy or girl who really understands how life begins would not want to make something cheap and ugly of it by using vulgar words or drawing vulgar pictures."[103]

Other curricula took a similar approach to defining intercourse. As the 1947 Minnesota guide explained the term, "The penis of the male is inserted into the vagina of the female in order that the seminal fluid containing sperms may be deposited where the sperms can enter the uterus."[104] In St. Louis, the phrasing with which Glassberg explained intercourse to ninth-graders was "in the sexual relationships of marriage the penis of the husband is introduced into the vagina of his wife to deposit sperm cells at the mouth of the womb."[105] The striking similarities in phrasing suggest that authors built on each other's texts, an explanation further supported by bibliographical citations.[106] Glassberg's reference to the womb's "mouth," however, reveals idiosyncratic wording that may have mystified the topic for students.

Minnesota's blueprint for sex education elaborated answers to more specific questions from young people, taking risks absent from the other curricula. The senior high school unit provided answers to questions those students might ask. Among them, "Can a doctor prove that a girl is a virgin?" involved discussion of the hymen. The response observed that assuming "that a girl is not a virgin simply because the hymen is absent or has been broken" is wrong.[107] Another question regarded a "safe period" when intercourse would not result in pregnancy, and yet another brought up the question of abortion. The suggested answers involved reference to studies that "indicate that fertilization may take place on any day of the menstrual cycle." Mention of abortion included reference to both "natural causes" and surgical procedures; surgical abortion, the authors noted, was illegal "for reasons other than the protection of the mother's life or health."[108] In a lesson suggested for senior high school or junior college, Minnesota educators recommended discussions of "erogenous zones" as well as three phases of intercourse, "preliminary love play," "the act of copulation," and "relaxation," among other sexual topics. Given that other authors declined to suggest such explicit information, it is highly improbable that the discussions occurred other than in a few scattered classes.[109]

Yet some curricula moved toward greater openness, taking a gentle approach so as not to upset the delicate psychological balance of appreciation of—but not premature indulgence in—intercourse. San Diego's approach continued to use the euphemistic de Schweinitz text into the 1950s, even as Wetherill and others acknowledged the more explicit questions that troubled young people. What, then, did it mean that the revised edition of "Growing Up" included a "Sex Relations" section in 1951? It was not an explicit discussion of facts but rather a great deal of moralistic proscriptions. Like the book *Human Growth,* "Growing Up" discussed the unloved, unplanned child. One should abstain from premarital intercourse, the text explained, so as not to produce a child who lacks the mother and father that "every family needs." Sex relations before marriage "almost always" cause "unhappiness," the lesson maintained, and potential pregnancy and "heartache" would be likely results. Sliding into moralizing, the lesson proclaimed that "if boys and girls really want to do what's right, they will be strong enough to control themselves and not take the chance of causing so much unhappiness."[110] At this point a brief mention of syphilis and gonorrhea further contributed to (and concluded) the discussion of sex relations and potential "pain and suffering."[111]

This discussion of so-called sex relations was not the last word on sex in San Diego's "Growing Up" curriculum. The sixth-grade lessons ended with a question-and-answer session, including anonymous questions, and there was also group counseling for junior and senior high school students. In group counseling, the topic of sex relations would again emerge, and peers could assert varied perspectives based on personal experience. Some of the more explicit topics contained in *Units in Personal Health and Human Relations* were potential subject matter, especially given group counselor Geneva Gordon's estimation that it was "a real text, the first good, usable one to appear."[112]

Most sex education courses did not include contraceptive information, although a surprising number discussed family planning. Whether it was the idea of family limitation or, more specifically, practices that controlled procreation remains unclear. Evidence is lacking over whether teachers discussed specific contraceptive devices or methods, but mention of family limitation would undoubtedly have prompted questions about how (and perhaps why). Those who felt such information was inappropriate included members of Michigan's State Department of Public Instruction, teachers at Arsenal Technical High School in Indianapolis, and individuals associated with the Denver, Colorado, city schools.[113] Minnesota authors explained that their state law prevented them from discussing contraceptive devices.[114]

Instruction related to contraception nevertheless occurred in a variety of educational contexts. Having engaged in limited discussion with his seventh-grade science classes in Winnetka, Babcock reported that he told students "that there is medical knowledge available from doctors which makes it possible for parents to control the size of their families." This, he maintained, was adequate information for students at that level.[115] A couple of classes had planned discussions of birth control, including family relationships courses in Tulsa, Oklahoma, and something called "units in bio-social relationships" at a public high school in Greeley, Colorado.[116] A survey of Pennsylvania public schools in the early 1950s noted that fewer than 20 percent of respondents with formal sex education programs covered planned parenthood, usually in separate boys and girls classes at the twelfth-grade level or in girls' home economics classes.[117] That percentage translated to forty schools, a small proportion of 477 replies the researchers received but nonetheless a notable number.

"Growing Up" considered the possibility and implications of sexuality outside the context of marriage and reproduction in a lesson that was to a great degree about physiology. It, like other material from this era, conveyed information—and misinformation—for supposedly psychological purposes. In providing information about sexual reproduction, educators were in a bind. How could they instill appreciation for intercourse in marriage or guide young people's attractions toward the other sex and yet discourage sexual activity? Educators relied on the premise that unhappiness is the likely outcome of premarital sex, as "Growing Up" insisted, and employed the psychological concept of adjustment in adolescence as well as marriage.

Conclusion

Female bodies and their relationship to the reproductive process were at the center of biological teaching about sex. But biological teaching contained as much "information" about gender expectations and conduct as it did about the physical body. Education about the sexed body—especially women's bodies—gave confusing and contradictory information to girls. In some cases the information was altogether inaccurate, and in many instances relevant information was omitted. Even as educators wanted to fortify girls with knowledge about their bodies, sexist distortions and omissions were common in sex education lessons.

When *Human Growth*'s teacher/actor beckons students who watched the film to ask any questions they wish, the onscreen questions reveal a degree of classroom decorum and wholesome curiosity that educators no doubt hoped viewers would emulate. The film's question-and-answer sequence encourages questions focused on reproduction and childbirth; it remains silent on intercourse and other sexual matters. According to the Hillsborough County report, discussion following screenings of *Human Growth* involved "answering all questions asked with respect and interest so the students will feel it perfectly proper to ask any kind of question they might have in mind."[118]

Was any question really "proper"? "Children throughout the county ask the same questions," the report's author noted, perhaps offering reassurance that question-and-answer sessions did not enter risqué territory. "The baby is the center of interest—freaks, disease, blue babies, sex, color of hair, twins (especially Siamese) are all discussed."[119] The report alleged that students inquired about the film's central emphases: sperm, eggs, fetuses, and infants. Other questions were no doubt voiced, although teachers ignored or minimized them in promoting sex education.

The perspective of *Human Growth* not only elided matters of sexual behavior but also rendered women passive or sometimes absent, even in the postconception stages of fetal development. Pupils' outside exposure to pregnant women might have led to curiosity about the female body, yet during the film's visual depiction of pregnancy and childbirth, the silhouette of the adult woman fades into the background. Meanwhile, the narrator describes the birth process from the perspective of the fetus. In essence, the film's narrative scripts a view that focuses on the infant and, to some extent, changes during puberty but steers viewers away from questions about adult women, men, and sexuality. Inquiring students nevertheless posed questions that educators might have wished to avoid.

Intercourse was neither the climax nor the main event of mid-twentieth-century sex education. The narrative of growth instead drew attention to the creation of life, often couching conception in celebratory terms and regaling students with pictures and stories of animal and human babies. Growth was a process that involved everything from puberty to childbirth, and educators sought to instill a wholesome regard for nature's plan and the responsibilities of "civilized" society. Curricula stressed both physical and psychological aspects of puberty, including the development of sexual organs and menstruation as well as their accompanying emotional consequences. In rare cases, they approached the topic of sexual pleasure.

Gender and heterosexual normativity, which guided boys and girls to become husbands and wives and fathers and mothers, was a common thread in discussions of sexual anatomy, masturbation, menstruation, and reproduction. Girls and women were rarely absent from the narrative of growth, but their relative insignificance compared to sperm, eggs, and fetuses sometimes displaced attention from girls' actual bodies onto diagrams and charts and stories of courting sex cells, yielding objectification if not objective facts. Yet the San Diego, St. Louis, and Minnesota plans—and offshoots of these sources—extended the potential for a more honest and relevant, if contradictory, discussion of anatomy, growth, and physical processes related to sex.

As they taught about the physical aspects of sex, teachers exposed young people to multiple ways of thinking about the body. Biology, health, and psychology were among the frameworks for presenting, maintaining, and modifying heterosexual gender norms. Mid-twentieth-century sex education curricula wavered between straightforward information and euphemism and complementary or parallel gender roles and asymmetrical gendered responsibilities. This perplexing set of viewpoints in sex education left girls (and boys) in a position to wonder about the contradictory "facts of life."

5

Gender and
Heterosexual Adjustment

"The emotional and social factors involved [in sex education] are of equal if not greater importance than the child's acquisition of information on the physiology of sex and reproduction," explained the authors of "The School's Responsibility in Social Hygiene Education" in 1940. "So conceived," they argued, "sex education is an inseparable part of the education of the total personality of the child."[1] In fact, teachers devoted a large proportion of the time spent in sex education and family living classes to matters that were only remotely connected to the physical body. As was especially apparent in teaching about menstruation, lessons often provided more advice about conduct and mental health than about physiology. Learning about the body, the sexual organs, and their reproductive capacities was one facet of learning what it meant to acquire maturity. But it was sexuality's mental and psychological components—how young people imagined and enacted gender and sexuality—that was at the heart of instruction and discussion in the public schools of the 1940s and 1950s.

During the mid-twentieth century, adolescence was perceived as a critical moment for adjusting to sex, gender, and heterosexuality. Educators sought to channel young people's interests according to gender, but they did not wish to turn interest in gender and sexuality into preoccupation or prurience. "To accept one's physique and masculine or feminine role" and "to develop new relations with age mates of both sexes," the Detroit, Michigan, source book for family life education in the late 1950s posited, were the first two "developmental tasks" of adolescence.[2] Accepting sex differences, or the distinctions between being male and female, was crucial to building an individual identity and wholesome relationships between the sexes during adolescence. Courses aimed at adolescents conveyed how gender roles and relationships with the other sex were significant to mental health as well as future life choices. Educators prepared young people to pursue marriage and parenthood, and they were prone to treat the nuclear family, consisting of a married couple and a few children living apart from extended family, as the ideal and norm. Their representations of married couples with children contained racial and class subtexts, idealizing the masculine and feminine features of white, economically advantaged men and women.[3]

This chapter explores how sex educators presented what they called "sex differences" as well as "boy-girl relationships"—topics linked to sexuality but more clearly about gendered behaviors and heterosexual identity. I maintain that educators exalted normative femininity, masculinity, and heterosexuality as tools for resolving the concerns and problems of adolescents. Teachers promoted adjustment to contemporary gender norms and heterosexuality in hopes of reducing individual anxieties among students of diverse backgrounds. In the process, they infused the curricula with a psychological framework that privileged adjustment and maturity but acknowledged a variety of experiences and realities. This psychological framework thus empowered young people to develop their individual personalities and preferences, but it invoked the fine line between "normal" gender and heterosexual interests and the extremes of disinterest or obsession. Teachers wanted to encourage respect for femininity, masculinity, and heterosexuality but sought to avoid making the realm of sexuality too enticing.

Although conservative beliefs about gender and heterosexuality pervaded classroom material and circumscribed teachers' perspectives, sex education's psychological bent helped weaken moral and biological absolutes.[4] On the one hand, sex education curricula's language of psychology, personality, fulfillment, and purpose encouraged girls' development of subjectivity and autonomy and therefore stood to empower girls. On the other hand, heterosexual gender roles and social ideals of the dominant culture, especially by the 1950s, prescribed a limited range of options for teenagers, in particular girls. As school material alternated between reinforcing the status quo and offering new options, girls gained opportunities to formulate their futures. Independent living and college campuses offered freedom for exploration and dissent in the 1960s, fueling the decade's sexual revolution.[5] Yet the possibilities for questioning sexual and gender norms emerged in earlier decades, and earlier in the life-cycles of mid-twentieth-century girls, through an unlikely source: public schools.

Femininity

As an ideal, femininity is a form of gender performance; women and girls are not inherently feminine but earn the label through enacting certain behaviors, many of which relate to outward appearances.[6] Along with contemporary feminist theorists, many sex educators in the 1940s and 1950s would have agreed that biology does not produce femininity but that social forces and personal efforts create it.[7] Mid-twentieth-century sex and family life educators saw femininity as variable and socially and culturally constructed, but they did not fully abandon biological explanations and hormonal motivations for feminine behavior and appearances. Unlike many late-twentieth-century feminists who argued that femininity was oppressive to women, students and teachers in mid-century classes tended to valorize it as an attribute that would contribute to a successful heterosexual future. In some instances resembling mass-market periodicals aimed at female consumers, self-help and self-improvement advice was rampant in sex and family life education curricula, especially material aimed at girls.

Sex education lessons contained both explicit and implicit messages about femininity, many of which derived from contemporary popular culture and psychological theories. In its most literal sense, "femininity" referred to traits belonging to women, but more commonly in sex education and popular usage the term encompassed acquired, culturally specific characteristics. Neither expressive of innate womanly charm nor simply a matter of possessing a female body, femininity entailed a certain kind of cultivated womanhood. A blend of conventional poise and mannerisms with commercial sexual allure, femininity in the 1940s and 1950s merged the attributes of white, middle-class respectability and glamour.[8] Popular magazines and cinema—and later television—helped recast femininity during the early to mid-twentieth century, building on the style young working women developed at the turn of the century.[9] Despite the efforts of working-class white women and women of color to fashion their own version of femininity, white, middle-class affluence and taste epitomized the feminine ideal. Teachers encouraged girls from lower-income families to seek beauty in their terms, disregarding financial constraints and the relevance of "ethnic" physical attributes for many.

Educational material identified anatomical as well as cultural and social components of femininity and masculinity. With regard to female and male identities and relationships, there were few facts and definitions to learn, and the preferred teaching method was discussion questions. The book version of Oregon's sex education movie *Human Growth*, for example, contained a glossary that defined "feminine" as "like a woman; having the qualities of a female" and "masculine" as "like a man; having the qualities of a male." Young readers learned in this book and elsewhere, however, that not just any characteristics of women and men counted as feminine and masculine.[10] Presuming that most people (even adolescents) knew what made a woman feminine and a man masculine, educators still felt compelled to teach young people to cultivate and respect such differences. They did so in several ways: showing correlations between physical and emotional changes during puberty; offering guidance on attitude, hygiene, grooming, and conduct; and modeling appropriate gender roles.

Educators taught junior high school classes that physical and emotional changes occur simultaneously. The body as well as emotions contribute to preparing young people for continuing the cycle of human growth and reproduction. Films instructed the adolescents that puberty and growth are natural, and the feelings accompanied by it are normal. If physical and emotional maturity did not harmonize perfectly during adolescence, *Human Growth* and *The Story of Menstruation* provided hope: Girls and boys could align their bodies and their feelings as they grew to be heterosexual adults.[11] Among the steps in that process were understanding puberty and reproduction and appreciating—but not exaggerating—the differences between the sexes.

To reassure adolescents and guide their development, educators offered advice for growing up, suggesting as incentives personal satisfaction as well as heterosexual success in dating and ultimately in marriage. They believed that visible secondary sex characteristics and menstruation could be troubling for young people emotionally and psychologically and adjusting to physical changes was part of becoming an adult. As the movie *Human Growth* phrased it, the development of secondary sex characteristics "usually make the boy feel more manly and the girl more womanly, which are perfectly normal feelings." At least that was the ideal scenario. Young people were supposed to begin to think of their bodies and selves as "manly" and "womanly," or masculine and feminine, in keeping with their biological sex. Such attributes were inseparable from heterosexual attraction; "manly" implicitly meant attractive to women and "womanly" attractive to men.

Illustrating the rewards more clearly, the Disney film *The Story of Menstruation* put a fairy-tale spin on its advice to girls. When the narrator admonishes, "Don't be droopy," she is referring to both standing up straight and not drowning in self-pity. Instead, girls learned that they should adjust their posture and develop a positive disposition. The application of cosmetics was one place to start. As a girl applies makeup onscreen in front of a mirror, the narrator points out that it is a good idea to "keep looking smart and well groomed to give you new poise and lift your morale." A feminine appearance and pleasing demeanor during menstruation were thus strategies for adapting to physical maturity. In another sequence a tearful girl who is frustrated with her tangled hair demonstrates a remedy for the situation. The narrator's advice to "stop feeling sorry for yourself" motivates her to become perky; she smiles, admires her new and improved reflection, and abandons the mirror for a dance with a young man.[12]

The movie's exhortations taught girls to downplay or disguise any physical or emotional discomfort experienced during menstruation, as historian Margot Elizabeth Kennard has argued. *The Story of Menstruation,* according to Kennard, suggested that "the solution to emotional changes is to put on a smile and change your attitude so other people in your life will not be affected by your unpleasant feelings."[13] "Changing a 'bad' feeling into a 'good' feeling so those you have to live around won't be affected" may have been one effect of this attitude adjustment, but not all potential interpretations of the film were degrading to girls.[14] It did, for example, acknowledge that they might experience physical or emotional discomfort.

Sex educators wanted to promote a healthy attitude toward menstruation, unencumbered by fears or anxiety. In this vein, the movie attempted to "minimize the mental handicap which hampers so many girls during their periods," as one reviewer commented.[15] Puberty was supposed to mark the onset of feelings of a heterosexually charged femininity replete with anticipation of dating and marriage, and self-pity could hinder those feelings and self-worth in general. While teaching girls to manufacture "good" feelings when they really felt bad verged on encouraging duplicity, filmmakers offered knowledge, advice, and sanitary hygiene products to minimize discomfort.

Mid-twentieth-century educators did not view menstruation or puberty as having deleterious effects on learning, as had some nineteenth-century predecessors.[16] But some effort to moderate activity during the menstrual period was a good idea, they claimed, as at any other time. *The Story of Menstruation* suggests that girls ought not to feel set back while menstruating in terms of being able to concentrate on schoolwork or perform regular daily activities—although nothing in extremes. Femininity in adolescence did not entail passivity or relegation to the domestic sphere, but neither did it grant girls and women license to live large or accentuate their sex appeal. The warning concerned taking activity too far. "When you come to think of it," the narrator reminds the audience, "most of your daily routine is on the mild side." Presuming that viewers were well-behaved girls, the narrative implies that moderation in athletics and social activities was the norm for girls at any time of the month, erasing altogether those who worked or played hard and stressing a middle-class code of docile gendered behavior.

Psychological problems and social adjustment plagued both adolescent boys and girls, judging by the material presented in sex and family life education classrooms, and all were counseled to gain control over unwieldy emotions. But there was no menstrual hygiene counterpart, no whimsical cartoon character modeling appropriate roles for boys in sex education films. The most comparable adjustment was perhaps learning to deal with nocturnal emissions and daytime erections and ejaculation. No films, however, were devoted to hygiene or advice in these areas. To be masculine, in part, was not to need such guidance.

Teachers and instructional material joined other media in fostering the development of femininity and masculinity from the onset of puberty, especially through guidance about attitude, hygiene, grooming, and conduct. As San Diego's "Growing Up" curriculum suggested, a well-adjusted adolescent gained emotional security by possessing pride—but not conceit—in his emerging manhood or her developing womanhood. Commenting on the implementation of sex education lectures in Lansing, Michigan, for instance, physicians Harold A. Miller and Robert S. Breakey noted that "the developing boy or girl should be led to feel pride rather than shame in his or her sexual characteristics and capacities."[17] Moderate satisfaction with one's sex and gender, in other words, could serve the aims of marital and heterosexual stability, whereas shame (repression) or audacity (libertinism) were threats to so-called normal adjustment.

Successful achievement of femininity could be a means to reduce awkwardness and curtail erratic behavior, the archetypal struggles of adolescence that had been linked to sexual development in the Western imagination since the beginning of the twentieth century.[18] To some extent, this required creating and fostering self-confidence and self-respect. Unemotional appreciation of the value of masculinity and femininity, educators thought, would bolster the confidence of adolescent girls without encouraging self-indulgence or premature sexual exploration.

An appreciation of masculine/feminine differences was not the exclusive terrain of girls; boys were also taught to value sex differences and what they contributed to heterosexual love and reproduction. A San Antonio, Texas, curriculum guide for family life education from the early 1950s showed how appreciation was imperative for both sexes. In mixed-sex classes, San Antonio teachers aimed to "help the student to understand the basic differences due to sex; to promote tolerant understanding of, and appreciation of the values in, the differences between boys and girls."[19] The latter type of appreciation reveals how gender differences were not distant features of adults but a framework relevant to how young people viewed themselves and their peers.

Just as San Diego schools offered what its curriculum advisors called an "appreciation lesson" on the process of reproduction, attempting to instill awe in young people about the beauty of nature's plan, their lessons also encouraged what contemporaries would call a "wholesome" recognition and appreciation of masculinity and femininity. Such appreciation, although generally based on physical anatomy and outward appearance, was not meant to vary with body size or the speed of development. Not so flexible as to permit girls wearing boys' clothing or vice versa (unless a girl was wearing her sweetheart's jacket), there nevertheless was some flexibility in masculinity and femininity. Classes acknowledged that boys and girls expressed gender along different timetables and in varying degrees. "Growing Up" lessons conveyed to boys' classes that masculinity is available to all and that penis size is not a measure of masculinity, nor is breast size indicative of femininity. "Small sex organs do not mean that the boy is less masculine than the boy with large sex organs," the guide instructed teachers to tell their classes; variations of breast size, the lesson plans contended, are also "normal differences."[20] Boys and girls experiencing anxiety about rate of growth or current size ought not to fixate on those aspects, lessons suggested, but consider the bigger picture: the cycle of human growth and the development of heterosexual interests in preparation for marriage.

Teachers invoked references to proper hygiene habits and self-awareness as practices also applicable to femininity. Boys and girls grew attentive to appearance as they developed feelings of manliness or womanliness, many materials purported.. According to *Human Growth,* boys shaved and combed their hair and girls coiffed their hair and applied lipstick. The book supplement to the film added that along with puberty came girls' "new interest in clothes" and desires to "experiment with a touch of lipstick or fresh-smelling cologne." "All this attention to how one looks," the authors wrote with regard to girls only, "is another stage in the process of reaching adulthood."[21] Without explaining why, the text asserted that self-awareness and concern about appearance, especially among girls, was to be expected.

Attempting to guide students' acceptance of teenaged and adult gender identities, teachers stressed that early- to late-bloomers and every size and shape between could achieve femininity or masculinity. Yet the insistence on this point suggests that at least some girls and boys were not readily convinced—and that success was relative to other variables, including race. Even though sex education material linked anatomical growth and gender socialization and touted conventional femininity as available to all, white girls and women, especially those with fair complexions, more easily achieved the ideal. One physical aspect of becoming an adult woman, *Human Growth*'s authors explained, was the development of hair on arms, legs, and, in some cases, the face. Facial hair was likely to be more noticeable on the upper lip and sides of the face among "girls with dark hair and skin." The book reassured girls that such hair growth should not concern them; it also continued to promote femininity as a state of mind rather than a measurable bodily feature. Alluding to white girls, the text pointed out, "This does not mean, however, that brunettes are any less feminine than blondes—body hair on the latter just doesn't show as much."[22]

Even as the book denied that certain adult features were more or less feminine, the authors reiterated contemporary ideals and supposed norms. In mentioning hair removal as an option elsewhere in the text, they contradicted the premise that having body hair does not detract from femininity. If naturally occurring features of the female body were considered within the realm of femininity, hair growth would require no special attention. And since *Human Growth*'s authors asserted that all women experience hair growth, for instance, it might logically be construed as characteristic of women and therefore feminine. Yet facial hair, more pronounced and socially acceptable in men, carried an unmentioned masculine association. Furthermore, women's practices of hair removal, noted in the book, suggested that many struggled against their bodies to be feminine—an inconsistency that must have been apparent to some girls. Seeking to encourage something between neglect and obsession about the body during adolescence, educators forwarded advice about hair removal to inquisitive female students.

Shaving was a rite of passage once boys entered puberty, but grooming facial hair, like the hygiene of seminal emissions, required no formal guidance. Although a Cleveland, Ohio, nurse teaching girls' personal hygiene, for example, discussed armpit hair removal methods, most girls' management of body hair did not warrant teacher input. Special techniques, however, were necessary for those unfortunate in having hair crop up in abundance or the "wrong" places.[23] "There are," the authors of *Human Growth* advised, "various ways of removing superfluous hair from the face and limbs. Hair can be plucked, cut, or even shaved—but before attempting any of these remedies, it is very important for a girl to consult her parents, the health teacher at school, or the family doctor, who can suggest the best ways to remedy unattractive facial hair." The book instructed boys, too, on removing unattractive hair, but their instructions were more terse and straightforward, suggesting that a boy should start shaving "whenever his beard starts to look unsightly."[24]

Recommended grooming rituals, a subject of discussion in both single-sex and mixed-sex classes, centered on gendered assumptions about self-perception and self-esteem. Scenes in *The Story of Menstruation* in which the girl studies her reflection in the mirror convey more than fixing one's hairstyle; they replicate advertising and popular culture's emphasis on glamour, especially so-called natural beauty. In matters of appearance, adults and peers expected adolescent girls to strike a balance between ostentation and heedlessness, which in turn encouraged them to remain perpetually aware of their looks but not to the point of vanity. In Virginia Milling's English class in Newark, New Jersey, boys offered suggestions to girls about how to win dates, illustrating peer ideals about girls' appearances. The suggestions implied that the ideal girl should carefully monitor her self-presentation to cultivate a desirable feminine appearance. She should exert some effort to maximize her beauty but not go to excess (no excessive makeup, no public application of makeup, no lipstick smeared on her teeth, and no lip liner); not wear "too much jewelry" and only "delicate" earrings; and appear in "well-chosen clothing," with slacks explicitly excluded.[25] Where, when, and how she made up her face and selected clothing and jewelry conveyed whether a girl was attractive and datable or unfeminine, gaudy, and overdone. Such prescriptions encouraged girls to base their dating potential—although not necessarily their self-esteem—on their looks.

Puberty demanded that young people—again, especially girls—pay closer attention to their behavior as well their hygiene and appeal. As educational theorist Robert J. Havighurst explained, boys' adjustment to the masculine role was "so easy to achieve that it hardly appears to be a task at all." Girls, however, needed more coaxing because there was "often much more hesitation among normally well-adjusted girls to assume the usual feminine role." Such hesitation, he maintained, derived from the belief that during adolescence women became "definitely the weaker sex" and also "attractive to men, and thus gain one kind of power while losing another."[26] The feminine role, then, entailed loss of strength and ability (relative to men) and newfound heterosexual allure. Applying such theories to educational practice, Havighurst asserted, "The school can *help girls to think through the problem of accepting the feminine sex role,*" which was one of the functions of sex and family living courses.[27]

A variety of courses, health- or relationship-based, promoted the idea that embracing feminine or masculine behavior was crucial to overcoming the psychological hardships of adolescence. Health classes in Oregon, for example, included study of the "development of heterosexuality," "sexual development and personality," and "sex as related to the mental-emotional problems of adolescents."[28] The family relationships course in Toms River emphasized psychology and behavior. Students in family living, social behavior, and even English courses at Toms River and elsewhere engaged in activities in which they established peer standards for adolescent appearance and conduct, particularly dating. Guided by teachers, students generated checklists for how adolescents could become popular—an attribute contingent on possessing appropriately feminine and masculine characteristics.[29]

Contributing to multiple and sometimes contradictory standards of conduct were the warnings and suggestions that teachers gave girls on other subjects, including contact with strangers and physical vulnerability. Warnings verged into the territory of "negative" sex education, and most educators preferred to emphasize a more uplifting view, as with the carefree cartoon girl in *The Story of Menstruation*. And yet, teachers, who wanted to talk sensibly with young people about sexuality, would have been remiss not to acknowledge the reality of girls' and young women's vulnerability to assault, rape, and pregnancy. Very little was said about perpetrators or consensual male sex partners in this regard; instead, girls learned that they had an extra responsibility to exercise self-control. The lesson plans for the first edition of San Diego's "Growing Up" classes, for example, instructed teachers to relay a story about "Jane," whose mother wanted to protect her from venturing out at night among young men in the military.[30] The message of the story was that girls should be careful and obey their mothers, not that men should exercise restraint.

Some references to protecting girls in "Growing Up" alluded to the health and safety of breasts and genitals, information that could be interpreted as protecting precious assets or sensitive areas of the body. In the first edition's first lesson for both girls and boys, teachers were to point out that brassieres protected the breasts from injury.[31] In this instance the warning was unnecessary. Teenaged breast injuries were not especially common, and the more usual justification for brassieres was to supply shape.[32] Also vulnerable (for unstated reasons) were girls' genitalia, the labia said to "protect the two body openings" of the pubic area in the second edition of "Growing Up."[33] By comparison, protective language was entirely absent from lessons plans related to boys' bodies and behavior. When they learned about the foreskin of an uncircumcised penis—an anatomic part with a relatively similar protective function to labia—no mention was made of its protective role.[34] The boys' lessons, like girls' lessons, mentioned keeping out of trouble but not with reference to protection.[35]

Conduct advice was not always gendered or based on a double standard, but often classroom material (and newspaper and magazine articles brought into classrooms) articulated different rules for men and women and boys and girls. Courtesy, for instance, was a trait to be admired in both sexes. Yet particularly in the realm of dating and engagement, male and female participants faced different expectations. When Newark students listed desirable traits, they labeled girls as objects (a "date-girl") whereas boys were described as subjects (an "escort"). According to peer-developed standards for dating, boys were obliged to deal with money and make decisions and girls were supposed to be pleasant companions.[36] "Acting like a boy" or seeming "hard boiled" were traits high school boys disliked in girls in Morely, Michigan— demonstrating that peers (specifically, boys) were more likely to criticize tomboyish traits than were teachers.[37]

As in dealing with most topics in sex education, teachers avoided focusing on aberrations when discussing femininity. Perhaps because they recognized the varied paths along which girls developed into heterosexual maturity, teachers typically did not include discussion of tomboys in lesson plans. Discouragement of girls who were tomboyish or resisted adopting feminine ways during adolescence was remarkably absent from planned sex education and family living curricula, including San Diego's lessons plans, Oregon's movie and book, and Toms River's course workbook. Especially given the extent to which femininity was tied to heterosexual attraction, and given teachers' belief that young people's heterosexual interests developed at different moments during adolescence, being a tomboy was likely interpreted as a form of arrested development that would correct itself with guidance and encouragement rather than criticism. Furthermore, precocious development of heterosexual interests in girls seemed more alarming to educators than reluctant development, although they worked to discourage both overeager and undereager heterosexual pursuits.[38]

On occasion, norms of conduct and gender roles were featured as static— emanating from an inner essence of men and women or acquired and fixed by adulthood—but more frequently teachers acknowledged fluctuation. Most obvious was the incremental and relative development at the individual level, but dialog about historical changes in gender roles of the white middle class were also part of a number of sex and family life education courses. These expanded roles removed some of the stigma for girls who found traditional feminine roles difficult to accept because, as Havighurst noted, they wanted a career and sought the freedom, power, and independence granted to their fathers and brothers.[39]

The increasing numbers of women who worked outside their homes became a topic of discussion in mid-twentieth-century classrooms.[40] Force's family living textbook from the mid-1950s indicated, for instance, that young women confronted a broader set of choices than had previous generations. The "Modern Girl's Dilemma" contrasted a contemporary white woman with an old-fashioned one; the pensive and ambitious female graduate who considered multiple options replaced the demure young woman in Victorian dress, pursuing a single road to marriage and motherhood. At the top of the modern girl's list of options were marriage and (relatively fewer) children, but three of the five roads led to a career, as represented by a large desktop with ink pen, telephone, and paper (absent was a typewriter, suggesting white-collar, not pink-collar, work). Although a career without marriage and children was one choice, its image was sparsely decorated and at the bottom of the list.[41]

The gulf between male and female roles became somewhat narrower in the middle decades of the twentieth century, and teaching devices sometimes reflected or even celebrated such change. In Force's text, the Victorian woman wears clothing that accentuates and embellishes her curves, whereas the modern woman's curves (if she has them) are disguised by her graduation gown. What marks her as a woman are her haircut (relatively short but bouncy and feminine), legs and shoes, small hands, and pearl necklace. She appears confident and serious, as would befit a middle-class high school or college graduate. Intended as a text for classes of boys and girls and circulated in communities that were likely more diverse than Toms River, the book invited readers to identify with the modern female character. Force, who had a career and no children, validated white, middle-class women's choices and changing opportunities.

Yet not all depictions of women's roles acknowledged choices. *Human Growth* depicted women's employment as ephemeral and slighted education while granting motherhood a position of prominence in the few frames of the movie focused on adult lives. Illustrating the narrative about life events accompanying sexual maturation, a male figure is shown with cap, gown, and diploma. Female and male forms are shown at work, but the narration "when they have completed their education [and] have steady jobs" is accompanied by images of a gendered workplace in which the man holds a professional job and the woman a subordinate one. Throughout the film, most women are shown as mothers and caregivers responsible for nurturing children.

Not intended as a point of discussion, the pictures in *Human Growth* are nonetheless striking for what they conveyed about women's place in the work-force. The image of a typist indicated women could pursue employment outside the home within certain parameters. In the drawing, a woman sits before a typewriter, her stiff form outlined by a fitted blouse and skirt, her arms extended toward the keys, and her legs exposed under the table. The man at the adjacent desk (solid and six times larger than the table on which her typewriter rests) leans to the side, occupying more space and signifying authority and comfort. In addition to representing a gender-segmented labor force, the illustration gave clues about how body posture and display factored into masculinity and femininity. Work and life outside the domestic sphere, as represented by the supposedly universal white woman, was temporary, somewhat awkward, and less relevant to an adult female identity than was motherhood.

Although teachers and texts sometimes circumscribed the available options for women, the ideas about femininity conveyed in classrooms enabled preteen and teenaged girls in sex and family living courses to develop opinions about certain conventions, including motherhood and heterosexual intimacy. Whether the prescriptions were subtle or overt, in the form of visual images or narrative passages, delivered as constructive criticism or positive reinforcement, rarely did questions of emotions, attitudes, hygiene, grooming, and conduct receive univocal responses. After all, the classes taught young people to value and accentuate their individuality.

As prescriptions about femininity make clear, however, compulsory heterosexuality was at its core. Contemporary women could more easily shake the necessity of bearing children than the imperative to participate in—or at least envision—dating, engagement, and marriage. The notion that feminine identities demanded an admiring male audience must have been difficult to resist, but a sense of self premised on a psychological rather than a physiological foundation helped open space for girls to question and imagine something different.

Heterosexuality and Gender Complementarity

Highlighting the virtues of femininity and masculinity, the differences between women and men, and male-female relationships, sex and family life curricula linked and reinforced gender and heterosexuality. Heterosexuality was not under siege during this period, but the parameters of normative heterosexuality were undergoing redefinition. The publication of the Kinsey reports, alarm about sexual "deviance" and juvenile delinquency, and rising divorce rates signaled a changing society in which sexuality appeared more mutable and transgressive than in the past.[42] How could educators make heterosexuality attractive, but not too attractive, to young people?

Fundamental to educators' understandings of sex differences was the union of male and female in marriage, a union that was both idealized and discussed in practical terms. The idea that marriage maximized the collaborative potential of complementary male and female traits was not unique to sex educators or to the era but reflected ideas in ascendance for decades past.[43] Teaching this understanding of gender and marriage to captive audiences of adolescents and teenagers through public schools, however, was new. The rise in divorce rates during the mid-twentieth century did not lead sex and marriage experts to conclude that marriage was becoming obsolete. Rather, they considered it to be a formula for successful integration of male and female characteristics and personalities, successful only when both parties made an informed commitment to the relationship.[44] Marriage was beleaguered in the mid-twentieth century, they thought, but not beyond recovery. By preparing young people for marriage, teachers encouraged students' consciousness of male-female roles and differences. Whether the emphasis was on difference or compatibility, and whether the foundation for differences was biological or cultural, teachers heightened students' attention to the significance of gender in adolescence and adulthood.

The contrast between male and female identities taught students to position themselves with their respective gender. Teaching devices geared toward mixed-gender classes, whether at the junior or senior high school level, tended to employ this comparative approach; the contrast appeared in visual representations and written (or spoken) terms. The first page of the adolescent development unit in the guide for family living from Detroit, Michigan, for instance, showed a boy and girl of high school age, holding hands. Exaggerating physical differences, art teacher Carl Owen's line drawings feature a rectangular-shaped male torso and an hourglass female figure. The teens sport a jacket (his) and skirt (hers) of matching pattern, and both appear white-skinned and fair-haired. But the resemblance ends there. The girl's waist is extremely narrow, but her shoulders, arms, legs, and buttocks are rounded; the male's shoulders, arms, and legs are rendered in straight lines, with the jacket covering his buttocks. In a gentlemanly fashion he carries the books and papers. Her arm, a bangle bracelet around the wrist, extends away from her body, and she is empty-handed.

The curricula also emphasized increasing complementarity between boys and girls as they reached adulthood. One figure in Force's *Your Family, To-*

day and Tomorrow renders the path toward marriage as one of growing compatibility, a progression illustrated by the image of a ladder. On the first rung, the sequence begins with "group friendships, no pairing off." That is followed by "group dating, crowd activities and fun, and no pairing off," and then "double dating, two or more couples sharing dates" for teenagers. The fourth rung, "single dating or going steady," is for "later teens near the adult line," and "engagement and marriage" "for mature people only."[45] Near the apex of the figurative dating ladder, teenaged couples maintained—yet also bridged—their differences through heterosexual romance, according to such illustrations.

Downplaying opposition and competition between the sexes was one way educators sought to reinvigorate matrimony. Sex and family life education reinforced differences between boys and girls, calling attention to male-female differences not so much as oppositional but compatible. The cliché that "opposites attract" was not, they believed, a sound foundation for marriage and sex education classes because it suggested the potential for marriage across such differences as race, ethnicity, class, or religion. Teachers often cautioned against "mixed marriages" between individuals of different religious backgrounds.[46] As Force noted, "Opposites sometimes attract, but strong marriages are built on similarities—in family and financial background, in religion, in education, in age."[47] Yet open-ended discussion questions, with no right or wrong answers, undermined the authority of such prescriptions as the dating ladder and cautions against mixed marriage.

As much as sex educators used terms that now seem conservative, they often viewed themselves as less traditional than other educators. Advocating a contemporary "liberal" perspective on gender—"that men and women need to accept each other as individuals with different capacities and potentialities"—sex education consultant Lester A. Kirkendall explained in 1951 that such a viewpoint departed from what he identified as two earlier understandings of gender. He maintained that feminist contentions that men and women were "exactly alike" and traditional beliefs about "opposite" sexes were losing favor. Enlightened individuals, he posited, "realize that each sex has an important and unique contribution to make to family and social life."[48] The perspective that Kirkendall articulated informed the sex and family life curricula of many mid-twentieth-century public schools.

Teachers possessed varying opinions about the nature of sex differences, which were, some believed, derived from nature or God-given. Others maintained that differences were established through culture. Most appear to have adhered to beliefs that straddled the spectrum. This question was not, however, a subject of major contention or discussion. Less concerned with origins and explanations of gender than outcome, sex and family life leaders leaned toward what is now called a "social constructionist" view. Kirkendall phrased the ideal attitude to convey in sex education as "a flexible, equalitarian [sic] regard for individual personality and an acceptance of the unique values of sex membership."[49] Being male or female was akin to being (or becoming) members of a particular club, relishing the perks and benefits that accrued to what he dubbed each person's "sex membership."

Complementary male-female relations reinforced a male-female division of labor. In response to the question, Why does a woman develop such a different shape from a man? for example, *Human Growth* referred to men's productive and women's reproductive capabilities. The book explained that as a girl grows, her body changes: "her hips become broader and her abdomen longer than those of a man in order that her body may have room for a baby. Her breasts fill out so that when she has given birth, she may provide her baby with milk." Male bodies are endowed with different capabilities and obligations, according to the text. "Men's bodies are able to perform heavy work, such as digging and building. For such activities they have broader shoulders and stronger muscles."[50] A remarkable flaw in this logic is that most men did not do heavy labor in the mid-twentieth century, and many women took on "men's jobs" with great success during the war. Despite a historically shifting relationship between gender, class, race, and work, however, the text seemed to uphold an ahistorical and universal gendered division of labor.

Some curricula conveyed how biological differences allegedly yielded compatible male-female needs and emotions. "Are there differences based solely on the fact that some people are born boys and some girls?" lessons queried in San Antonio. "Are boys treated differently in the home from girls?" "Should boys be treated differently?" "Should you be glad you are a boy or a girl?"[51] Such questions, and their affirmative answers, contributed to the unit's objectives to "stimulate thinking about actual ways and means of getting along better with himself [intended as a gender-inclusive pronoun], his family, and his girl or boy-friend" and inculcate appreciation and acceptance of gender differences. The teachers' guide itemized four categories in response to a question regarding the differences between boys and girls: physical, mental, emotional, and spiritual. According to this text, boys are larger and stronger than girls; boys and girls are of equal intelligence but boys react more logically; boys have greater emotional stability and stronger emotional reactions; and boys and girls are similar when it comes to prayer but girls attend church more than boys.[52] To interpret the significance of these differences, the instruction guide had a column in which one could "check those [differences and similarities] that help boys and girls to get along."[53] Differences in size and strength and similarities in intelligence and prayer were selected in the guide. The only category not marked was emotional differences, indicating that the real challenge of gender differences was to bridge men and women's different emotions and attitudes—the realm of psychology.

Sex education often invoked gender-specific emotions and attitudes, and in this arena some teachers and class material maintained that gender roles were learned, especially in civilized society. These ideas were prominent among family life educators who embraced psychological explanations for behavior. Various experts in the field of marriage and family life education, including Kirkendall and Force, contended that boys and girls behaved in certain ways because of their socialization. Certain tendencies may have resulted from biology, but more pertinent, given the growing authority of cultural anthropology and social psychology, were the ways that children learned to interact. After more than a decade of experience teaching family relationships, Force explained why girls were more interested in marriage. Boys "have not been oriented to marriage as girls have been. A girl practices her future homemaking role from the time she is a child by holding the baby and helping her mother cook. To be a bride is a goal constantly held up before her," she noted. "The boy, in contrast, plays soldier and reads in the funny papers that husbands are poor, browbeaten creatures, and hears about the high cost of rearing a family and caring for a wife."[54] Without directly critiquing this system of gender training, Force remarked on its pervasiveness; implicit were its potential flaws. She hoped her course would moderate some of the extremes of the gender spectrum, such as girls fixating on finding a marriage partner and focusing on the pageantry of weddings while boys supposedly remained unconcerned about finding a mate and heedless of a need to plan for successful marriages and families. Force was not arguing for a rejection of gender roles, but by revealing their social construction she pointed to their malleability.

In-class discussions and exercises made gender divisions more prominent in young people's consciousness. Not all aspects of family living classes focused on gender differences, but many topics did. In the adolescent development unit of the Detroit schools' family life education program, gender differences were everywhere. "Psychosexual" growth was one of five kinds of development on which the unit focused, with subsections on understanding growth, adolescent developmental tasks, military service, differences between men and women, adolescent problems, and relationships with the other sex.[55] Teachers used the family life course to address the roles of men and women in contemporary society—growing up, serving the country, or getting along with others. Gendered differences and contributions to society may have seemed common sense to many adults, but the lessons reveal that gender roles were not self-evident or did not reproduce automatically. They merited instruction in secondary schools.

Writing assignments in various classes contributed to helping understand modern society and articulate the importance of gender. When read aloud in class, such compositions enhanced peer awareness of gender norms and encouraged individual subjectivity. Helen Randolph, who taught senior problems at North Hollywood High School, advised teachers in 1950 to assign such topics as "The Kind of Husband (or Wife) I Intend to Be" and "The Kind of Girl (or Boy) I Want to Marry."[56] A suggested activity in Minnesota's 1947 *Units in Personal Health and Human Relations* likewise asked students to "outline a plan of activity for a week that would meet the need for well-rounded development (1) for a high school boy, (2) for a high school girl."[57] ("How can we develop happy and wholesome relationships with people of the other sex?" rated an entire section.)[58] Yet another instance of itemizing male and female traits in separate categories occurred in Mildred Sanders Williamson's 1950 family life course at Five Points High School in Alabama; boxes and posters labeled either "orchid" or "onion" listed traits that boys considered positive or negative in girls and vice versa.[59]

Promoting heterosexual relationships during adolescence did not mean advocating intercourse or other types of sexual activity to achieve psychosexual development. Instead, teachers perceived dating as a desirable way for young people to practice relationships with members of the other sex and thereby move beyond the homosocial phase of childhood and toward marriage. Although *Units in Personal Health and Human Relations* authors posited that "physical changes" during adolescence "form the basis for their new interest in each other," guidance in the areas of emotions and behavior remained necessary at both the junior and senior high school levels.[60]

Sex and family life educators for the most part promoted ideas about heterosexual relationships in two phases. At puberty, they sought to inform students about anatomical changes related to reproduction. While teaching about subjects such as menstruation, nocturnal emissions, and childbirth, they fostered gender consciousness and noted the onset of heterosexual attractions at puberty (but did not yet recommend dating). Toward the end of high school, teachers had other goals. In classes for students on the verge of graduating, they emphasized preparation for engagement and marriage. They accepted and assumed that most teenagers were dating by that age and offered an opportunity for them to improve current relationships, as well as dating or marriage potential, by contemplating their personalities and communication skills.

Some assumed that young people needed little stimulation to develop interest in the other sex. "One girl in my class said she had been 'engaged' to four different fellows in two years," Force commented. "The boys pounced on her for being fickle. I pointed out that adolescents, in the first flush of their sexual awakening, tend to fall wonderfully in 'love' with the whole opposite sex. Only gradually do they discriminate on the basis of such mature considerations as companionship and character."[61] *Marriage and Family Living* contributor Louise Ramsey likewise noted that most young people easily developed interest in heterosexual dating and marriage but needed guidance in applying those sentiments. According to Ramsey, that interest could assist teachers in a variety of projects, including psychological development and the acquisition of healthful behavior. "Fortunately," she claimed, "where youth is thinking in terms of making himself or herself attractive to the opposite sex and later into a parent worthy of fine children, he or she will give heed to instruction on improving health, posture, and appearance. A boy will adopt new habits of food, exercise, and even bathing if acne has threatened his popularity. A girl will part company with coco-colas when she finds that her skin responds favorably."[62] Ramsey's assertions reveal her confidence that heterosexual attraction in youth needed no prompting but ought to be channeled into self-improvement.

Whether in junior high school and just learning the ropes of boy-girl relations or in senior high school and preparing for marriage, students seem to have been receptive to messages about how to be liked and become popular.[63] Popularity may have been the immediate goal for young people, but teachers saw an opportunity to lend dignity to self-improvement strategies as part of the process of heterosexual adaptation and eventually mate selection. In an eighth-grade social hygiene class in Rock Island, Illinois, students were encouraged to study self-improvement, with books on personality and etiquette at their disposal. "The positive approach to sex education was carried forward through the *do's*. The pupils were encouraged to become interested in any activity which could help an adolescent become socially popular in an acceptable manner."[64]

Yet educators' efforts to enhance heterosexual inclinations risked overstimulation. "Growing interest in the other sex springs from normal impulses which need to be understood by the adolescent," Mabel Grier Lesher, a sex education authority, observed in a guide for parent education. "But this sex-interest is complicated by family attitudes, parent restrictions, morality-defying companions, passion-teasing movies, sexy stories, and lures to questionable adventure. Much explaining and guidance is needed if the boy and girl are to steer through the complications successfully." Furthermore, she noted, "The natural attraction between boys and girls should be recognized by both as a normal part of growing up. But it calls for self-control and chivalry by the boy, and for fair-play by the girl in not increasing his problem of control through thoughtless or deliberate familiarities."[65] Conventional gender roles, then, held the potential to prevent premature heterosexual activity.

One obstacle to boy-girl relationships at the junior high school level was the discrepancy between when most boys and most girls reached puberty—a problem for teachers who wanted to stress mutuality and compatibility. They attempted to resolve the issue by suggesting that boys and girls would catch up with one another eventually. Acknowledging that the pace of puberty and emotional development occurred slightly earlier in girls than in boys, teachers nevertheless tried to assert that there was parity between the sexes; neither had the advantage. While describing the physiological changes that young people ordinarily experience as they grow, a pair of silhouette forms—male and female—illustrated the film *Human Growth.* The narrator conveys that physical changes in males and females during puberty are relative to one another, comparable, and noncompetitive. At one point the narrative implies that the fluctuation in male and female height achieves resolution in the end, with the "boy again being appreciably larger than the girl." As another statement of reassurance, the narrator explains that on reaching the late teens and early twenties, "the differences in sexual maturity will have disappeared." According to such teaching material, the imbalance of maturity between the sexes during puberty was temporary.

While emphasizing the uniqueness of the two sexes, teaching material usually avoided fueling a boys-against-girls mentality so as not to alienate pupils from developing attractions to the other sex. At least two strategies were commonly employed. One was to note the relative progress of each sex during the course of maturation. Although the young man had physical advantages by the end of *Human Growth,* that occurred in conjunction with the age at which many people married and thus at a point where collaboration—in the institution of marriage—settled the differences. In the event that members of the audience, usually seventh- and eighth-grade students, lacked affection or allegiance to those of the other sex, a future of heterosexual attraction and consummation in marriage would beckon by the late teens and early twenties, the film asserted.

A second way in which teachers attempted to promote heterosexual attraction was by calling boys' and girls' attention to the positive traits of the
other sex. Seniors in Milling's American literature course in Newark discussed
popularity after they had read a short story. "A wave of interest and eagerness
swept the class" as the teacher asked, "What, in your estimation, makes a girl
sought after; a boy popular? The girls will discuss the boys only and the boys
the girls only."[66] The outcome of the discussion was "How Do You Rate on a
Date?" The mimeographed pamphlet, in multiple colors, featured columns
on "attributes of the perfect escort" and "the perfect date-girl." The youth-
generated list of ideal qualities demonstrates that young people contributed
to shaping gender differences and that girls' expectations for boys varied
from boys' expectations for girls. Girls favored boys who were courteous and
sincere, whereas boys expressed preferences (in a much longer list) for girls'
physical appearance. Boys also indicated that control of dating situations was
important to them, and they objected to assertive girls. The list of traits reveals
that young people participated in imagining gender roles in classrooms but
rarely questioned social and gendered norms in a collective way.

Heterosexual interests in the latter teenaged years, teachers thought, could
be channeled into future-minded concern with marriage. Mid-twentieth-
century educators prompted students near graduation to engage in preparation for marriage and family life because many would have no further
formal education and were likely to marry in the few years following high
school graduation. In 1950, women, on average, married at twenty and men
at twenty-three. In the 1940s and 1950s, high school graduates were less likely
to delay marriage than their parents' generation had.[67]

Instructors of marriage and family living courses for high school juniors
and seniors employed language from psychology, including models of heterosexual development. Explicit discussion of homosexuality and heterosexuality focused not on sexual activity but on the orientation of attraction.[68] In
other words, the homosexual phase that they sometimes discussed did not
imply sexual activity with persons of the same sex but rather interest and
pleasure in interactions with same-sex companions—or, even more common,
hero worship. Heterosexuality similarly meant appreciation and desire for
interactions with the other sex—which, upon maturity and marriage, should
include heterosexual intercourse.

Educators were confident that the study of marriage and family relationships—and placing male-female relationships within that framework—during the high school years would contribute to reduced divorce rates. Teachers
and administrators in Denver public schools agreed that "education for home

and family living," as they called their course, offered young people an opportunity to "meet marriage and the responsibilities of a home with more than romantic, superficial notions about marriage."[69] Also focusing on potential conflict in marriage was a course offered at Garfield Heights High School in Cleveland, Ohio: "social relations—premarriage problems."[70] Observing that most of her thousand former students from Toms River had married and were parents, Force recognized that some unions would fail no matter the amount of training and preparation. As one former pupil reported, "I know I am handling my failure better than I would have had I not had the opportunity to think so seriously about such matters when I was in high school years ago."[71] Knowing that not all marriages would succeed, educators nevertheless found comfort in the thought that young people would take matrimony seriously.

Gender antagonism was not entirely missing from sex and family life education classrooms, and a small amount of competition could be fruitful. Exercises that might engender a battle of the sexes, however, were not about defeating the other side but coming to a clearer understanding of different perspectives. Such discussions were a healthy form of debate that might give young men and women more insight about one another. "The boys admit that they do kiss and tell," Force observed. "The girls have a pretty good idea of what the boys discuss in their bull sessions. This is all thrashed out in the classroom, and it is fun to hear the boys and girls tell one another off. After the heated discussion is over, each sex has a better understanding of the other's viewpoint. This leads to more respect for one another, too."[72] Especially because her class consisted of older teenagers in their last years of high school, when the majority had long since abandoned any homosocial inclinations, Force was confident that there was no danger in stimulating a little controversy. As reported by a teacher in Greeley, Colorado, a student noted that "sex instruction could not be taught in a better manner than in a mixed group [of boys and girls]. Sometime in life we are going to have to face these problems together, and not alone." The Greeley students wished only that instruction would begin at the junior rather than the senior high school level.[73]

When courses focused on gender differences and male-female relationships in the 1940s and 1950s, prescriptions of appropriate gender norms and normal heterosexual interests tempered the more liberatory messages about gaining maturity and expanding autonomy. Young people might make more independent choices as they approached adulthood, but they ought to remain alert to the consequences youthful behavior could have for the future. Sexual behavior was mostly unspoken in classrooms, but heterosexual interests and developing an attractive appearance and personality were om-nipresent. Teachers encouraged the discovery and cultivation of interest in the other sex, especially using exercises that guided students' thinking about male-female relationships. Social norms, however, differed from biological absolutes. Emphasis on identity and psychology drew attention to variations in socialization and cultural norms, and, indeed, their vulnerability in times of social upheaval.

Conclusion

Appealing to young people's desires to attain maturity and acceptance, sex educators sought to stabilize society by reinforcing what they thought were complementary female and male characteristics. Sex and family life educa-tion showed boys and girls how to avoid abnormality and suppress undesir-able personality traits in the interest of becoming ideal candidates for mar-riage. At times ambiguous about distinctions between biological imperatives and social norms, teachers led girls to believe that appropriate gendered choices, behaviors, and interactions—"boy-girl relations"—in adolescence had ramifications for identities as wives. Even though teachers sometimes acknowledged a range of possible futures, the emphasis on femininity and heterosexuality began at puberty to influence girls' self-consciousness and interactions with others.

Cooperation and harmony between boys and girls was critical during adolescence, and coed courses allowed young people to practice gender-appropriate courtesies and roles. In the movie *Human Growth,* the teacher selects a boy (Dick) to operate the film projector and a girl (Carolyn) to record questions from the class on the blackboard. From behind the projector, Dick asks a classmate (Nancy) to please turn out the lights. Classroom dynamics modeled in the film concerned how to establish gender-appropriate conduct during adolescence, whether viewing a film or operating equipment. When sex education is studied as lessons about reproduction only, the broader contemporary meanings of sex and the central relevance of gender to this instruction are missed. Yet repeated messages about heterosexuality and femininity probably made a greater impression than did the physiology of menstruation or conception.

The language of cooperation between the sexes often distorted the power differential in future options. In *Human Growth,* for example, the narrator stresses the compatibility of men and women and their mutual achievement of maturity, but he indicates separate tracks for male and female adulthood—

at least in their ideal configuration. As the narrator explains that differences in sexual maturity dissipated around the age of twenty, an image depicting adult roles appears on the screen. The four frames showing a model family consist of a white, middle-class man with a diploma, a desk job, a wife on his arm, and children by their side. Suggesting acceptable roles for white, respectable women were a perky young secretary, a bride latched onto her groom, and a mother holding an infant and surrounded by three additional children. While intending to illustrate the "normal" adult roles available upon sexual maturity, the film's images also hint at distinct gendered privileges and conventions, marked by race and class as well, that ultimately unite man and woman in a common goal: family-building.

Sex and family living classes thus revealed and justified sex differences and gender expectations to students, sometimes projecting traditional roles and at others suggesting new interpretations and possibilities. Rationales for gender roles were not exclusively grounded in physical anatomy, nor were they polarized as opposites or extremes. Yet the differences were more than benign forms of cultural variation in which boys and girls could choose attributes of personality to their liking. One North Carolina teacher referred to the part of the curriculum in which students learned to understand and value their new identities as young men and women as "self-analysis."[74] Amid rhetoric of choice and democracy, which was pervasive in postwar secondary education, a powerful system of social norms that encouraged introspection and self-improvement promoted adolescent development and acceptance of one's sex. Despite the constraints of appropriate psychological development, girls and boys were empowered to consider the kind of person they wanted to become. They also discussed in each others' presence such topics as career choices, marriage potential, and traits they found attractive.

Taking pride in one's maleness or femaleness was a central message that teachers conveyed to students in sex and family life education. To the extent that adolescent problems derived from sex and gender, educators were able to grasp an easy solution: promoting heterosexual femininity and masculinity along with marriage preparation. But educators alone did not create sex education, and formal sex education was certainly not the last word. Young people were active participants in educating one another, and as the next chapter explores more fully, in- and out-of-school activities were instructive as well, sometimes reinforcing and other times contradicting the ideas about personalities and heterosexual romance they received in formal sex education.

6

Sexuality Education
beyond Classrooms

When educators talked about sex education in the 1940s and 1950s they typically meant formal sex education conducted by adults. They thought about sex talks by teachers, parents, and the clergy; books and pamphlets; and visual aids such as anatomical charts and movies. Their conception of sex education also included instructor-supervised classroom discussions about puberty, dating and engagement, and marriage and the family. Although teachers and administrators were quick to acknowledge that young people derived misinformation from a variety of unreliable sources, incidental learning about sexuality did not, for them, "count" as sex education. Yet young people in the mid-twentieth century encountered knowledge and ideas about sexuality—and not all of it inaccurate—in many places beyond the realm of formal education.

The premise that sex education occurs within and outside classrooms is not unique to the period discussed in this book. The confluence of rising rates of high school attendance and a growing national youth-oriented popular culture in the mid-century decades, however, meant that more young people were encountering similar experiences across the country. A particular youth culture—or youth cultures—solidified during and after World War II was tied to consumerism, the popular media, and collective identity as "teen-agers," a term widely adopted in the 1940s. Teenagers experienced growing independence, autonomy, and collective identity, particularly as participants in school-based extracurricular activities and consumer culture off campus.[1]

Youth culture and teenage identity, however, fail to encompass the experience of many in the mid-twentieth century; in fact, historian William

Graebner has noted that the concept of "youth culture" is a mythical invention rather than a social reality.[2] The tensions within the concept were similar to those operating in society more generally: Boundaries and limits usually corresponded to class, race, ethnicity, and sexuality. Like the fictional Cleaver family of television fame, the mythical bobby-soxers provide a limited portrait of the lives of mid-century young people, especially those of color and those from low-income families. Nevertheless, the idea of youth culture, continually reiterated in popular culture, shaped the imaginations, styles, behaviors, and experiences of adolescents who came of age in the mid-twentieth century.

High schools were instrumental in solidifying an age-segregated teen culture, the contours of which were shaped by region, race/ethnicity, and class.[3] Much highlighted in the popular press was the growing spending power of young people, usually coupled with greater independence from parents. World War II brought military and job opportunities not previously available, and parental supervision declined in many homes. Parents and teenagers alike heeded the call to join the Armed Services, the industrial workforce, or the volunteer corps. Paychecks, babysitting money, and allowances flowed into the hands of young people, whose spending produced a niche market. Manufacturers, retailers, and advertisers seized the opportunity to cater to youths and construct tastes and fads. Teen consumer culture was born, and adolescents' participation in it, and their school attendance, shaped their sense of belonging among peers. As sociologist Amy L. Best has maintained, parents, administrators, and advertisers place a great deal of pressure on teenagers to recall proms as meaningful events, nights to remember, occasions for countless photographs, and, especially more recently, causes for spending hundreds of dollars.[4] Although mid-twentieth-century proms were not nearly as consumer-driven as they have been in more recent decades, they remain part of a school's informal curriculum. They continue to center on the formation and celebration of heterosexual dating couples.

This chapter identifies prominent sources and messages that contributed to informal sex education, in particular the ways in which schools and popular culture championed and reinforced the gendered and heterosexual realm of dating. Ideas about sexuality in popular culture multiplied the concerns—and contradictions— in school curricula about sex, gender, puberty, and reproduction. While "human relations" classes provided students with tools to think about and understand themselves and their relationships with others, most experiences of identity and relationships occurred outside classrooms. Young people formulated understanding of gender and sexuality at venues that included school activities, libraries, dances, summer camps, slumber parties, soda fountains, movie theaters, and parked cars. Attending to appearances and participating in recreational activities in the 1950s fostered and refined awareness of what it meant to become heterosexual adolescents.

Appearances

In Western culture of the past century, awareness and concern about image—especially attractiveness—has tended to develop during adolescence. This self-consciousness had gendered dimensions as well as sexual significance that must be situated in its social context. Advertisers, moviemakers, teachers, nurses, and parents contribute to training young people to monitor their looks, odors, manners, and their associates. School culture, too, contributes to young people's self-awareness about appearance. From peers in particular they learn expectations and norms related to beauty, popularity, and heterosexual success.

Appearances were often deceiving. Teens had to look no further than the wildly popular novel *Peyton Place* and its movie counterpart to appreciate that things were often not what they appeared.[5] The best-selling novel's depiction of a New England town and its varied sexual intrigues—extramarital affairs, rape, incest, abortion, and teenaged sexual encounters, to name a few—indicated that even a quiet, seemingly respectable community harbored many secrets. And if the book was merely fiction and not a true representation of sexual noncomformity and hypocrisy in American society, then at the very least it indicated Grace Metallious's rebellious imagination and the reading public's eagerness for stories that challenged conventional morality.

Many youths in the 1950s turned to books to understand sexuality. A wide array of perspectives could be found, whether in libraries or on drug store and train station bookstands, including everything from literature to pulp fiction, comic books, *True Romance* magazines, daily newspapers, sexology, and the Kinsey reports. Some sought facts and information, like Miranda Clark and her friend, Selena, with whom, she remembered, she would "spend hours after school talking about what sex would actually feel like and reading Krafft-Ebing aloud to each other."[6] Others sought fiction such as *Peyton Place* and the novels of D. H. Lawrence, which attracted controversy and, in the case of Lawrence, censorship. Girls did not always sneak around to read such books in private. Toms River educator Elizabeth Force reported witnessing them reading *Lady Chatterly's Lover* on the subway, for example.[7]

Girls seeking information about same-sex love typically did so more furtively, and yet explicit tales of lesbian love found an avid readership. First among the lesbian-themed pulp fiction novels was Vin Packer's *Strange Fire* (1952), whose cover teased, "A story once told in whispers, now frankly, honestly written."[8] Having discovered Packer, novice writer Ann Bannon—a newlywed with no lesbian experience—began writing novels of her own, ultimately culminating in the Beebo Brinker series. The first title in the series, Bannon's *Odd Girl Out,* dealt with a sexual intrigue between sorority sisters Beth and Laura, and it was the second-best-selling paperback in 1957.[9] Yet many who might have found self-recognition in such books never discovered them. While growing up in the 1950s, Jill Morris found only Radcliffe Hall's *Well of Loneliness,* which, despite its literary value, she read "with a newspaper wrapped around it."[10]

If Greenwich Village and lesbian relationships were distant from many girls' growing-up experiences in the 1950s, school annuals or yearbooks more directly reflected young people's realities. These books provide illustrated and annotated guides to the teen culture that schools fostered in the mid-twentieth century. Assembled by a yearbook staff of student editors and photographers, annuals appeared each spring at schools across the country. Students would autograph each other's copy, recounting memories or composing clever if not very original sayings. The official account of the year was embedded in pictures and commentaries usually scrutinized and approved by faculty and administrators, but yearbooks also preserve an unofficial account of good times, ambitions, secrets, conflicts, and desires.[11]

The more official, school-sanctioned representations of high school culture reveal that young people were in the process of crafting gendered identities and heterosexual relationships on school grounds. Individual portraits, pictures of clubs and sports stars, and images from activities such as dances and plays demonstrate the ways they displayed their maturing personalities through appearance. The posed photographs capture how gender and heterosexuality pervaded the informal processes of learning and fitting in. Without invoking sexual activity, the images and words reveal the ubiquity of gendered and heterosexual expectations.

As Wini Breines recounts in her memoir and sociological examination of growing up white and female in the 1950s, concern about appearance shaped the lives and self-esteem of many. Beauty standards that privileged white features—such as fair skin and ponytail-length hair—had significant bearing on ideals of femininity. In popular women's magazines of the 1950s, Breines points out, not just whiteness but also "idleness" and "childishness" were valued.[12]

While many teen girls assimilated to white beauty standards they also sought to represent accomplishments and maturity—not idleness and childishness—in yearbook photographs. Whether organizing events, excelling in sports or baton twirling, or posing for homecoming queen photographs, girls communicated initiative and activity as well as aspirations to be viewed as mature and heterosexually attractive. Young people assembled their own ideas of what it meant to be mature and an eligible dating partner, piecing together messages from teachers, parents, media, and their peers.

School-sponsored girls' beauty pageants began in junior high schools, and photographs featured the winners modeling feminine heterosexual attractiveness. Some variation on homecoming, prom, or May queen contests occurred at many junior and senior high schools around the country. Yearbook features on the competitions added further glamour to the honor of being selected. San Diego's Roosevelt Junior High School yearbooks from the 1950s featured photographs of the smiling May queen and her court, dressed in their best gowns and with their hair coiffed. Homecoming queens at San Diego High School in the 1950s were similarly featured.[13] Whether pictured from the waist or shoulders up, their semiformal and formal dresses showcased their developing bodies.

Girls learned how to be alluring and attractive not just from adult movie stars and magazines but also from peers and youth-oriented publications such as *Seventeen* magazine. Advertisers promoted fashions and cosmetics that promised sex appeal, although teens in the early-twenty-first century would probably have been unable to detect what was "sexy" about such styles. Even though it was not a new trend among adolescent girls in the 1950s, wearing lipstick was associated with glamour and heterosexual allure. According to a survey of more than a thousand readers conducted by *Seventeen* in the mid-1940s, 93 percent of girls regularly used lipstick, second only to soap and toothpaste (both rating 100 percent) among popular toiletries.[14] Certain brands of lipstick made girls' lips kissable, they learned from advertising; other products, such as a perfume called "Beaux Catcher," suggested that they could improve prospects for dating.[15]

White beauty queens predominated in racially integrated high schools as they did in all-white schools, but there were exceptions. In San Diego, a district with significant numbers of black and Mexican American students and a number of Asian Americans as well, competition winners and runners-up were usually but not always white. The mixed-race student body at San Diego High School elected some Latina and African American girls during the 1950s. Queens were chosen for good looks as well as personalities, popularity, and other attributes. Casting anonymous ballots permitted some white students to express attraction across the color line with little consequence and in the midst of a climate hostile to interracial dating.

A more elaborate system of beauty queens and popularity contests existed at the mostly upper-middle-class, and all white, Webster Groves, Missouri, High School for most of the 1950s. An elite school with many aspiring debutantes and socialites, Webster Groves distributed more than the usual share of titles and tiaras. The student body voted on football "maids" (one for each of the five grades) and queen; Paper Doll maids and queen; and *Echo* maids and queen. Six pages of the school's annual, the *Echo*, were devoted to large pictures of the winners. The beauty contest winners' family names were significant factors in popularity, along with personality, poise, and attractiveness. The ten categories in the 1953 superlatives ("senior class poll") listed the top three vote winners for boys and girls each. Among them were three pairs elected as "best couple."[16]

High school girls were active alongside boys in selecting prom queens, and on occasion they created opportunities to honor attractive boys as kings. Competitions for boys were less common and demonstrated the differences in standards of popularity and desirability based on gender. A double standard for male and female attractiveness accorded with ideals of masculinity and femininity. Electing a "king" or hosting a dance for which girls invited boys reinforced the "normal" pattern. Girls waited for boys to ask them on a date, and boys exercised the privilege of being in charge. These gendered roles were inverted, however, during the 1950s in Webster Groves when the Girls' Athletic Association (GAA) would crown the "Kampus King" at the "backward" dance. The event was far less prominent in the yearbook than the various queens elected during the year and received only brief mention, although it gained prominence over time. Like the queens, the 1956 and 1957 kings (and "jacks," the equivalent of maids) were dressed in formal attire, jacket and tie.[17] Unlike the girls' adultlike clothing, which had plunging necklines and tight bodices, formal attire for males did not call attention to sexual attributes.

Other school-sponsored competitions named winners in a variety of categories other than beauty, and those sometimes earned photo spreads as well. Such awards, too, contributed to gender and heterosexual socialization. "Superlatives," usually voted on by the senior class, honored students deemed best dressed, most likely to succeed, and possessing the best personality, to give several examples. In all cases there were separate competitions for boys and girls in each category. Some categories used gender-specific titles for similar traits, especially when it was a measure of attractiveness. The 1958 competition at San Diego High School recognized the "prettiest" girls, "most handsome" boys, "best figure" for girls, and "best physique" for boys.[18]

When featuring the winners of superlative or popularity contests, some yearbook editors opted to show the winning pairs posed as a couple, encoding messages about sexuality, race, and gender into the pictures. In such cases, students were deciding how to photograph winners and expending extra effort to do so. Although not consciously attempting to reinforce heterosexual pairing, such representations conveyed heterosexuality as natural, normal, and expected among graduating students. During the 1959–60 school year, for example, San Diego High School seniors selected by student government as the male and female leader of the month appeared in the yearbook posed together as a couple. So did the students winning senior superlative awards.

In integrated school districts, like San Diego's, white students and those of color were sometimes paired as winners of superlatives.[19] Such pictures suggested the possibility of interracial coupling, something to which administrators, teachers, and parents tacitly objected. Because white-black and white-Latino and Latina romances remained taboo among high school students in the 1950s, sexual attractions and tensions were not often openly expressed. In the several instances in which mixed-race pairs were photographed as winners of superlatives noticeably more space appears between the figures. No doubt the fact they were photographed together at all made some administrators and defenders of racial segregation uncomfortable. Separate competitions based on gender were appropriate; separate competitions by race and ethnicity were not, especially in a school that championed democracy, "brotherhood," and intercultural cooperation among various racial, ethnic, and national groups.[20]

Gender hierarchies were also established and maintained through the photographs, although not always in obvious ways. Even though girls and boys did not compete against one another directly—in sports or in popularity contests—male privilege and domination seeped into youth culture in subtle and not-so-subtle ways. Competitive sports for boys were, not surprisingly, accorded more space in yearbooks than those for girls and also had bigger budgets, better equipment, and more prestige. Even in popularity competitions, girls were not supposed to outdo boys or undermine the appearance of masculine control. When one girl superlative winner was taller than her male counterpart at San Diego High School she was photographed seated, the boy standing beside her so she would not appear to outsize him and thereby disrupt the appearance of male superiority.[21]

Gender-differentiated rules for behavior on dates was another way in which young people learned about—and constructed—appropriate conduct. The rules, like the photographs, reinforced the importance of appearances. Blending formal and informal curricula, students enrolled in the social behavior course at Toms River High School in 1955 developed a series of brochures for teenagers who dated. The lists of rules reveal how students were actively formulating norms, but stating which practices were undesirable indicated what required regulation or intervention. In other words, some girls and boys did not know—or did not choose to abide by—the rules other students wished to establish.

The brochures indicated that courtesies applied to all but in gendered ways. Whether "escorted" or "unescorted" to a dance or party, girls, for example, were instructed to greet their hosts. Boys who went "stag" had no such obligation, and those "with date" were told to take her to greet the hosts. Single boys and girls were both urged to "circulate." Girls' special instructions were to "be gracious and friendly to all [and] have a cheerful manner," whereas boys were advised to "dance as many dances as possible" to ensure a successful experience.

The pamphlet doled out advice for couples on dates and in so doing advocated particular gender norms. Two of the five points of advice for girls related to pleasing parents and teachers: secure understanding with parents about a curfew and greet hosts. One concerned dress etiquette. And then two points dealt with being submissive to their date's wishes: "Allow escort to find a seat for you and be an agreeable companion," and "Be willing to exchange dances with others if he suggests it." Girls were also advised not to choose seats, be disagreeable, suggest switching dancing partners, or refuse to dance if the date proposed doing so.

Boys were perceived to be more unruly than girls, and the list of expectations pertaining to them was longer. Most reinforced the notion of being the "leaders" in dating. Three concerned making arrangements: asking with advance notice, calling her at her house, and learning about her curfew. After taking the date to greet the hosts, the boy was to initiate the first dance with her and save the last for her as well. In between, the pamphlet commented, "It is a good policy to exchange dances with other couples." Other courtesies surrounded the act of dancing. Boys were to "thank her for the dance and escort her to the dance floor" and "obey all dance rules." Finally, it was plausible to the pamphlet creators that boys might behave in disruptive or uncouth ways at a school dance, so they stated, "Conduct yourself so that no unfavorable attention is drawn to you and your partner."

Youth-produced advice pamphlets, like youth-produced yearbooks, offer a glimpse of what student leaders believed normal and ideal among their peers. As adult-supervised publications they were unlikely to deviate too far from the rules and behaviors that teachers and administrators valued. They reveal that students and school personnel collaborated in recognizing and encouraging dating and heterosexual interests among teenagers. The artifacts indicate consensus among young people and adults about holding school events for heterosexual couples, where feminine beauty was prized and gendered dating behavior was the norm. Open challenges to unspoken rules, such as taboos on interracial dating, sexual activity, or standards of respectability, are missing from the documents and images. Rather than conclude that such challenges did not occur, it seems likely that young people tested the limits of race, sexuality, and gender expectations in more subtle ways. As Breines suggests, "Dissemblance, even hypocrisy, were coping strategies for girls engaged in experimentation and rulebreaking," especially when it came to sexuality.[22]

Activities

There was perhaps no bigger social expectation for teenagers in the mid-twentieth century than to go on their first date. By the time a teenager was old enough to graduate from high school it was likely that he or she would have dated at least once..[23] Schools facilitated the opportunity for doing so by sponsoring proms and other dances, and dating also occurred away from school property, for example at ice cream parlors, movie theaters, parks, and other commercial venues. "Teen canteens" grew popular during the 1940s, and other adult-sponsored social activities provided space for young people to socialize, dance, and flirt. As an alternative to commercial establishments, community-organized youth events were especially attractive to parents and teachers. According to an article in the *California Parent-Teacher,* parents were enthusiastic to note that "San Diego is out in front with its Friday Flings; Santa Barbara, Oakland, and Santa Paula are organizing teen-age clubs. In fact, the desire to give youth a wholesome good time has spread like wildfire all over California."[24]

Young people, however, often preferred less-supervised commercial dance-halls and concert venues, amusement parks, and drive-ins. African American young people in Portland, Oregon, for example, in the mid-1950s initially attended a "Coed Inn" program on Thursday nights at the local YWCA. When attendance dropped off precipitously, adults discovered that the young people had found other, more alluring activities. On one particular Thursday night, many were probably at McElroy's Ballroom, where "a name band was playing." That did not answer the larger question of "where the kids were on other Thursday nights." In the report explaining why the canteen was discontinued, organizers listed a variety of competing events and complications, from calypso dance lessons and youth dances at a commercial studio, an increase in teenaged pregnancies and "hasty marriages," and allegations of the rape of girls who were "picked up" following a Y dance.[25]

In Portland, young people were enticed or coerced into activities beyond the purview of well-meaning YWCA organizers and adults. A youth forum about programming changes indicated that some remaining teenaged council members were interested in "charm class" or early-afternoon club meetings. Ultimately, however, weekly Y dances lacked appeal (other than one at which girls invited a particular group of boys), and the young people wanted to be free for commercial recreation in the evenings. The dances had also troubled local law enforcement officers who complained about "obstreperous" behavior and "delinquency" as the young people came and went from the venue. Whether racism or police harassment was at issue, the YWCA committee concluded that "the girls of the Williams Avenue Area need much help in becoming mature and socially acceptable in their behavior, especially since many do not have the kind of home background which would give them this training. Every possible effort should be put into helping the Teen-age girls to handle the pressures of growing up."[26]

Girls apparently welcomed such advice and input, especially during their early teenaged years. Classrooms incorporated discussion of "boy-girl relations" into the curriculum during the same period, and students launched forums of their own through clubs or even more informally, especially among girls, at such activities as slumber parties. At Webster Groves High School, the seventh- and eighth-grade girls' clubs linked to the YMCA (the "Tri-Hi-Y") held a combined meeting in 1955 for extending such conversations beyond classrooms. According the to the *Echo,* they met and "discussed dating and other boy-girl relations." They also invited the boys' club from the St. Louis suburb of Maplewood and "discussed these things" with their male guests as well.[27]

For girls, forming a heterosexual identity in adolescence was vital to attracting dates and participating in youth culture. Boys seem to have faced less pressure, in part attributable to the supposition that they enter puberty later than girls and in part due to male privilege. Although girls were often eager to learn more about relationships—boy-girl relations in particular—it was common for boys to remain indifferent to or even defiant of social pressures to date and still retain status among peers. A number of St. Louis boys complained in the early 1950s that their parents pressured them to ask girls to go on dates but they would rather spend money some other way. As one said, "It is too expensive for what I get."[28] Likewise, when Mac Eagle was a junior at Toms River's South High School, he and three friends created what they called the Bachelor's Club. They celebrated the idea of not pairing up with or settling down with a girlfriend or wife, much in keeping with the idea of being a playboy. "There were four of us," Eagle recalled, "that claimed we'd be the last one married. Each of us *knew* we wouldn't be the first one to fall." Included in the Bachelor's Club was Mark Jahnke, whom Eagle labeled "a neat looking blond guy with a great personality" and "the most popular in the class." Jahnke "probably could have dated many of our female classmates," Eagle claimed, but "the rest of us were not ladies' men at all; in fact none of us had to my knowledge dated anyone."[29]

Like their YWCA counterparts, school officials and student leaders were proud of the opportunities they provided young people to dress up, arrange dates, and dance to a live band or records. Such dances ranged from casual to formal affairs. In a decorated school gym or another venue, young people socialized, consumed refreshments, and danced to a band or music played by a deejay. Some would attend solo (called "stag" if they were male or "unescorted" if female), but there was a great deal of social pressure, particularly for girls, to have a date, and those who did not were far less likely to be popular.[30] The etiquette for securing one involved boys asking girls, unless the event was a "reverse," "backward," or "Sadie Hawkins dance," all names that indicated role reversal. It was a tradition at San Diego High School for an administrator to "marry" couples at the Sadie Hawkins dance—a prospect that must have added more pressure to girls when they chose dates. As the 1958 *Gray Castle* feature explained, partners were "laden down with their marriage licenses and shower-curtain wedding rings."[31]

For many, the excitement of their teenage years—especially those memorable, early experiences of sexual desire and flirtation—took place elsewhere. In public, girls gravitated to rock 'n' roll concerts in the 1950s. According to *Variety* magazine, girls, especially those under sixteen, dominated the crowds at racially mixed music halls. They seemed enthusiastic about the shows, commentators observed, even though the music explicitly alluded to sexual acts, including prostitution and homosexuality.[32] Although, as Breines points out, rock 'n' roll music was "sanitized for white audiences, [it] was charged with sexual meaning." Combined with the advice of experts and popular culture, rock 'n' roll "provided a national frame of reference against which to measure oneself," in particular, one's sexual identity.[33]

Many rebelled in small ways when it came to music, recreation, dating, and flirting. As a self-described "high-achieving, Jewish" girl in Brooklyn, New York, in the 1950s, Alix Berns recalled that she and her friends did not choose to date boys in their own crowd but gravitated to the "'bummy' Italian or Greek boys, the street corner hoods that we'd meet in the movies from time to time." These were not, she explained, people she and her friends would date—"that would have been too scary"—but they shamelessly flirted with them. "Even at the time I knew it was a learning thing," Berns admitted. "I was learning how to act sexual with boys and also how to deal with them, how to keep them at a distance. It was a way to get validation for our sexuality because we thought the guys we hung around with didn't notice those things."[34]

For some girls dates involved conforming to strict gender expectations about sexuality and other forms of adolescent troublemaking—drinking, for example. A date in the 1950s meant sipping soft drinks at a roadhouse with boys who drank beer explained Sheila McCarthy, who grew up in suburban Indianapolis. Sexual experiences could be had, however, especially with a steady boyfriend. McCarthy found a steady, a non-Catholic, she stressed, as quickly as she could. "We kissed continuously," she recalled. "I was tremendously interested in sex. Over the course of two years, we progressed down from the lips. I remember the moment his hand touched my pale blue cashmere-covered breast because I was immediately stricken with the first migraine headache of my life." The couple did not have sexual intercourse, and McCarthy was oblivious to the fact that some girls did, but "there was tremendous tension and fondling and heavy breathing."[35] "Going all the way" or losing one's virginity might separate promiscuous girls from more cautious ones, but the fact was that those engaging in fondling and other forms of sexual intimacy were having sexual experiences, only avoiding intercourse.

Because people often think of "sex" as intercourse, they have tended to overlook other sexual experiences or assume that ultimate sexual gratification equals vaginal intercourse and male ejaculation and orgasm. This heterosexual, male-centered view of sexuality and pleasure neglects the ways girls and women experience pleasure, especially as their bodies begin to respond sexually for the first time. After hours and hours of necking with her boyfriend Vince, Kay D'Amico, explained how "incredibly turned on" both she and her partner were, remarking, "Oh God, I remember feeling as if the whole lower half of my body, from the waist down, had turned to liquid."[36] Only after she got to college did Tyler Barrett understand, thanks to her dermatologist, "why *I* was having a discharge" while "petting" with Ned. The doctor explained to her that she was lubricating and that it was normal (and then, she noted, the doctor "made a pass at me").[37]

Rarely did girls in the 1950s have much understanding or appreciation of orgasms and pleasure, which is not surprising given how little spoken or printed information was available. Miranda Clark, raised by bohemian parents in Greenwich Village, recalls learning from her mother at eleven that she should "never let a man make you come because then he'll have power over you." Although her mother's exact meaning was ambiguous, Clark "had an idea," and she knew after having intercourse for the first time that she had not when her partner asked, "Did you come?"[38] Other tales from Clark's teenaged years indicated further ignorance. When she and a friend went to be fitted for diaphragms and were completing a form about their frequency of intercourse, they reported twelve times a week so as "not to look like amateurs." They also heard one woman in the waiting room say to another, "My husband doesn't like the taste of jelly." The girls "were convulsed at the stupidity of this man *eating* the jelly."[39]

Before most girls became aware of contraceptive options they encountered a youth culture in which male-female relationships were accorded special status. Several studies of dating during the 1950s indicate that the majority of first dates resulted from pressure to participate in the dating system rather than a desire to go out with a particular individual.[40] Girls and boys were supposed to start noticing each other in early adolescence, according to social norms. Many attempted to project that consciousness of heterosexuality when inscribing friends' and acquaintances' yearbooks.

By junior high school, girls learned that paying attention to boys and dating were ways of fitting in. "The higher the mountain / The cooler the breeze / The younger the couple / The tighter they squeeze" wrote Stephanie Freeman in Carol Ortman's 1955 yearbook from Roosevelt Junior High in San Diego. More boldly, Terry Chamberlain contributed "Roses are red / Violets are blue / A low neckline / Would look good on you."[41] These students, most of them thirteen, were expressing a type of heterosexual awareness. Allusions to tight hugs and plunging necklines conveyed sexual curiosity and even a hint of subversiveness, implying that adolescents more fervently seek physical intimacy than adults and converting a romantic ditty to a poem that involved a sexual gaze rather than the usual ending to the roses and violets rhyme, "sugar is sweet / and so are you." Less subversive but as emphatic about the significance of heterosexuality, was Millie Schnell's contribution: "When Cupid shoots I hope he Mrs. you."

More personal inscriptions generally wished luck, alluded to a shared experience in a club, or mentioned summer plans. It was, however, just as common for the notes to invoke heterosexuality—and, quite often, its asymmetries. The ubiquitous phrase "good luck with the boys" appeared in girls' yearbooks, whereas wishes for boys were more likely to convey best wishes for success with school, sports, or their futures without references to girls. Girls needed luck to experience dating success because of the gendered norm that mandated boys to ask and girls to angle to be selected and wait by the telephone.

Brief entries throughout Ortman's seventh-grade yearbook demonstrate how commonplace it was for girls to comment on one another's date prospects, even when most had barely begun to date. Colleen Leafdale wished Ortman happiness in the eighth grade and "with the boys." Eloise, also known as "Duck," wished Ortman good luck in her love life. Girls were more likely to include references to dating when they signed other girls' yearbooks, but boys who signed girls' yearbooks did so as well. John Frabotta, for example, wrote, "Lots of luck! Best wishes and may all of your good dreams come! true (boys)."[42] It is not clear whether the exclamation point after the word *come* was deliberate, but Frabotta clearly wanted to voice enthusiasm for heterosexual success—likely his and Ortman's.

Boys often exhibited a certain amount of bravado in their yearbook inscriptions that did not necessarily reflect their self-confidence but more often indicated norms of adolescent masculinity. In some cases they expressed open admiration for a boy they perceived to be lucky in love. In a Webster Groves High School *Echo* yearbook from 1952, seventh-grader David Steinmeyer wrote a three-sentence inscription to classmate Cy Perkins, whom he addressed parenthetically as "lover." Not only did Steinmeyer compliment Perkins's "swell personality" but he also penned, "I think you can have any of the women you want."[43] The idea of a thirteen-year-old boy attracting "women" is amusing given typical mid-century dating patterns; girls tended to date older boys, and boys were likely to date younger girls.

The yearbook inscriptions of older teenaged boys were bolder in the latter years of high school. In 1954, Ronnie Stein wrote to Cy Perkins, "Don't do anything I wouldn't do and if you do name it after me."[44] Insinuating that rebellious behavior might result in getting a girl pregnant, Stein made light of the potential consequences of heterosexual intercourse. He also playfully signaled appreciation of the sexual license that many teenage boys enjoyed, especially those from white, upper-middle-class backgrounds such as theirs.

Boys' friendships allowed them to assert masculinity and learn the social norms surrounding gender and sexuality. Some were more awkward in doing so than others, and standards of masculinity varied across social contexts. At Webster Groves it was not unorthodox for seventh-grader Bill Canfield to include sentimental lyrics to a popular song of the time (ending with the line "so let your hair down and go on and cry!") along with "best wishes to a swell guy."[45] Bob Younger expressed appreciation for Perkins's friendship in the eighth grade and also commented "your [sic] cute"; in the tenth grade, Younger wished "good luck to a cute Cy!"[46] Such compliments were common and apparently did not convey sexual attraction.

In these unofficial records of high school friendships and romantic relationships young people expressed feelings in a peer-controlled forum. Occasionally, teachers would autograph the books as well, and young people might suspect that curious parents would want to read and decipher the commentaries. But adult surveillance or self-censorship was less here than in other artifacts of school culture. If anything, young people were most self-conscious about the fact that peers might read what they wrote.

At a racially integrated high school like San Diego's, teachers, parents, and many students generally frowned on interracial intimacy, yet such bonds could find expression—however muted—in personal inscriptions and occasionally in photographs, however carefully cropped.[47] When popular newspapers and magazines covered the racial integration of schools, race "amalgamation" was an openly expressed concern of many segregationists. A *U.S. News and World Report* article in 1958 tapped into precisely those fears. One white teenaged girl reported that it was the norm for white girls to have crushes on boys of color. As Renee C. Romano points out, 96 percent of all whites opposed interracial marriage in 1958, and articles such as the one in *U.S. News* could lead to the conclusion that through integration, "Young girls were bound to see black boys either as exotic experiments or, worse [in the estimation of segregationists] ordinary guys."[48]

Racial subtexts remained hidden even as generic comments and rhymes in junior high school yearbooks evolved into more lengthy paragraphs about the quality of friendships and hopes for the future as well as references to particular heterosexual relationships. In this way, young people cooperated with adult expectations that different-sex friendships would attain greater significance during the teenaged years—from friendships to double or casual dating to steady dating as graduation approached. Students, for example, were acting in accordance with peer norms rather than imposed rules when they reserved a full page for their girl or boyfriend, as many did. Same-sex friends—especially in girls' yearbooks—would sometimes write several pages of comments but nearly always attribute significant space to heterosexual experiences: their various crushes on boys, dating successes and failures, and serious relationships.

Conclusion

As adolescents progressed through high school they encountered increased pressure, from adults as well as peers, to exhibit heterosexual interests. Teachers, youth group leaders, yearbook advisors, and parents helped construct an informal sexuality education curriculum. Like its formal counterpart, informal sex education developed with significant input from young people. They led and participated in school-based and out-of-school activities that centered on gendered maturity and heterosexual coupling. Although many young people worked to develop heterosexual recreational opportunities that pleased parents and teachers, there is evidence of dissent as well. Some challenged adult expectations by seeking companionship and love with same-sex partners or with different-sex partners from other racial, ethnic, religious, or class backgrounds, although such rebellions were not as common as they would be in subsequent decades.

Girls, thought to mature earlier than boys in both a sexual and an emotional sense, faced stronger imperatives to conform to and maintain the gendered expectations of adolescent heterosexuality. Striking an appearance of heterosexual interest—without entering into the realm of unacceptable promiscuity or inappropriate selection of dating partners—remained, however, difficult for many. A sociological study from 1956 found that more than half—163 of 262—of the first-year college students in Indiana recalled experiences of male sexual aggression as a senior or in the summer following high school graduation.[49] Untold numbers of girls encountered sexual harassment, a concept that lacked a name in the 1950s. However much educators sought to promote a single standard of sexual conduct and complementary, egalitarian gender roles through curricula and school activities, double standards and gender asymmetries persisted.

Concern about body image was another source of insecurity for many, and in the absence of feminist understanding of objectification and the male gaze critics tended to blame media influences rather than sexism or male entitlement as problems. Making note of teenage pregnancies and an alleged case of a teenaged girl who contemplated suicide on account of dissatisfaction with her breasts, a medical doctor in Oregon, Goodrich C. Schauffler, expressed outrage during the 1950s over "bosom inferiority complex" and the fact that "girls scarcely into adolescence" wore "falsies."[50] Schauffler's account lapses into sensationalism, but the underlying issues concerning pregnancy and body image were real for many. Teasing was common, and it especially frustrated girls as they developed mature bodies and encountered sexual attention, sometimes appreciated but often unwanted.[51]

Memoirs, yearbooks, and oral history interviews, along with sex education material, show how intensely schools and youth culture encouraged girls to monitor their appearance and display interest in being pretty and popular with boys. Yet because of the social norms of dating, they encountered a double bind. Gender ideology suggested that girls were to remain passive and let boys ask and pay for dates, yet sex and family life education encouraged girls to be assertive about making decisions that suited their personalities and relationship preferences. Public schools and popular media were not entirely dissimilar in their attempts to sexualize—or heterosexualize—teenaged culture. Adolescent adjustment guided by school officials and shaped by participation in peer culture virtually mandated that girls be agreeable to dating.

As girls developed sexual subjectivity and were rewarded for demonstrating interest in boys, pressures to be sexually interested but not sexually permissive left many confused. Girls sought advice and answers in a number of places, from adults and peers, family and friends, and the popular media and professional experts. For those who experienced guilt and frustration about feelings and desires it would take another decade of social upheaval, the turbulent 1960s and the movement for women's liberation, to do justice to their adolescent—and adult—struggles with sexuality.

Conclusion

"What a relief to learn that all my worries and my problems are normal!" Commenting on Elizabeth S. Force's family relationships class in Toms River, New Jersey, one teen girl wrote in the 1940s, "The course made me realize that all girls go through the same things."[1] Family relationships and similar courses gave students an opportunity to learn about customs and norms as well as a chance to hear from their peers. In an informal classroom setting they could gather on couches and comfortable chairs and collectively discuss the challenges of being a teenager, gaining independence from parents, dating and going steady, choosing a mate, planning a wedding, and ultimately marrying and forming families of their own. Judging by students' enthusiastic reports on family relationships, it was an enlightening, reassuring, and bonding experience.

After taking the American Social Hygiene Association course in a Cincinnati, Ohio, public school in the mid-1940s, girls revealed that the unit eliminated their unnamed concerns and worries about subjects their parents had not discussed.[2] Similar to the New Jersey students and Cincinnati girls, female high schools students at a laboratory high school affiliated with the University of Florida commented favorably about their experiences of sex education in home economics, stating that "knowing the truth" eliminated fears. They welcomed the new vocabulary that permitted them "to talk about sex without it seeming vulgar." Only three of the one hundred surveyed felt that schools should leave sex education to parents.[3]

Sex education and family living courses in public schools contributed to a process of removing sex and relationships from the realm of privacy. Lessons on puberty at the later elementary and junior high level or, in senior high school, conversations about family living were opportunities for frank and honest discussion about questions and problems. Such topics as growing up, secondary sex characteristics, dating, and reproduction became subjects of collective discussion, helping minimize taboos about sex talk among adolescents and contributing to a view of bodies, heterosexuality, and relationships as public concerns rather than individual, private matters. In addition to reducing the potential for self-consciousness, the discussions encouraged young people to evaluate and develop perspectives on male-female relationships and related topics.

Many students expected no less than a straightforward approach from teachers. The relieved Toms River student was probably one of many in sex education and family living classrooms across the country who insisted that teachers not "beat around the bush."[4] Responding to what they liked best about a sex education talk in the late 1950s, eighth-grade girls praised a visiting sex education lecturer who "didn't beat around the bush," "got to the point," and was "blunt, frank, and understanding." The words *frank, straight out, direct,* and *matter-of-fact* predominated in explanations of what students liked about the talk. One girl pronounced, "He talked to us, not at us, and answered our questions well."[5]

Preference for straightforward facts and guidance, however, was not universal. When physiology instructor Cecil M. Cook of Van Nuys High School near Los Angeles, California, asked twelfth-grade students to respond to a sex questionnaire in the late 1950s, his frankness courted trouble. At the state Board of Education hearing on Cook's conduct, "The state's star witness, blond Patricia Mather, thought the quiz itself 'shocking,'" reported *Newsweek.* Mather's "distaste increased when Cook's tabulation showed that nearly half the class had gone a long, long way in 'near intercourse' and that a fourth had gone all the way." To her chagrin, the witness relayed, some students were laughing during the presentation of the data. Another female student asserted that "all the kids sort of gasped" on learning the results.[6]

Explicit discussion of sex could prompt blushing and shame among girls (and possibly boys), but it could also dignify discussion of sexual norms, practices, and values in contemporary society. When Judy Kessler, a "self-possessed brunette miss," testified before a largely adult audience of parents and Board of Education members, her opinions resembled those of students who insisted that teachers not beat around the bush. Kessler articulated her need for answers and commented, "The teacher's manner was dignified. . . . There was never any feeling of vulgarity or dirtiness," she maintained. "In my opinion, the conduct of the class was above question. I was never embarrassed at all."[7]

Many young people were curious about questions of conduct and norms and willing to announce that concern. Countless students expressed curiosity through anonymous questions to instructors or lecturers. "Do you happen to know what percentage of men and women in the U.S. have sexual intercourse before marriage?" asked a teenager in St. Louis, Missouri, in an unsigned question submitted in advance of a 1958 sex education lecture. Another queried, "Do you believe that modern literature tends to dwell too significantly on sexual relations and sexual promiscuity? Is it an accurate representation of true life?" Other questions included, "What does society think of petting by teenagers? (In this day and age) Also: What do you think about the same subject?" and, "How do you feel about intercorse [sic] in a whorehouse?"[8]

Others, similar to Kessler, raised questions and concerns to a broader audience. Taking a public stand, Ruth Clarke, a seventeen-year-old from Erasmus Hall High School in New York City, proposed requiring sex education for schools at the Hi-Y "City Council" in 1946. She "encountered no difficulty with the sex education measure for which she was sponsor," and the vote was unanimous, unlike the unsuccessful measure to raise subway fares. All students who spoke on the provision for mandatory sex education favored the proposal.[9]

Young people's commentaries about sex and the problems of teenagers in the 1940s and 1950s reveal an active pursuit of knowledge and insight about sex, bodies, conduct, and relationships. For many girls, sex did not remain a taboo topic, in part because they learned to discuss it in classrooms, often in mixed company. "At one time I never could have talked so without blushing like a beet," a pupil in Force's class reportedly explained.[10] Yet Toms River courses—and others similar to them—enabled students, both boys and girls, to talk in mixed company about matters often viewed as personal. Embarrassment and awkwardness were likely to limit the ways that girls negotiated physical and/or sexual contact in heterosexual relationships. Learning to talk about sex without fear of being labeled precociously sexual or a slut, however, was a step forward and empowered girls to assert their perspectives and priorities in becoming physically intimate or choosing a dating partner or spouse.[11]

Previous scholars have not investigated mid-century girls' roles and experiences in sex and family living education, missing the fact that girls were in many ways the instigators and beneficiaries of such courses. Girls' bodies mature earlier than boys', which makes information about menstruation and pregnancy more immediately pertinent to their lives. Their interest in relationships occurs at a younger age than their male counterparts, and many girls are disposed to seek advice and input from teachers as well as peers on such questions as dating and engagement. Girls benefited from the courses because teachers sanctioned their introspection and analysis of relationships and guided them to useful ends. Female students learned about the significance of their reproductive organs and the process of menstruation; they learned how reproduction occurs and fetuses grow; and, in some instances, they learned about sexual feelings and masturbation as normal aspects of growing up for many.

As much as teachers included unexpected material in their lesson plans, they did not fully demystify the physical body, and much of what girls learned perpetuated sexist and heterosexist norms. That was especially the case when teachers conveyed outmoded ideas about women's physical capacity or grooming standards or when material focused on the fetus to the exclusion of the pregnant mother. Teachers commonly remained convinced of the legitimacy of social limitations on women. Psychological perspectives on relationships were as amenable to holding women back as to liberating them from the binds of domesticity and subordination. Nevertheless, in the process of covering material about the body and relationships and offering a psychological perspective on that information, teachers enticed adolescent girls to explore new terrain.

Educators' broad conception of sex in the 1940s and 1950s led them to focus on a wide variety of subjects, including some seemingly remote from sexuality. Educators' definition of sex as involving male-female differences and attractions meant that such topics as dating and finding a mate were essentially sexual. Although not usually about heterosexual intercourse or even sexual contact of other sorts, these topics amounted to teaching and advising about heterosexual lifestyles. Equally evident are the ways in which the lessons hinged on discussion and analysis of gender. Gendered heterosexuality was relevant course material for adolescents, both from their perspectives and from the perspectives of their teachers. Dating in particular was a subject for classroom discussion and an institutionalized rite of passage.

Rather than asserting gender as a given, a number of teachers and texts explained its historical and cultural variations; they were, however, less likely to recognize heterosexuality as a social construction. Many mid-century teachers believed that the division of roles and responsibilities along gender lines was acceptable and even ideal. They did not always respond to variation from gender norms as problematic, and furthermore they attempted to place boys and girls on an even footing with regard to interest in marriage and family. Yet rarely were lifestyles that did not include heterosexual partnerships granted serious consideration.

Sex education nevertheless had several positive outcomes during the 1940s and 1950s. First, it won the support of the public, student body, and administration in a number of locales, contributing to more openness of discussion, less shame about the body, and diversity of opinion. Although comprehensive sex education later came under attack for its explicitness, numerous classes participated in discussions before the backlash in the 1960s. Second, mid-century sex education shifted attention from negative repercussions of sexual contact—the emphasis of earlier projects—onto the positive elements of sex and gender, including the emotional satisfactions that romantic and sexual relationships ought to entail. Third, and least examined in scholarly literature, sex and family living education supplied girls with critical tools for questioning exploitation and male dominance, whether in relationships, in family dynamics, or in society.

Believed by proponents to be a "democratic" undertaking, sex education and family living courses were not exclusively offered to girls but rather to male students as well. Oregon's *Human Growth* demonstrated how to offer sex education to coed groups of young adolescents, but equally as important it was a launching point for further discussion and premised on the kinds of questions to which students sought answers. Interactive curricula at the high school level, especially group counseling in San Diego and family relationships courses in Toms River, organized successive classes around the concerns of each set of students. Methods of group discussions and panels, as well as other activities, redistributed power in classrooms and made the learning process one of exchange rather than lecture.

Discussion-oriented pedagogy helped embolden young people to be critical thinkers about sexual conduct and gender expression. Open-ended questions about desirable qualities in a mate held out the possibility that each student would formulate a unique agenda for heterosexual and marital success not dictated by the wisdom of adults or scholarly research. In coed classes in particular, gender did not differentiate the possibilities for marital happiness; teachers promoted complementary rather than hierarchical male-female relationships. It is not clear that parents and community members sought to empower young people in these ways, but few objected to promoting their emotional maturity and thoughtful conduct.

In the mid-century decades Parent-Teacher Associations commonly favored and promoted sex education, as did the National Education Association and various professional organizations. They faced little to no organized opposition although commentators frequently cited Catholics as holding back progress in sex education.[12] A Chicago school cancelled its family life curriculum in a home economics course after a newspaper headline claimed in 1948 that "Chicago High School Offers Sex Instruction" and unnamed special interest groups pressured the school administration to drop the course.[13] But such incidents were rare, and few interest groups mobilized around the issue at the time.

In the mid-twentieth century, upstanding administrators, teachers, and PTA leaders were in many cases able to convince parents and communities of the merits of sex education in schools. The degree of openness, however, had limits, both in sex education curricula and in public forums and discussions among adults. The personal (even professional) lives of leading sex researchers and educators were not subjected to scrutiny as has been the case with public figures more recently. Even publicity surrounding the case of the Van Nuys educator who chose to measure students' sex experience, a decision that brought him censure, did not extend into his personal life other than mentioning that he was married and had three children.

Nevertheless, popular endorsement of sex education was often passive, and it only took a small minority of mobilized opponents to eviscerate programs. Most classrooms permitted open discussion, but there were considerable constraints to what could be said. Cautions and warnings about sexual activity, which mid-century educators claimed to have eliminated from their "positive" sex education, were not entirely absent, especially as gendered notions of sex drives and misogyny persisted in the larger culture. Whatever critical tools they provided to young people, teachers rarely demonstrated how they might be used to upset the status quo of gender, race, class, or heterosexual privilege.

Although Alfred Kinsey's sex research raised the hackles of many commentators who were outraged and disgusted by his seeming endorsement of sexual diversity and "immorality," few parents and communities of the 1940s and 1950s sought to stop sex education or dictate what could be taught. What are we to make of such as discrepancy? By the end of the 1950s a few sex educators were rethinking traditional sexual values and abandoning proscriptions against premarital heterosexual intercourse, but their viewpoints were little known beyond the readership of professional journals. The anomalous Van Nuys case indicated the limits of what parents and community members would tolerate. Outlying cases notwithstanding, sex education—as the public imagined it—entailed factual knowledge that promoted stable families and gender and sexual conformity. Popular media did not contradict that view, yet professional literature and archival sources reveal that much more was going on in the field.

Sex education came under greater scrutiny from concerned parents during the 1960s, interest often mobilized by anticommunist organizations and the early beginnings of an organized religious right.[14] In the decade several programs developed in the 1940s and 1950s eventually caught the attention of the right, which decried what it considered the communist, humanist, and anti-Christian values of leading sex education authorities. In 1969, twenty years after the San Diego program's inauguration, the author of a pamphlet published by Sword of the Lord Publishers bemoaned the fact that children learned about sex in the sixth grade and viewed the film *The Story of Menstruation*.[15] Conservatives became more active when the Sex Information and Education Council of the United States (SIECUS) and Planned Parenthood Federation of America became active during the 1960s and 1970s and promoted "comprehensive" sex education that included such topics as premarital sex, contraception, and abortion, as Janice Irvine has detailed.[16]

By the end of the twentieth century, sex education had become a hotly debated topic, and conservative approaches were triumphant in the realm of publicly funded education. Welfare reform legislation in 1996 offered massive federal funding to states for use in abstinence-only education or education that stressed abstaining from sexual activity; all fifty states applied for such funds.[17] State and federal governments' allocation of $440 million for abstinence-based sex education bolstered the conservative agenda to remove contraceptive and "safe sex" information from schools. Although some states found ways to continue offering comprehensive education, one study revealed that more than a third of the nation's schools prohibited discussion of contraception other than highlighting its failures.[18]

Despite polls indicating that nearly all parents want their children to learn about sex and birth control at school, abstinence-only sex education has gained ground. Among the most outspoken proponents of abstinence only was Texas governor and U.S. president George W. Bush.[19] Whereas mid-century parents and adults tended to favor sex education, the main obstacles to creating such programs were inertia and lack of training. The current predicament seems quite different. One explanation for the discrepancy between popular support of school sex education and public policy limiting it is the mobilization of advocacy groups that wield influence beyond their numbers and set the terms of the debate.

Another distinction concerns the degree of sexual explicitness in the schools' surrounding environments. In the decades separating the 1950s and the new century, such controversy-inspiring topics as condoms, sexual harassment, HIV and AIDS, and gay, lesbian, bisexual, and transgender communities have become part of popular culture and permissible subjects of discussion in some classrooms.[20] Half a century earlier, prophylaxis, contraception, sexual assault, and homosexuality were uncomfortable subjects for many adults, and only infrequently did school children receive planned instruction in these areas. Yet the absence of planned discussions of such topics did not ensure their omission in classrooms of the 1940s and 1950s, and it was at students' prompting that teachers adopted a broader program of sex education. Numerous opportunities for young people to place anonymous questions in question boxes or voice personal concerns in mid-century class discussions compelled teachers to address premarital sexual activity, masturbation, rape, and abortion, among other topics. So, too, did anecdotes in the media, and stories relayed to doctors and school nurses.

Mid-century discussions and peer exchanges were not free from prescriptive and sometimes moralizing messages. Even teachers whose presence in classrooms was less than pedantic had numerous opportunities to shape discussions and information to suit particular adult agendas. In some instances instructors supported restrictive gender codes of etiquette, as when they instructed girls in methods of secrecy during menstruation or when discussions of dating reasserted girls' obligations to be heterosexually attractive but not tempting. Teachers helped girls develop greater self-awareness and the ability to monitor themselves using notions fully saturated with heterosexuality and gender. Instructors frequently abstracted women's bodies from their lives and isolated the process of pregnancy—as a tale about the growth of babies—from the experience of being pregnant. The possibilities for women's lives, presented through textbooks, movies, and classroom discussions, reinscribed heterosexual marriage and procreation as the ultimate satisfactions. Jobs, education, and other ambitions, in some instances, were valued as contributions to household needs rather than as individual goals.

The discussion method employed in almost all sex and family living courses mid-century involved dialog, which meant that students' perspectives found expression and often predominated. An ethic of fairness in discussions of dating pervaded both youths' and adults' assessments of boy-girl relationships, and that had the potential to be egalitarian with respect to gender. Yet much of what boys and girls said in class reiterated social prescriptions for a gendered division of labor and responsibilities. It might be only fair that a boy who paid for a date could determine the restaurant at which the couple would eat, but fairness was not just a matter of purchasing power. In the abstract, girls and boys had equal rights and responsibilities to ensure dating success but often those responsibilities were gendered and therefore placed special burdens on girls. As an example, allowing intimacies and exciting male "weaknesses" illustrates that "fairness" was not always fair. Girls were expected to attempt to control both their own conduct and their dates' behavior as well.

As a necessary precursor to feminist consciousness, the gender consciousness instilled in girls by sex education and family living curricula in some ways enabled them to recognize their collective identity and gain awareness of gender inequality. Pupils studied gender and examined the relevance of those lessons to their development and plans. The curricula's historical comparisons of family living in particular helped situate gender as a social and historical construct, mutable and subject to change. At the same time, through sex and family living courses as well as other aspects of the curricula, schools taught young people to embrace democratic idealism and be optimistic about human progress. A rhetoric of fairness and democracy was incompatible, in a number of instances, with prescribed heterosexual gender roles and expectations, for example, rules for dating and school dances. Gender dichotomies and restrictions cemented by school policies and cultures contradicted the democratic and antipatriarchal ideology expressed in classrooms.

Teachers encouraged young people to be introspective and strive for self-improvement. At a superficial level, Dallas educators suggested that students in twelfth-grade home and family living classes develop a scorecard to rate their personal appearances.[21] But introspection typically involved an examination of personality and adjusting to heterosexual maturity—including the ability to exercise self-control, balance work and leisure, establish independence from parents, and participate in the peer culture surrounding dating.

As the historian Ellen Herman has noted, the women's liberation movement and other movements of the New Left gained from concepts originating in psychology, which allowed them to see the connection between the personal and the political.[22] Among the resources psychology offered feminism was the ability to distinguish public and private as well as psychological and social.[23] Women's liberation activists took these resources into different territory and collectively used them to critique systemic gender discrimination and male dominance. A similar dynamic was at work in sex education classes, where group discussions united students in exploring sexual and gender-related topics, examining personal and family problems, and identifying individual needs, desires, and inclinations in the context of peers, families, and society. They learned about the process of adjustment to social norms, including the fact that the process was not natural or uniform but required certain amounts of effort that one might or might not choose to exert.

Disconnected from a feminist movement, sex and family life educators nevertheless conveyed to their pupils a critique of male-dominated households. The ideal democratic household did not depend on a patriarch; it was cooperative relationships that gave the democratic family the stamina it needed to survive the trials and tribulations of the World War II and postwar era. In the 1940s and 1950s the model of cooperative families and relationships extended to girls and women the possibility of autonomy, respect, and equal treatment even as some gendered and heterosexual norms remained beyond question. Yet social norms were changing, in part because of the efforts of young people to reconcile contradictory messages about sex, gender, and sexuality in and out of school.

Notes

Introduction

1. Important recent works on the history of sex education include Jeffrey P. Moran, *Teaching Sex: The Shaping of Adolescence in the Twentieth Century* (Cambridge: Harvard University Press, 2000); Julian B. Carter, "Birds, Bees, and Venereal Disease: Toward an Intellectual History of Sex Education," *Journal of the History of Sexuality* 10, no. 2 (2001): 213–49; Janice M. Irvine, *Talk about Sex: The Battles over Sex Education in the United States* (Berkeley: University of California Press, 2002); and Claudia Nelson and Michelle Martin, eds., *Sexual Pedagogies: England, Australia, and America, 1879–2000* (New York: Palgrave Macmillan, 2004).

2. David B. Tyack, *Seeking Common Ground: Public Schools in a Diverse Society* (Cambridge: Harvard University Press, 2003).

3. Michel Foucault, *History of Sexuality*, vol. 1: *An Introduction*, trans. Robert Hurley (New York: Pantheon, 1978).

4. Stephanie Coontz, *The Way We Never Were: American Families and the Nostalgia Trap* (New York: Basic Books, 1992); Joanne Meyerowitz, ed., *Not June Cleaver: Women and Gender in Postwar America, 1945–1960* (Philadelphia: Temple University Press, 1994).

5. "High School Graduates by Sex: 1870 to 1970," series H 598–601, *Historical Statistics of the United States, Colonial Times to 1970*, part 1 (Washington: GPO, 1975), 379.

6. Kelly Schrum, *Some Wore Bobby Sox: The Emergence of Teenage Girls' Culture, 1920–1945* (New York: Palgrave Macmillan, 2004); Deborah L. Tolman, *Dilemmas of Desire: Teenage Girls Talk about Sexuality* (Cambridge: Harvard University Press, 2002); Lois Weis and Michelle Fine, eds., *Construction Sites: Excavating Race, Class, and Gender among Urban Youth* (New York: Teachers College Press, 2000); Sherrie A. In-

ness, ed., *Delinquents and Debutantes: Twentieth-Century American Girls' Culture* (New York: New York University Press, 1998); Joan Jacobs Brumberg, *The Body Project: An Intimate History of American Girls* (New York: Random House, 1997); Susan J. Douglas, *Where the Girls Are: Growing Up Female with the Mass Media* (New York: Times Books, 1995); Marion de Ras and Mieke Lunenberg, eds., *Girls, Girlhood, and Girls' Studies in Transition* (Amsterdam: Het Spinhuis, 1993); Wini Breines, *Young, White, and Miserable: Growing Up Female in the Fifties* (Boston: Beacon Press, 1992).

7. Adrienne Rich, "Compulsory Heterosexuality and Lesbian Existence," *Signs* 5 (Summer 1980): 631–60; see also Jonathan Ned Katz, *The Invention of Heterosexuality* (New York: Penguin, 1995); and Mary Louise Adams, *The Trouble with Normal: Postwar Youth and the Making of Heterosexuality* (Toronto: University of Toronto Press, 1997).

8. Jennifer Terry, *An American Obsession: Science, Medicine, and Homosexuality in Modern Society* (Chicago: University of Chicago Press, 1999); Anne Fausto-Sterling, *Sexing the Body: Gender Politics and the Construction of Sexuality* (New York: Basic Books, 2000); Joanne Meyerowitz, *How Sex Changed: A History of Transsexuality in the United States* (Cambridge: Harvard University Press, 2002).

9. Wallace H. Maw, "Fifty Years of Sex Education in the Public Schools of the United States (1900–1950): A History of Ideas," Ed.D. diss, University of Cincinnati, 1953; James R. Cook, "The Evolution of Sex Education in the Public Schools of the United States, 1900–1970," Ph.D. diss., Southern Illinois University, 1971; Lawrence D. Klein, "Three Areas of Contention in Sex Education: The Policy Problem for American Public Schools," Ed.D. diss., Indiana University, 1971; Bryan Strong, "Ideas of the Early Sex Education Movement in America, 1890–1920," *History of Education Quarterly* 12, no. 2 (1972): 129–61; Michael Imber, "Analysis of a Curriculum Reform Movement: The American Social Hygiene Association's Campaign for Sex Education, 1900–1930," Ph.D. diss., Stanford University, 1981; Michael Imber, "Toward a Theory of Curriculum Reform: An Analysis of the First Campaign for Sex Education," *Curriculum Inquiry* 12, no. 4 (1982): 339–62, Michael Imber, "Toward a Theory of Educational Origins: The Genesis of Sex Education," *Educational Theory* 34, no. 3 (1984): 275–86; Judith Rabak Wagener, "A Social Epistemology of Sex Education in the Milwaukee Public Schools: 1910–1960," Ph.D. diss., University of Wisconsin-Madison, 1991; Christabelle Laura Sethna, "The Facts of Life: The Sex Instruction of Ontario Public School Children, 1900–1950," Ed.D. diss., University of Toronto, 1995; Jeffrey P. Moran, "'Modernism Gone Mad': Sex Education Comes to Chicago, 1913," *Journal of American History* 83, no. 2 (1996): 481–513; Adams, *The Trouble with Normal;* Moran, *Teaching Sex;* Carter, "Birds, Bees, and Venereal Disease."

10. Moran, *Teaching Sex,* 61. Less surprisingly, dissertations and theses written at mid-century display a disinterest in gender issues.

11. Mariamne Whatley, "Male and Female Hormones: Misinterpretations of Biology in School Health and Sex Education," in *Women, Biology, and Public Policy,* ed. Virginia Shapiro (Beverly Hills: Sage Publications, 1985), 67–89; Michelle Fine,

"Sexuality, Schooling, and Adolescent Females: The Missing Discourse of Desire," *Harvard Educational Review* 58, no. 1 (1988): 29–53; Susan Shurberg Klein, ed., *Sex Equity and Sexuality in Education* (Albany: State University of New York Press, 1992); James T. Sears, ed., *Sexuality and the Curriculum: The Politics and Practices of Sexuality Education* (New York: Teachers College Press, 1992); Bonnie Nelson Trudell, *Doing Sex Education: Gender Politics and Schooling* (New York: Routledge, 1993); Janice M. Irvine, ed., *Sexual Cultures and the Construction of Adolescent Identities* (Philadelphia: Temple University Press, 1994), Janice M. Irvine, *Sexuality Education across Cultures: Working with Differences* (San Francisco: Jossey-Bass Publishers, 1995); Robert Eberwein, *Sex Ed: Film, Video, and the Framework of Desire* (New Brunswick: Rutgers University Press, 1999).

12. Trudell, *Doing Sex Education*, 7, 8.

Chapter 1: Momentum and Legitimacy

1. Harold Isaacs, "Youth: Shall Our Schools Teach Sex?" *Newsweek*, 19 May 1947, 100–102.

2. Lester A. Kirkendall, *Sex Educations as Human Relations: A Guidebook on Content and Methods for School Authorities and Teachers* (New York: Inor, 1950), chap. 4.

3. "The Battle over Sex Education Films," *Look*, 30 August 1949, 34–35.

4. Issacs, "Youth," 102.

5. Bob Gilmore, "Sex Goes to School in Oregon," *Better Homes and Gardens*, September 1947, 41; "Sex in the Schoolroom in Oregon," *Time*, 22 March 1948, 71–72; "Sex Education . . . San Diego Pioneers," *Ladies' Home Journal*, April 1948, 23, 273, 275–77; Karl Kohrs, "They Study How to Live: Toms River Youngsters Face the Problems of Living in a Special—and Significant—High School Course," *Parade*, 9 May 1948, 5–7. For a local newspaper story, see Velma Clyde, "Sex Education: Oregon Takes Lead over Rest of Nation," *Portland Oregonian*, 4 May 1947.

6. Isaacs, "Youth," 101.

7. Lester A. Kirkendall, "Sex Education in Nine Cooperating Schools," part 1, *Clearing House* 18, no. 7 (1944): 387.

8. Kohrs, "They Study How to Live," 5.

9. Alfred C. Kinsey, Wardell B. Pomeroy, and Clyde E. Martin, *Sexual Behavior in the Human Male* (Philadelphia: W. B. Saunders, 1948).

10. Myron M. Stearns, "The ABC's of Happy Marriage," *Today's Woman*, February 1948, 32–33, 131–35; "Where Babies Come From: University of Oregon Program of Education on Family Life," *Newsweek*, 22 March 1948, 90; "Sex in the Schoolroom"; "Sex Education . . . San Diego Pioneers"; Stella B. Applebaum, "A School That Prepares for Living: Toms River, N.J. Revamped Its High School Program to Satisfy the Students' Real Needs," *Parents' Magazine* 24 (May 1948): 36–37, 106; "They Study How to Live"; "Sex Education: Oregon Film Provides New Approach to Delicate Problem," *Life*, 24 May 1948, 55.

11. According to the *Readers Guide to Periodical Literature* index between 1935 and 1960, articles focused on "sex instruction" peaked between May 1947 and April 1949, with thirty-two titles listed during those two years. The "sex instruction" category encompassed teaching sex education at school, educating children at home, and answering adults' questions about sex.

12. See, for example, "The Battle over Sex Education Films"; and "More Candid Attitude toward Sex Education," *Nation*, 24 December 1949, 607.

13. For a recent example of the controversy thesis in mid-century sex education, see Ginia Bellafante, "Facts of Life, for Their Eyes Only," *New York Times*, 6 June 2005.

14. See, for example, Letters to the Editor, *Life*, 14 June 1948, 17–18.

15. Janice M. Irvine, *Talk about Sex: The Battles over Sex Education in the United States* (Berkeley: University of California Press, 2002).

16. The best sources on social hygiene and sex education are Alan M. Brandt, *No Magic Bullet: A Social History of Venereal Disease in the United States since 1880*, 2d ed. (New York: Oxford University Press, 1987); and Jeffrey P. Moran, *Teaching Sex: The Shaping of Adolescence in the Twentieth Century* (Cambridge: Harvard University Press, 2000). See also John C. Burnham, "The Progressive Era Revolution in American Attitudes toward Sex," *Journal of American History* 59, no. 4 (1973): 885–908; and Michael Imber, "Analysis of a Curriculum Reform Movement: The American Social Hygiene Association's Campaign for Sex Education, 1900–1930," Ph.D. diss., Stanford University, 1981.

17. See especially Julian B. Carter, "Birds, Bees, and Venereal Disease: Toward an Intellectual History of Sex Education," *Journal of the History of Sexuality* 10, no. 2 (2001): 220–24. On eugenics in the twentieth-century United States see Wendy Kline, *Building a Better Race: Gender, Sexuality, and Eugenics from the Turn of the Century to the Baby Boom* (Berkeley: University of California Press, 2001).

18. Grace F. Ellis and T. Dinsmore Upton, "Sex Instruction in a High School," *Social Hygiene* 1 (March 1915): 271–72; Mildred E. Reeve, "Gifts of Spring: An Experiment in Social Hygiene," *Journal of Social Hygiene* 12 (March 1926): 137–43.

19. William T. Foster, "Statewide Education in Social Hygiene," *Social Hygiene* 2 (July 1916): 309–29, esp. 318–20.

20. Brandt, *No Magic Bullet*; Moran, *Teaching Sex*; Robert Eberwein, *Sex Ed: Film, Video, and the Framework of Desire* (New Brunswick: Rutgers University Press, 1999).

21. Newell W. Edson, *Status of Sex Education in High Schools* (Washington: GPO, 1922); Lida J. Usilton and Newell W. Edson, *The Status of Sex Education in Senior High Schools of the United States in 1927* (Washington: GPO, 1928). Although difficult to quantify, one calculation suggests that 2,500 senior high schools offered sex education, covering the following topics: "eugenics and heredity" (1,306 schools), "reproduction" (1,154), the ambiguous "'social aspects' of sexuality" (850), venereal diseases (571), "'internal secretions' and menstruation" (420), and "seminal emissions" (171). Moran, *Teaching Sex*, 105–7.

22. Thomas Parran, foreword to Benjamin C. Gruenberg, with the assistance of J. L. Kaukonen, *High Schools and Sex Education* (Washington: GPO, 1939), xvi.

23. Anita D. Laton, "Approaches to Sex Education in the Schools," *University High School Journal* 16 (April 1938): 147–55.

24. University of Chicago education professor Robert J. Havighurst was tremendously influential. Many teachers employed his model of developmental tasks of adolescence, and in 1950 Havighurst wrote the foreword to Kirkendall's *Sex Education as Human Relations*. Although few educators directly articulated their intellectual debts, such luminaries as G. Stanley Hall and Sigmund Freud clearly shaped their understanding of adolescence.

25. The influence of current events and academic scholarship in shaping mid-twentieth-century sex education appears in introductions, forewords, and bibliographies to contemporary books on the subject. A useful guide to the constellation of interest groups associated with progressive education is the afterword to a scholarly study in the history of education: Herbert M. Kliebard, *The Struggle for the American Curriculum, 1893–1958*, 2d ed. (New York: Routledge, 1995), 231–52.

26. The child study movement, dating to the late nineteenth century, offered advice on parenting, including sex education; mostly dismissed by twentieth century psychologists and social scientists, the field became dominated by "professional guidance counselors." Joseph F. Kett, *Rites of Passage: Adolescence in America, 1790 to the Present* (New York: Basic Books, 1977), 230. In addition to the Child Study Association, such organizations as the Society for Research in Child Development and the National Society for the Study of Education published reports and studies, many with a psychoanalytic bent. William Walter Greulich, *Handbook of Methods for the Study of Adolescent Children* (Washington: National Research Council, 1938), esp. chap. 21; Nelson B. Henry, ed., *The Thirty-Third Yearbook of the National Society for the Study of Education, Part 1: Adolescence* (Chicago: National Society for the Study of Education, 1944), esp. chap. 13. Attention to "normal" adjustment instead of problem children developed during the mid-twentieth century. See Frances Bruce Strain, *The Normal Sex Interests of Children from Infancy to Childhood* (New York: Appleton-Century-Crofts, 1948).

27. "The Matter and Methods of Sex Education," *Social Hygiene* 2 (October 1916): 573–81, quotation on 574.

28. Maurice A. Bigelow, "The Established Points in Social-Hygiene Education, 1905–1924," *Journal of Social Hygiene* 10 (January 1924): 2–11, quotation on 3.

29. John Newton Baker, *Sex Education in High Schools* (New York: Emerson Books, 1942); Lester A. Kirkendall and Mark Fleitzer, "Recent Findings on Sex Behavior: The Facts Speak for Sex Education," *Clearing House* 22 (September 1947): 27–31; Margie Lee Robinson, "Measuring the Sex Knowledge of Junior High School Pupils," master's thesis, University of Oregon, 1949; Thomas Poffenberger, "Responses of Eighth Grade Girls to a Talk on Sex," *Marriage and Family Living* 22 (February 1960): 38–44.

30. Maurice A. Bigelow, "Sex Education in School Programs on Health and Human Relations," *Journal of Social Hygiene* 30 (February 1944): 84–87.

31. See, for example, guidance for discussing "mixed marriage" in Elizabeth S. Force and Edgar M. Finck, *Family Relationships: Ten Topics toward Happier Homes,*

a Handbook for Administrators and Teachers Who Use the Accompanying Study Guide (Elizabethtown: Continental Press, [1949]), 32–33.

32. Division of Instruction, Department of Family Life Education, Detroit Public Schools, *Family Life Education in the High School: A Source Book for Teachers* (Detroit: Board of Education of the City of Detroit, 1958), 33. Notably, the guide recommended that the class might bring a "minister, rabbi, and priest to discuss with the class: a. Some problems of mixed marriages (religion and race) [and] b. How religion prepares young people for marriage."

33. More often than not, educators conveyed concern about choosing a socially rather than biologically compatible mate. Heredity, then, was also related to social characteristics, educational background, and lifestyle choices and therefore had as much to do with social class and racial/ethnic communities as with genes. Bert Y. Glassberg, lecture for twelfth-grade students, "The Choice of a Marital Partner," St. Louis Board of Education Program on Personal and Family Living, [March 1957,], box 7, folder 183, Bert Y. Glassberg Papers, Becker Medical Library, Washington University School of Medicine, St. Louis, Missouri.

34. Purity reformers deployed a moral and religious approach to social ills earlier in the century, and although social hygiene's messages were laden with Victorian morality, their tendency was to focus on disease. Burnham, "Progressive Era Revolution."

35. On companionate marriage, see Christina Simmons, "'Marriage in the Modern Manner': Sexual Radicalism and Reform in America, 1914–1941," Ph.D. diss., Brown University, 1982.

36. Teachers in publicity about sex education were almost two times more likely to be female than male, and the widely viewed film *Human Growth* cast a female teacher as well. Surveys of Pennsylvania and Wisconsin educators, however, each found that men slightly outnumbered women as teachers of sex or family life education, with women comprising 45 and 44 percent respectively. Warren H. Southworth, "A Study in the Area of Family Life Education: The Nature of Sex Education Programs in Wisconsin High Schools," *High School Journal* 38 (December 1954): 104; Allan A. Glatthorn, "Family Life Education in the Public High Schools of Pennsylvania, 1957–1958," Ed.D. diss., Temple University, 1960, 148.

37. Elizabeth S. Force, *Teaching Family Life Education: The Toms River Program* (New York: Teachers College, Columbia University, 1962), chap. 1.

38. Lawrence Arthur Cremin, *The Transformation of the School: Progressivism in American Education, 1876–1957* (New York: Knopf, 1961), chap. 9; Kliebard, *The Struggle for the American Curriculum,* chap. 9.

39. William E. Vickery, "Ten Years of Intergroup Education Workshops: Some Comparisons and Contrasts," *Journal of Educational Sociology* 26 (March 1953): 292–302.

40. Clara Lee Cone, "A High School Course in Family Living," *Marriage and Family Living* 13 (November 1951): 154–55.

41. Jacob A. Goldberg, "Sex Education or Social Hygiene Education in Schools in

Forty Cities" *Journal of Social Hygiene* 33 (December 1947): 437–44, quotation on 444.

42. G. Gage Wetherill, *Human Relations Education: A Program Developing in the San Diego City Schools* (New York: American Social Hygiene Association, 1946).

43. Kenneth E. Oberholtzer and Myrtle F. Sugarman, "Denver Educates for Home and Family Living," *Journal of Social Hygiene* 37 (February 1951): 51–61. On Denver Superintendent Oberholtzer's philosophy of education and his role in updating the city's curricula, see the column "Education," *Time*, 2 February 1950, 66–72.

44. S. P. Marland Jr., "Placing Sex Education in the Curriculum," *Phi Delta Kappan* 43 (December 1961): 132–34; Calvin R. Benefiel and Helen U. Zimnavoda, "Pupil Reaction to Family Life Education," *California Journal of Secondary Education* 28 (November 1953): 363–65; "What Are Some Promising Administrative Practices in the Junior High School?" *Bulletin of the National Association of Secondary-School Principals* 42 (April 1958): 227–29.

45. Marjorie Cosgrove, "School Guidance for Home and Family Living: A Required Course for Seniors in Highland Park, Michigan High School," *Marriage and Family Living* 14 (February 1952): 26–31; Una Funk, "A Realistic Family-Life Program—One Approach to the Problem of Teenage Marriage," *National Education Association Journal* 44 (March 1955): 163–64; Fannie B. Masten, "Family Life Education at Central High School, Charlotte, North Carolina," *Marriage and Family Living* 15 (May 1953): 105–8; Francis Bruce Strain and Chester Lee Eggert, "Framework for Family Life Education: A Sourcebook," *Bulletin of the National Association of Secondary-School Principals* 40 (December 1955): 62–67.

46. Kirk Fox, "Sex Education in the Schools," *Successful Farming*, April 1938, 14–15.

47. "Public Opinion Polls," *Public Opinion Quarterly* 7, no. 4 (1943): 748.

48. "Companion Poll Question: Do You Favor Special Courses in Sex Education in High Schools as One Means of Reducing Juvenile Delinquency?" *Woman's Home Companion*, November 1943, 32.

49. Statistics appear in "Parents Demand Sex Education in Schools," *Family Life* 6 (September 1946): 1–2. Apparently, *New York Tribune* reporters mentioned the survey. "Sex in the News," *Sexology* 14 (January 1948): 328; see also Kirkendall, *Sex Education as Human Relations*, 45–46.

50. Kenneth Fink, "Public Thinks Sex Education Courses Should Be Taught in the Schools," *Journal of Social Hygiene* 37 (February 1951): 62–63.

51. Cecil Thomas Paddack, "Public Opinion of the People of Washington Regarding the Teaching of Sex Education in the Public Schools," master's thesis, State College of Washington, 1951, 14–15.

52. Paddack, "Public Opinion of the People," 23.

53. "What about Sex Instruction?" *Nation's Schools* 33 (June 1944): 49.

54. "Sex Education Has Place in Junior, Senior High Schools," *Nation's Schools* 65 (March 1960): 94.

55. "Urge More Sex Teaching," *New York Times*, 26 June 1947, 17.

56. "Parents Held Lax in Sex Education," *New York Times*, 5 December 1948, 77.

57. "Boys Urge Sex Classes," *New York Times*, 20 June 1949, 16.

58. Donald Kaiser cited in "Sexological News," *Sexology* 17 (April 1951): 609.

59. Cited in "Sexological News," *Sexology* 15 (October 1952): 200.

60. "Hi-Y Rejects Ban on Minors' Liquor," *New York Times*, 10 December 1939, 36; "Youth 'Legislate' on Varied Lines," *New York Times*, 10 December 1944, 52; "Teen-Age Council Shelves Subway Fare Rise but Votes for a Course in Sex Education," *New York Times*, 27 April 1946, 19; "Pupils Run City Council," *New York Times*, 3 April 1948, 16.

61. American Association of University Women, *Report of a Parent Education Survey Conducted by the Branch Chairmen of the American Association of University Women* (1932), cited in Joseph K. Folsom, *Youth, Family, and Education* (Washington: American Council on Education, 1941), 142, see also 144, 209–11; Mabel Grier Lesher, *Meeting Youth Needs* (Trenton: New Jersey Congress of Parents and Teachers, [1944]); "Notes on Recent State Activities Relating to Sex Education," *Journal of Social Hygiene* 31 (April 1945): 220–27; Betty A. Murch, "Rhode Island Offers Lecture Series on 'Love and Marriage Today,'" *Journal of Social Hygiene* 24 (December 1948): 438–40.

62. William F. Snow, *Social Hygiene in Schools: Report of the Subcommittee on Social Hygiene in Schools, White House Conference on Child Health and Protection* (New York: The Century Co., 1932), 40; National Congress of Parents and Teachers, *Proceedings: Forty-Eighth Annual Convention*, New York, 22–24 May 1944 (Chicago: National Congress of Parents and Teachers, 1944), 181–84, 339–40, 361, 402.

63. National Congress of Parents and Teachers, *Forty-Eighth Annual Convention*, 339; see also Eleanor Shenehon, "Colorado: State PTA Favors Social Hygiene Instruction in Schools," *Journal of Social Hygiene* 32 (June 1946): 264–65; Mabel Grier Lesher, "Education for Family Life (New Jersey)," *Journal of Educational Sociology* 22 (March 1949): 440–49; and Ray H. Everett, "Sex Education in Washington," *Journal of Social Hygiene* 40 (June 1954): 222–25.

64. Payton Kennedy, "Family Life Education in San Antonio," *Journal of Social Hygiene* 39 (April 1953): 156–64, esp. 164.

65. Mildred Morgan, "The Hillsborough Study: A Grass Roots Development of a County-Wide Family Life Program Which Includes Sex Education," unpublished manuscript, 1962, American Social Hygiene Association Papers, box 12, "Florida-Hillsborough" folder, Social Welfare History Archives, Minneapolis, Minnesota.

66. "'Jury' of 350 Mothers Approves Sex Education Films in Schools," *New York Times*, 22 March 1949, 27; "Audiences Approve Sex Education Film," *New York Times*, 31 March 1949, 23; *Human Growth*, 16 mm, 20 min., E. C. Brown Trust and Eddie Albert Productions, Portland, Ore., 1947; *Human Reproduction*, 16 mm, 21 min., McGraw-Hill, New York, 1948. The latter film correlated with Harold S. Diehl's *Textbook of Healthful Living*, 3d ed. (New York: McGraw-Hill, 1945). It was intended for a college or adult audience or for senior high school students.

67. Helen Manley, "Sex Education: Where, When, and How Shall It Be Taught?" *Journal of Health, Physical Education, and Recreation* 35 (March 1964): 21–24.

68. Ewell G. Pigg, "Sex Education in High School Science," *Science and Mathematics* 41 (December 1941): 851–54, quotation on 853.

69. See, for example, Ruth Farnham Osborne and Lester A. Kirkendall, "Family-Life Education in Illinois High Schools," *School Review* 58 (December 1950): 516–26.

70. Anna M. W. Wolf, *When Children Ask about Sex* (New York: Child Study Association of America, 1943); Frances Bruce Strain, "Sex Education at Different Ages," *Parents' Magazine*, April 1945, 34–35+; Benjamin Spock, *The Pocket Book of Baby and Child Care* (New York: Pocket Books, 1948); Howard Whitman, *Let's Tell the Truth about Sex* (New York: Pelligrini and Cudahy, 1948); Milton L. Levine, "What Do Our Adolescents Really Want to Know about Sex?" *Ladies' Home Journal*, September 1955, 68–69, 194, 197–98.

71. Dollie R. Walker, "The Need of Sex Education in Negro Schools," *Journal of Negro Education* 14 (Spring 1945): 174–81, esp. 177.

72. Beth L. Bailey, *From Front Porch to Back Seat: Courtship in Twentieth-Century America* (Baltimore: Johns Hopkins University Press, 1988), esp. 119–40. Descriptions of such courses abound; see, for example, Winston W. Ehrmann, "Preparation for Marriage and Parenthood," *Journal of Higher Education* 24 (March 1953): 141–48, 167–68.

73. Students enrolled in University of California, Berkeley's popular course on youth and marriage voted 99 percent in favor of sex education in high school for students aged sixteen and up. Dean Jennings, "Sex in the Classroom," *Collier's*, 15 September 1945, 22–23, 51.

74. "District of Columbia: Board of Education Approves Sex Instruction," *Journal of Social Hygiene* 29 (November 1943): 551; "California: South San Francisco School Board Acts," *Journal of Social Hygiene* 35 (May 1949): 226.

75. Howard Stanley Hoyman, *Health-Guide Units for Oregon Teachers, Grades 7–12* (Portland: E. C. Brown Trust, 1945); "Michigan Adopts Law Proving for Social Hygiene Education," *Journal of Social Hygiene* 35 (October 1949): 346.

76. The "Tenny Bill" (S.R. 1026) would have limited sex education to senior students and mandated its instruction by a physician only, but with PTA opposition and state legislators' inaction the initiative died. Greta Willis Slater, "An Historical Study of the Social Health Program in the San Diego City Schools, 1937–1966," master's thesis, University of California, Los Angeles, 1966, 61–62.

77. Imber, "Analysis of Curriculum Reform," chap. 5; Moran, *Teaching Sex*, 73–75.

78. Gladwin Hill, "Hearing Is Ended on Sex Teaching," *New York Times*, 9 August 1959, 63; "Sex in the Classroom," *Newsweek*, 10 August 1959, 84.

79. Richard Kline, "Should Sex Education Be Taught in Schools?" *Los Angeles Examiner*, 2 August 1959, sec. 1, 2.

80. Lester A. Kirkendall, "Values and Premarital Intercourse—Implications for Parent Education," *Marriage and Family Living* 22 (November 1960): 317–22; Ira L.

Reiss, *Premarital Sexual Standards in America: A Sociological Investigation of the Relative Social and Cultural Integration of American Sexual Standards* (Glencoe: The Free Press, 1960).

Chapter 2: Reconstructing Classrooms and Relationships

1. For a critique of present and past conceptualizations of adolescent development, see Nancy Lesko, *Act Your Age! A Cultural Construction of Adolescence* (New York: RoutledgeFalmer, 2001).

2. Beth L. Bailey, *Sex in the Heartland* (Cambridge: Harvard University Press, 1999).

3. Fannie B. Masten, "Family Life Education at Central High School, Charlotte, North Carolina," *Marriage and Family Living* 15 (May 1953): 105–8; see also Nancy C. Wimmer, "Trends in Family Life Education in the Schools," *Journal of Social Hygiene* 19 (February 1953): 69–78.

4. Linda Ann Gray, "Family Life Education Courses: A Survey of Selected High Schools of Illinois," master's thesis, Illinois State Normal University, 1955, 54.

5. Donita Ferguson and Carol Lynn Gilmer, "Sex Education, Please!" *Coronet,* January 1949, 73–80.

6. Margaret Schilling, "Evaluation in a Family Life Education Program," *Marriage and Family Living* 23 (August 1961): 297–99.

7. Payton Kennedy, "Family Life Education in San Antonio," *Journal of Social Hygiene* 39 (April 1953): 156–64, esp. 156.

8. Moran dates this type of innovation to the 1960s. Jeffrey P. Moran, *Teaching Sex: The Shaping of Adolescence in the Twentieth Century* (Cambridge: Harvard University Press, 2000), chap. 6, esp. 174.

9. Maurice A. Bigelow, "The Established Points in Social-Hygiene Education, 1905–1924," *Journal of Social Hygiene* 10 (January 1924): 5–6.

10. John Newton Baker, *Sex Education in High Schools* (New York: Emerson Books, 1942), 58.

11. Elizabeth S. Force, "What Teen-Agers Want to Know about Sex and Marriage," *American Magazine* 155 (January 1953): 34–35, 103–6, quotations on 34, 103–4.

12. Eva Kirby, "Family Life Education in Biology," *California Journal of Secondary Education* 25 (January 1950): 34–37, quotation on 36.

13. Howard M. Bell, *Youth Tell Their Story* (Washington: American Council on Education, 1938), 40–42, 88–91.

14. Bell, *Youth Tell Their Story,* 42.

15. Ibid.

16. Ibid., 91.

17. Thomas Poffenberger, "Family Life Education in This Scientific Age," *Marriage and Family Living* 21 (May 1959): 150–54, quotations on 152.

18. Bell, *Youth Tell Their Story,* 40. The sample was 84.6 percent "White" and 15.4 percent "Negro." Ibid., 257.

19. Ibid., 90. Bell's emphasis on "admitted" suggests that he assumed the number to be greater than admitted. On unwed motherhood and race during this period, see Rickie Solinger, *Wake Up Little Susie: Single Pregnancy and Race before Roe v. Wade* (New York: Routledge, 1992).

20. Viola I. Lampe, "Growing Up: Lessons in Health and Human Relations for Sixth Grade Boys and Girls," in G. Gage Wetherill, *Human Relations Education: A Program Developing in the San Diego City Schools* (New York: American Social Hygiene Association, 1946), 39. The second edition was less condemnatory of parents but retained the notion that many parents were immature or too poorly adjusted themselves to provide guidance for their children. Viola I. Lampe, "Growing Up: Lessons in Social Hygiene Education for Sixth-Grade Boys and Girls," in G. Gage Wetherill, *Human Relations Education: A Report,* 2d ed. (New York: American Social Hygiene Association, 1951), 40.

21. Lampe, "Growing Up," 39.

22. Quoted in Ruth Strang, *The Adolescent Views Himself: A Psychology of Adolescence* (New York: McGraw-Hill, 1957), 342.

23. Strang, *The Adolescent Views Himself,* 341.

24. "Sex Education . . . San Diego Pioneers," *Ladies' Home Journal,* March 1948, 275.

25. Geneva E. Gordon, "First Annual Report to the Superintendent, San Diego City Secondary Schools," unpublished outline, 14 June 1948, quoted in Lloyd S. Van Winkle, "The Teaching of Sex Education in the Elementary School," Ed.D. diss., Colorado State College of Education, 1949, 54.

26. Gordon, "First Annual Report," 55.

27. Catherine Marsman Jones, "A Resource Guide for the Establishment of a Social Health Program at the Secondary Level," master's thesis, San Diego State College, 1960, 52; *Name Unknown,* 16 mm, 10 minutes, Los Angeles, Calif., Sid Davis Productions, 1951.

28. Thomas H. Knepp, "The Need for Sex Education in the High School," *The Science Teacher* 19 (March 1952): 60–63.

29. Roscoe G. Bernard, "An Investigation of the Possibility of Teaching Sex Education as an Integral Part of a Mental Hygiene Program on an Elementary School Level," master's thesis, Kansas State Teachers College of Emporia, 1955, 4–10.

30. James A. Michener, "Sex Education: A Success in Our Social Studies Class," *Clearing House* 12 (April 1938): 461–65; Dorothy Wertman, "Our Successful Lecture Series on Sex Education," *Clearing House* 19 (November 1944): 174–76; Clara Lee Cone, "A High School Course in Family Living," *Marriage and Family Living* 13 (November 1951): 154–55.

31. Wendell P. Hill, "A Study of a High School Marriage and Family Course," master's thesis, University of Michigan, 1952, 34, 40.

32. Elva Horner Evans, "Sex Education: It Can Be Taught as a Separate Course," *Health and Physical Education* 17 (May 1946): 268–70, quotations on 269.

33. Gordon, "First Annual Report," 54.

34. Fannie B. J. Masten as told to Jack Harrison Pollack, "What I Teach Teen-Agers about Love, Sex, and Marriage," *Woman's Home Companion,* February 1955, 87–88.

35. G. Gage Wetherill, "Who Is Responsible for Sex Education?" *Journal of School Health* 29 (December 1959): 361–64, quotation on 364.

36. G. Gage Wetherill, "Sex Education in the Public Schools," *Journal of School Health* 31 (September 1961): 235–39, quotation on 235.

37. Harl R. Douglass, *Trends and Issues in Secondary Education* (Washington: Center for Applied Research in Education, 1962), 39.

38. Douglass, *Trends and Issues,* 19–20, 74.

39. "Sex Education Question up to S.D. Round Table," *San Diego Union,* 2 November 1937, 12; "Sex Education Put Forward as Public Problem," *San Diego Union,* 4 November 1937, 6; "Third Annual State-Wide Conference on Social Hygiene," 4 February 1944, in *Oregon Health Bulletin,* 2 February 1944, 6–7.

40. Katherine L. Arnold and Virginia L. Gleason, "Discussion Methods with New Variations," *Marriage and Family Living* 21 (May 1959): 180–81.

41. Mention of this method was ubiquitous; for a few examples see Baker, *Sex Education in High Schools,* 58–59; Roanoke City Public Schools, *Family Life Education Resource Guide, Grade 1 through 12* (New York: American Social Hygiene Association, 1958), 71; and Mildred Morgan, "The Hillsborough Study: A Grass Roots Development of a County-Wide Family Life Program Which Includes Sex Education," unpublished manuscript, 1962, 4, box 12, "Florida—Hillsborough" folder, American Social Hygiene Association Papers, Social Welfare History Archives, Minneapolis, Minnesota (hereafter ASHA Papers).

42. Elliott E. Kigner, "Girls in Junior High School Analyze Their Problems," *Clearing House* 31 (April 1957): 466–69, quotations on 466–67.

43. Kigner, "Girls in Junior High School," 469.

44. Virginia Milling, "How Do You Rate on a Date?" *Clearing House* 19 (November 1944): 165–66, quotation on 165.

45. Masten as told to Pollack, "What I Teach Teenagers," 87.

46. H. Edmund Bullis and Emily E. O'Malley, *Human Relations in the Classroom, Course 1* (Wilmington: Delaware State Society for Mental Hygiene, 1947), 217.

47. Bullis and O'Malley, *Human Relations,* 5.

48. On the authority of social scientists, see Moran, *Teaching Sex;* Ellen Herman, *The Romance of American Psychology: Political Culture in the Age of Experts* (Berkeley: University of California Press, 1995); Regina G. Kunzel, *Fallen Women, Problem Girls: Unmarried Mothers and the Professionalization of Social Work, 1890–1945* (New Haven: Yale University Press, 1995); and Solinger, *Wake Up Little Susie.*

49. Moran, *Teaching Sex,* 157–58, makes a similar argument.

50. Alfred C. Kinsey, Wardell B. Pomeroy, and Clyde E. Martin, *Sexual Behavior in the Human Male* (Philadelphia: W. B. Saunders, 1948); Alfred C. Kinsey et al., *Sexual Behavior in the Human Female* (Philadelphia: W. B. Saunders, 1953).

51. Lester A. Kirkendall, *Sex Education as Human Relations: A Guidebook on Content and Methods for School Authorities and Teachers* (New York: Inor, 1950).

52. Elizabeth S. Force, "Toms River Looks Back—1951–1941," *Journal of Social Hygiene* 38 (January 1952): 2–10.

53. Gertrude Burgess, "Development and Results of a Sex Hygiene Course in a Consolidated High School," *Michigan Public Health* 23 (September 1935): 170–77, esp. 174–76; Lillian L. Biester, William Griffiths, and N. O. Pearce, *Units in Personal Health and Human Relations* (Minneapolis: University of Minnesota Press, 1947), 166–68.

54. Kennedy, "Family Life Education," 161.

55. Van Winkle, "Teaching Sex Education," 26.

56. Ibid., 28.

57. Elizabeth S. Force and Edgar M. Finck, *Family Relationships: Ten Topics toward Happier Homes* (Elizabethtown: Continental Press, 1948), 66; Elizabeth S. Force and Edgar M. Finck, *Family Relationships: Ten Topics toward Happier Homes, a Handbook for Administrators and Teachers Who Use the Accompanying Study Guide* (Elizabethtown: Continental Press, n.d. [1949]), 34.

58. Force and Finck, *Family Relationships*, 66.

59. Barbara Newman, completed workbook, *Family Relationships: Ten Topics Toward Happier Homes*, 1956, 66, box 1, Elizabeth Sculthorpe Force Papers, Ocean County Historical Society, Toms River, New Jersey (hereafter Force Papers).

60. Force and Finck, *Family Relationships Handbook,* 37, and Force and Finck, *Family Relationships,* 71.

61. Alice V. Keliher, with the Commission on Human Relations, *Life and Growth* (1937; reprint, New York: D. Appleton-Century, 1938), 205.

62. Esther Emerson Sweeney and Roy E. Dickerson, eds., *Preinduction Health and Human Relations* (New York: American Social Hygiene Association, 1953), 121, 132. On schools that employed the 1952 test curriculum, see the correspondence in box 83, folders 1, 2, ASHA Papers.

63. Marjorie Cosgrove, "School Guidance for Home and Family Living: A Required Course for Seniors in Highland Park, Michigan High School," *Marriage and Family Living* 14 (February 1952): 26–31, quotation on 31.

64. Eugene J. Kanin, "Male Aggression in Dating-Courtship Relations," *American Journal of Sociology* 63 (September 1957): 197–204.

65. Evans, "Sex Education Can Be Taught," 318, 319.

66. Poffenberger, "Family Life Education," 152.

67. Thomas Poffenberger, "Responses of Eighth Grade Girls to a Talk on Sex," *Marriage and Family Living* 22 (February 1960): 38–44, quotations on 39.

68. The emotionally mature man "displays a readiness to protect a girl against her own weakness or poor judgment and an unwillingness to take any advantage of her." Roy E. Dickerson and Esther Emerson Sweeney, eds., *Pre-Induction Health Education Manual (For Use with High School Seniors)* (New York: American Social

Hygiene Association, 1952), 141, 124; see also Sweeney and Dickerson, *Preinduction Health and Human Relations*, 123, 134.

69. Poffenberger, "Responses of Eighth Grade Girls," 44.

70. Ibid., 39. The author's claim, in a coauthored pamphlet from 1953, that "more sexual advances to children are made by people they know (including relatives) than by strangers," suggests some ability to separate facts from myths about sexual violence, yet this quotation in a later publication has the opposite effect. Lester A. Kirkendall and Thomas Poffenberger, "Parents, Children, and the Sex Molester," in Kirkendall, *Kirkendall on Sex Education* (Eugene: E. C. Brown Center for Family Studies, 1970), 34.

71. Dickerson and Sweeney, *Pre-Induction Health Education Manual*, 120, 131; Sweeney and Dickerson, *Preinduction Health and Human Relations*, 119, 129.

72. Lester A. Kirkendall and Curtis E. Avery, "Ethics and Interpersonal Relationships," *Coordinator* 3 (March 1955): 1–7, esp. 5–6.

73. [Questions on Sex Education, Normandy Hi-Y Group,] postmarked 3 March 1958, Bert Y. Glassberg Papers, box 3, folder 70, Becker Medical Library, Washington University School of Medicine, St. Louis, Missouri.

74. Bullis and O'Malley, *Human Relations*, 51.

75. Ibid., 84.

76. Division of Instruction, Department of Family Life Education, Detroit Public Schools, *Family Life Education in the High School: A Source Book for Teachers* (Detroit: Board of Education of the City of Detroit, 1958), 9.

77. Kenneth E. Oberholtzer and Myrtle F. Sugarman, "Denver Educates for Home and Family Living," *Journal of Social Hygiene* 37 (February 1951): 51–61, quotations on 60.

78. Detroit Public Schools, *Family Life Education*, 29.

79. Bert Y. Glassberg, "The St. Louis Board of Education Program on Personal and Family Living," March 1957, grade 9, lecture 2, box 7, folder 183, Glassberg Papers.

80. Thomas Poffenberger, "A Lesson for Group Leaders from *Palmour Street*," *Coordinator* 4 (December 1955): 5–11; *Palmour Street*, 16 mm, 27 min., Georgia Department of Health, 1950, available at http://www.archive.org/details/PalmourS1957, accessed 24 June 2005. See also Ken Smith, *Mental Hygiene: Classroom Films, 1945–1970* (New York: Blast Books, 1999).

81. Poffenberger, "Lesson for Group Leaders," 11.

82. Thomas Millard Poffenberger, "A Technique for Evaluating Family Life and Mental Health Films," Ed.D. diss., Michigan State College, 1954, 118–19.

83. Barbara Newman, "*Palmour Street:* Film Study Guide and Work Sheet," n.d., in Newman, completed workbook, 80, Force Papers.

84. "*Palmour Street* Film Discussion Guide," *Coordinator* 4 (September 1955): n.p.

85. New Jersey Secondary School Teachers' Association, *The Family Relationships Primer for Secondary Schools* ([Trenton]: New Jersey Secondary School Teachers'

Association, 1949), 13; Evelyn Millis Duvall, *Family Living* (New York: Macmillan, 1950), 276; Paul H. Landis, *Your Marriage and Family Living*, 2d ed. (New York: McGraw-Hill, 1954), 218.

86. Landis and Landis, *Personal Adjustment*, 252.

87. Payton Kennedy, *A Source Book for Teachers of Family Life Education*, rev. ed. (San Antonio: San Antonio Independent School District, [1951]), 4.

88. Wellington G. Pierce, *Youth Comes of Age* (New York: McGraw-Hill, 1948), 228–30, quotation on 230.

89. Landis, *Your Marriage*, 218.

90. Landis, *Your Marriage*.

91. ElizabethS. Force, *Your Family, Today and Tomorrow* (New York: Harcourt, Brace [1955]), 131.

92. Force and Finck, *Family Relationships*, 80.

93. Newman, completed workbook, 80, Force Papers.

94. Ibid., 81.

95. Cosgrove, "School Guidance," 28.

96. Lampe, "Growing Up," 45, 51.

97. Newman, completed workbook, 29, Force Papers.

98. Ibid.

99. Ibid., 84.

100. Sweeney and Dickerson, *Preinduction Health and Human Relations*, 124.

101. Ibid., 134–36.

102. Anita D. Laton and Edna W. Bailey, *Suggestions for Teaching Selected Material from the Field of Sex Responsiveness, Mating, and Reproduction* (New York: Teachers College, Columbia University, 1940), 73.

103. Force and Finck, *Family Relationships*, 19.

104. Ibid., 13, 22.

105. Force and Finck, *Family Relationships Handbook*, 18.

106. Ibid., 16.

107. Coined by Philip Wylie, "momism" blamed mothers for social problems. Philip Wylie, *Generation of Vipers* (New York: Holt, Rinehart, and Winston, 1942). On mother-blaming, see, for example, Molly Ladd-Taylor and Lauri Umanski, eds., *"Bad" Mothers: The Politics of Blame in Twentieth-Century America* (New York: New York University Press, 2000).

108. Helen Manley, "Sex Education in the Schools," *Journal of School Health* 21 (February 1951): 62–69, quotation on 69.

109. American Association of School Administrators, *Character Education*, Tenth Yearbook (Washington: Department of Superintendence of the National Education Association, 1932), esp. 189–97; see also Moran, *Teaching Sex*, 104.

110. Stephanie Coontz, *The Way We Never Were: American Families and the Nostalgia Trap* (New York: Basic Books, 1992); Steven Mintz and Susan Kellogg, *Domestic Revolutions: A Social History of American Family Life* (New York: Free Press, 1988);

William Henry Chafe, *The Paradox of Change: American Women in the Twentieth Century*, rev. ed. (New York: Oxford University Press, 1991); Sonya Michel, "American Women and the Discourse of the Democratic Family in World War II," in *Behind the Lines: Gender and the Two World Wars*, ed. Margaret Randolph Higgonet et al. (New Haven: Yale University Press, 1987), 154–67.

111. Jack Gould, "Programs in Review," *New York Times*, 7 December 1947, section 2, 13.

112. Newman, completed workbook, 7, Force Papers.

113. Barbara Newman, "Family Circles" worksheet, 17 February 1956, Force Papers, 80.

114. Wini Breines, *Young, White, and Miserable: Growing up Female in the Fifties* (Boston: Beacon Press, 1992), 12; see also Wini Breines, "Postwar White Girls' Dark Others," in *The Other Fifties: Interrogating Midcentury American Icons*, ed. Joel Foreman (Urbana: University of Illinois Press, 1997), 53–77.

Chapter 3: Experiments in Sex Education

1. Gertrude Burgess, "Development and Results of a Sex Hygiene Course in a Consolidated High School," *Michigan Public Health* 23 (September 1935): 170–77; Maude M. Firth, "Teaching Family Relationships to Mixed Classes," *Journal of Home Economics* 29 (March 1937): 151–53; James A. Michener, "Sex Education: A Success in Our Social Studies Class," *Clearing House* 12 (April 1938): 461–65; Mary Helen Stohlman, "Sex Education in the Public Schools of the District of Columbia," *Journal of Social Hygiene* 25 (October 1939): 330–39.

2. The *New York Times* covered developments in this debate. "Sex Education Urged in City High Schools," 18 May 1937, 25, and Maude Dunlop, "Sex Education in Schools Again Provokes a Debate," 5 February 1939, sec. 2, 5; see also Ellsworth B. Buck, "Our Public Schools and Sex," *American Mercury*, May 1939, 30–36; "Information Please! E. B. Buck Thinks Instruction in Sex Ought to Be Introduced into High School Courses," *Collier's*, 17 June 1939, 82; and Jacob A. Goldberg, "Arousing Teacher Interest in New York City," *Journal of Social Hygiene* 25 (October 1939): 340–45.

3. "Ohio—Sex Education in Cleveland Secondary Schools," *Journal of Social Hygiene* 27 (November 1941): 412; Alma M. Volk, "Rock Island's Program of Sex Education," *School Executive* 65 (May 1946): 53–54; R. S. Cartwright, "Marriage and Family Living," *NEA Journal* 45 (February 1956): 92–93.

4. John Newton Baker, *Sex Education in High Schools* (New York: Emerson Books, 1942).

5. Baker, *Sex Education*, chap. 3. Maryland and Virginia did not participate in the survey, and Alaska and Hawaii were not yet states, making the number of states surveyed equal forty-six.

6. On Illinois, see Russell B. Babcock, "A Seventh Grade Course in Sex Education," *Progressive Education* 13 (May 1936): 374–82; "Volk, "Rock Island's Program"; and Cartright, "Marriage and Family Living." On Michigan, see Burgess, "Development

and Results." On Minnesota, see William Griffiths, "An Investigation of the Present Status of Social Hygiene Education in the Minnesota Public Schools," *Research Quarterly* 12, no. 2 (1941): 189–97. On Missouri, see Helen Manley, "Sex Education in the Schools," *Journal of School Health* 21 (February 1951): 62–69. Of the six programs Baker neglected, only Babcock, Burgess, and Griffiths were published at the time of his research.

7. "Notes on Recent State Activities Relating to Sex Education," *Journal of Social Hygiene* 31 (April 1945): 220–27, esp. 223–24; Betty A. Murch, "Educational Notes," *Journal of Social Hygiene* 34 (November 1948): 392–94; and Samuel Tubbe Robbins, "Education for Responsible Parenthood (Mississippi)," and Wayne J. Anderson, "Education for Happy Family Living (Utah)," *Journal of Educational Sociology* 22 (March 1949): 468–74, 450–56.

8. Adelaida Teves Bautista, "Family Life Education for High School Seniors in the Philippines," master's thesis, San Francisco State College, 1955; Christabelle Laura Sethna, "The Facts of Life: The Sex Instruction of Ontario Public School Children, 1900–1950," Ed.D. diss., University of Toronto, 1995. The American Social Hygiene Association created links with educators in Puerto Rico, and St. Thomas, Virgin Islands, in the 1950s. See box 83, folder 8, American Social Hygiene Papers, Social Welfare History Archives, Minneapolis, Minnesota (hereafter ASHA Papers).

9. *Human Growth*, 16 mm, 20 min., E. C. Brown Trust and Eddie Albert Productions, Portland, 1947.

10. G. Gage Wetherill, foreword to Augustine Escamilla, *Guide for Secondary Social Health Education* (San Diego: San Diego City Schools, 1966), iii.

11. The OSHS began as a subcommittee of the Physical Department of the Portland Young Men's Christian Association (YMCA) in 1911; as an independent organization, its funding and activism fluctuated between the 1910s and 1950s. Curtis E. Avery, "Toward an Understanding of Sex Education in Oregon," in *Sex Education: Concepts and Challenges, A Collection of Readings from "The Family Life Coordinator,"* ed. Curtis E. Avery, with David S. Brody and Margie R. Lee (Eugene: E. C. Brown Center for Family Studies, 1969), 17–19; Minutes of the Oregon Social Hygiene Society, 7 August 1940, and E. C. Brown to President and Executive Committee, 26 March 1929, box 1, file 15 and box 1, file 5, Oregon Hygiene Society Records, Oregon Historical Society, Portland (hereafter OHS Records).

12. Harry Beal Torrey, *Biology in the Elementary Schools and Its Contribution to Sex Education* (New York: American Social Hygiene Association, 1928), 3–5.

13. OSHS members expected Brown's will to enable their work to continue, as he had suggested in a 1929 letter to the organization when he initiated financial support of $5,000 per year. Upon their benefactor's death in 1939, society members learned from Brown's lawyer that no more funds would be forthcoming, essentially disabling the organization. Brown to President and Executive Committee, 26 March 1929; and Curtis E. Avery, *Meet the E. C. Brown Trust Foundation* (Portland: E. C. Brown Trust, [1969?]), 4–5.

14. Brown believed the University of Oregon president would be "most likely to possess the breadth of understanding and depth of educational experience" required for the job, according to *A Brief History of the E. C. Brown Trust* (Portland: E. C. Brown Trust, 1958), 2–3. On the value of the estate, see Velma Clyde, "Sex Education: Oregon Takes Lead over Rest of Nation," *Portland Oregonian,* 4 May 1947. The $500,000 value of the Brown estate was equivalent to $6.9 million in 2006.

15. Howard C. Stearns to Reverend Raymond B. Walker, 12 July 1938, box 1, file 5, Multnomah County Medical Society Committee on School Health, "Report of the Committee on School Health Concerning Sex Instruction in the Public Schools," [December 1937?], 1, and M. A. Bigelow to F. B. Messing, 20 July 1943, box 2, file 3, and box 1, file 7, OHS Records.

16. Multnomah County Medical Society Committee on School Health, "Report of the Committee," 1, OHS Records.

17. Torrey, *Biology in Elementary Schools,* 3.

18. Quotations from Orlando Hollis, paper read at the third annual Oregon State Conference on Social Hygiene, 1944, in Avery, "Toward an Understanding," 20. On the beginnings of Brown Trust activities, see Michael E. Pajot, "Guiding Principles for the Revision of *Human Growth,*" [1974], 1–3, box 1, "*Human Growth*" folder, E. C. Brown Trust Papers, Division of Special Collections and University Archives, University of Oregon, Eugene (hereafter ECBT Papers). Erb was university president and trust administrator between 1939 and 1943, and Weinzirl directed the trust from 1941 to 1948. *A Brief History of the Trust,* 11.

19. Pajot, "Guiding Principles," 2, ECBT Papers; Stearns to Walker, 12 July 1938, and [Oregon Social Hygiene Society,] untitled and undated typescript, box 1, file 5, both in OHS Records.

20. House Bill 53, "An Act to Provide for Programs of Health Instruction and Physical Education," was first read 16 January 1945. The text of the bill is contained in box 96, Legal Reference files, "Sex Education Legislation, Oregon, 1945," ASHA Papers. See also Rex Putnam, "Social Hygiene in Oregon Schools," *Phi Delta Kappan* 29 (March 1948): 303–4, and Rex Putnam and Dorotha Massey, "Social Hygiene Education in the Oregon Schools," *National Education Association Journal* 37 (November 1948): 498–99.

21. Hundreds of letters attest to this interest. See boxes 18 and 19, Health and Physical Education, 1945–53, General Correspondence, Department of Education (General) Papers, Oregon State Archives, Salem (hereafter Oregon Education Papers). One of several sources giving incorrect information about the law was Bob Gilmore, "Sex Goes to School in Oregon," *Better Homes and Gardens,* September 1947, 41.

22. Howard Stanley Hoyman, *Health-Guide Units for Oregon Teachers, Grades 7–12* (Portland: E. C. Brown Trust, 1945); Putnam, "Social Hygiene in Oregon Schools"; Putnam and Massey, "Social Hygiene Education in Oregon Schools"; Curtis E. Avery, "The Oregon Program of Sex Education," [1964], box 1, file "Miscellaneous Published Papers," ECBT Papers.

23. Avery, *Meet the Trust*, 9.

24. Clyde, "Sex Education."

25. Avery, *Meet the Trust*, 8.

26. Publicity was widespread. See, for example, Clyde, "Sex Education"; Gilmore, "Sex Goes to School"; "Sex Education: Oregon Film Provides New Approach to Delicate Problem," *Life*, 24 May 1948, 55; Margaret Hickey, "Parents Want Help," *Ladies' Home Journal*, April 1948, 23; "Sex in the Schoolroom," *Time*, 22 March 1948, 71–72; "Where Babies Come From: University of Oregon Program of Education on Family Life," *Newsweek*, 22 March 1948, 90; Ann Sullivan, "Touchy Sex Subject Handled Objectively in New Film," *Portland Oregonian*, 15 February 1948, 24; "'Jury' of 350 Mothers Approves Sex Education Films in Schools," *New York Times*, 22 March 1949, 27; "Audiences Approve Sex Education Film," *New York Times*, 31 March 1949, 23; "Use of Sex Films in Schools Urged," *New York Times*, 12 May 1949, 26; and Dorothy Barclay, "Doctors Give Ideas on Sex Education," *New York Times*, 22 November 1950, 29. According to an obituary for Lester F. Beck ("Pioneer Filmmaker in Education Dies," undated newspaper clipping, [1977?], personal collection of Sy Wexler), *Human Growth* "garnered more national and international awards than any other documentary film." Negative publicity was comparatively slight. "Catholics Attack School Sex Films," *New York Times*, 14 October 1949, 31; "Catholic Boycott of Sex Film Urged," *New York Times*, 5 December 1949, 20; "Catholics Warned on School Trends," *New York Times*, 9 January 1950, 17. The New York state commissioner of health rejected Catholic complaints regarding the screening of *Human Growth*. "Catholic Protest on Film Rejected," *New York Times*, 29 November 1949, 23; see also Robert Eberwein, *Sex Ed: Film, Video, and the Framework of Desire* (New Brunswick: Rutgers University Press, 1999), chap. 3.

27. Sullivan, "Touchy Sex Subject," 24.

28. "Sex Education: Oregon Film," 55; "Sex in the Schoolroom," 71.

29. Howard Stanley Hoyman, *Health-Guide Units for Oregon Teachers, Grades 7–12*, rev. ed. (Portland: E. C. Brown Trust, 1948). See especially the letters dated between January and December 1949 in boxes 18 and 19, Health and Physical Education, 1945–53, General Correspondence, Oregon Education Papers.

30. Avery, "Toward an Understanding," 24.

31. The film did not touch on the subject of family planning. Not only did they reason that mention of birth control was illegal, but Brown Trust leaders also felt it would have been inappropriate because it would suggest to pupils that "they do need such knowledge" and might also "encourage its use in illicit sex experiences that would violate legal, moral and religious codes." Howard Stanley Hoyman, "Basic Issues in School Sex Education," *Journal of School Health* 23 (January 1953): 14–22, quotation on 16. Screenings of *Human Growth* in Catholic areas, such as Hillsborough County, Florida, might have put into relief the depiction of the contemporary Protestant family ideal of few children as opposed to the mid-twentieth-century Catholic norm of larger families.

32. New Jersey Department of Education's Advisory Committee on Social Hygiene Education, "An Approach in Schools to Education for Personal and Family Living," *Journal of Social Hygiene* 38 (February 1952): 63; Harold Isaacs, "Youth: Shall Our Schools Teach Sex?" *Newsweek,* 19 May 1947, 100.

33. Sy Wexler of Los Angeles, California, provided access to a print of the 1947 film and promotional materials, which remain in his possession. [Lester F. Beck], *Human Growth: Film Guide for Teachers and Discussion Leaders* (Portland: E. C. Brown Trust, [1949]); *Human Growth,* 3d ed., promotional pamphlet (Highland Park: Perennial Education, 1976); see also Eberwein, *Sex Ed.*

34. Marcille Harris, Berlan Lemon, and Lester F. Beck, "Sex Instruction in the Classroom," *Educational Leadership* 6 (May 1949): 519–24; "'Jury' of 350 Mothers"; "Audiences Approve"; Sullivan, "Touchy Sex Subject"; Marcille Hurst Harris, "Parent-Teacher Attitudes toward Sex Education and the Film *Human Growth,*" master's thesis, University of Oregon, 1949.

35. Hoyman, *Health-Guide Units;* see also Putnam, "Social Hygiene in Oregon Schools"; Putnam and Massey, "Social Hygiene Education in Oregon Schools"; and Gilmore, "Sex Goes to School."

36. Gilmore, "Sex Goes to School."

37. Avery, *Meet the Trust,* 8–9.

38. Curtis E. Avery and Lester A. Kirkendall, *The Oregon Developmental Center Project in Family Life Education* (Portland: E. C. Brown Trust, 1955), 2.

39. Hoyman, "Basic Issues," 22.

40. Bigelow to Messing, 20 July 1943, OHS Records.

41. The population of Dover Township (including Toms River schools) increased from 3,970 in 1930 to 17,414 in 1960, with migration stepped up after the end of the war and a marked increase in the birthrate in the township after 1944. In 1943, 465 pupils attended Toms River High School; by 1947, there were 631 students. Engelhardt, Engelhardt, and Leggett, Educational Consultants, *School Building Needs, Toms River School District, New Jersey* (Trenton: New Jersey Department of Education, 1952), 1–5, 2–5, 4–2. Approximately one-third of 1940 Ocean County residences were inhabited by their owners. U.S. Bureau of the Census, Housing, vol. 1, Data for Small Areas, 1940, table 5. As the local Jewish population grew in the 1940s, more Jewish students attended Toms River High School. Jeanne Littman and Mildred Robinson, eds., *History of Pioneers: Reminiscences and Personal Histories of the Jews of Toms River* (Toms River: Council of Jewish Organizations, 1976).

42. Most African Americans in the county resided outside of Dover Township. U.S. Bureau of the Census, Population by Municipality, Ocean County, 1930–1980; U.S. Bureau of the Census, New Jersey, Characteristics of the Population, 1940, table 28, 60.

43. School Segregation, Toms River, N.J. Case, Papers of the NAACP, part 3, series A, microfilm collection; Donald F. Martin, "A History of the Public Schools of Dover Township, New Jersey, from 1900 through 1955," Ed.D. diss., Rutgers University, 1957, 216.

44. Martin, "Public Schools of Dover Township," 205–7, citing *New Jersey Courier* (Toms River), 1 July 1927; Minutes of the Dover Township Board of Education, 7 July 1927.

45. "Some Say Toms River Is Next Objective of the Ku Klux Klan," *New Jersey Courier* (Toms River), 22 June 1923, 1; "Spectacular Visit of Ku Klux at Toms River M. E. Church," *New Jersey Courier* (Toms River), 23 August 1923, 1.

46. Martin, "Public Schools of Dover Township," 216.

47. Ethel Lewis, Robert R. Riegle, and Dorothy Jameson (chair) compiled the original course guide under Finck's supervision. *Tentative Course of Study: Family Relationships* (Toms River: Toms River High School, 1939), 1, box 1, Elizabeth Sculthorpe Force Papers, Ocean County Historical Society, Toms River, New Jersey (hereafter Force Papers).

48. Elizabeth S. Force, "What Teen-Agers Want to Know about Sex and Marriage," *American Magazine* 155 (January 1953): 34–35, 103–6, esp. 106.

49. Educator Helen Manley claimed in 1964 that the Toms River program "is perhaps best known" among pioneers in school sex education. Helen Manley, "Sex Education: Where, When, and How Should It Be Taught?" *Journal of Health, Physical Education, and Recreation* 35 (March 1964): 21–24, esp. 22. For national publicity, see Force, "What Teen-Agers Want"; Elizabeth S. Force, "Toms River Meets a Challenge," *Progressive Education* 24 (April 1947): 202–5; Elizabeth S. Force, "Toms River Looks Back—1951–1941," *Journal of Social Hygiene* 38 (January 1952): 2–10; Elizabeth S. Force, "High School Education for Family Living," *Annals of the American Academy of Political and Social Science* 272 (November 1950): 156–62; Elizabeth S. Force, "Family Life Education: Are We Passing the Buck?" *National Parent Teacher Magazine* 53 (February 1959): 24–26, 36; Myron M. Stearns, "The ABC's of Happy Marriage," *Today's Woman*, February 1948, 32–33, 131–35; Stella B. Applebaum, "A School That Prepares for Living: Toms River, N.J. Revamped Its High School Program to Satisfy the Students' Real Needs," *Parents' Magazine* 24 (May 1948): 36–37, 106; and Karl Kohrs, "They Study How to Live: Toms River Youngsters Face the Problems of Living in a Special—and Significant—High School Course," *Parade*, 9 May 1948, 5–7. Finck boasted letters of inquiry from every state as well as Australia, England, and Canada. Kohrs, "They Study How to Live," 5.

50. Elizabeth S. Force, *Teaching Family Life Education: The Toms River Program* (New York: Bureau of Publications, Teachers College, Columbia University, 1962), 1.

51. Force, *Teaching Family Life Education*, 6, 3. The classroom resembled "the environment of a very pleasing living room, with pine paneling, comfortable lounge chairs and sofas, and a small kitchenette. Both individual and group work can be carried on here in an atmosphere which is most conducive to friendly understanding and learning." Engelhardt, Engelhardt, and Leggett, *School Building Needs*, 4–10.

52. Elizabeth S. Force and Edgar M. Finck, *Family Relationships: Ten Topics toward Happier Homes* (Elizabethtown: Continental Press, 1948). Although the workbook was not published until 1948, it is likely that a mimeographed version was in use before that date.

53. Force, *Teaching Family Life Education*, 6.

54. Force recalled that Renee Ewart, who taught French and was a native of France, also occasionally taught the course. After Force left to work for the ASHA in 1957, a male instructor took charge. Elizabeth S. Force, interview by author, New York City, 7 August 1999.

55. Finck published columns in newspapers and education publications to lay the groundwork for the new courses. Martin, "Public Schools of Dover Township," 316. On expanding curriculum and statistics of college-bound students, see Applebaum, "School Prepares for Living," 37.

56. *Ten Topics toward Happier Homes*, promotional brochure, box 2, file 12, Force Papers.

57. New Jersey Department of Education, *A Guide for Health Education in the Secondary School* (Trenton: New Jersey Department of Education, 1955), 45.

58. New Jersey Department of Education, *A Guide for Health Education*, 46.

59. Elizabeth S. Force and Edgar M. Finck, *Family Relationships: Ten Topics toward Happier Homes, a Handbook for Administrators and Teachers Who Use the Accompanying Study Guide* (Elizabethtown: Continental Press, [1949]), 1. A California writer proposed that failed marriages resulted from two factors: "poor marital selection" and "lack of skill *and will* in adjustment after marriage"—both addressed in the Toms River curriculum. Ray E. Baber, "Youth Can Be Trained for Successful Marriage and Parenthood," *California Parent-Teacher* 19 (February 1943): 6.

60. For a recollection of Toms River from the perspective of a 1953 high school graduate, see Mac Eagle, *Raised in Toms River and Darn Proud of It* (Grand Rapids: Mac Eagle, 1996), esp. 17–36, 65–90, 119, 136, 143. Although Eagle never took the family relationships course, his parents were friends with Force and occasional guests in her classes. Ibid., 78.

61. Force and Finck, *Family Relationships Handbook;* "Sex Education: Oregon Film Provides New Approach to Delicate Problem," 58–62.

62. Force and Finck, *Family Relationships Handbook*, 29.

63. Force did not recall any black pupils in her class, had little memory of foreign-born students, and recalled a few Jewish youths in her classes. Force interview. A photograph of four young women—two apparently white and two African American—working on a family living project appeared in "Purposeful Education for Tomorrow's Citizens," *Annual Report of the Toms River Schools, 1949–1950*, 11; see also Esther Emerson Sweeney to Conrad Van Hyning, memo, 18 October 1965, 3, box 30, file 1, ASHA Papers. The inclusion of photographs of black students in the annual report may have signaled liberal sentiment of inclusion or a more problematic assumption that students of color exemplified the need for family life education.

64. Kenneth Fink, "Public Thinks Sex Education Courses Should Be Taught in the Schools," *Journal of Social Hygiene* 37 (February 1951): 62–63.

65. Stearns, "ABC's of a Happy Marriage," 132. No evidence of personal consultations remains, and in 1999 Force dismissed the idea that she counseled individual students. Force interview.

66. Kohrs, "They Study How to Live," 5; Stearns, "ABC's of a Happy Marriage," 132; Applebaum, "School Prepares for Living," 106.

67. Force, *Teaching Family Life Education*, 15.

68. Force and Finck, *Family Relationships Handbook*, 34. Visitors to Force's 1956 family relationships class included a rabbi, an insurance agent, and a lawyer but no physician. Barbara Newman, completed workbook, *Family Relationships: Ten Topics toward Happier Homes*, 1956, box 1, Force Papers.

69. Force, *Teaching Family Life Education*, 23.

70. Ibid., 10, 21.

71. In 1950, Harcourt, Brace asked Force to produce a textbook. She eventually used the high school textbook in her course along with several other texts. Ibid., 29.

72. Ibid., 19.

73. Force and Finck, *Family Relationships Handbook*, 15.

74. A psychiatric team favorably evaluated family relationships and social behavior, lavishing praise on Force as instructor (and source of "maternal support and sympathy") for both courses. Committee on Preventive Psychiatry, *Promotion of Mental Health in the Primary and Secondary Schools: An Evaluation of Four Projects* (Topeka.: Group for the Advancement of Psychiatry, 1951), esp. 6–8, quotation on 8. On Group for the Advancement of Psychiatry, see Ellen Herman, *The Romance of American Psychology: Political Culture in the Age of Experts* (Berkeley: University of California Press, 1995), chap. 9.

75. Force and Finck, *Family Relationships Handbook*, 1–2. Finck's staff distributed the survey to 166 graduates and received answers from 35 men and 123 women. One hundred percent of the men were still married, and 66 of 68 women had successful marriages, an overall rate of 73 of 75 (97 percent). Two couples had separated. Kohrs, "They Study How to Live," 5; *Ten Topics* promotional brochure, Force Papers.

76. Force and Finck, *Family Relationships Handbook*, 2.

77. Ibid. Also emphasizing the class's success, a journalist noted that the schools' statistics demonstrated far fewer couples splitting up during the first three to five years following marriage, which according to this article, amounted nationally to 500,000 divorces for 1.6 million marriages in 1945. Stearns, "ABC's of a Happy Marriage," 33.

78. Force, "High School Education," 159.

79. The city of San Diego's population increased between 1940 and 1950 by 64.4 percent, compared with 14.5 percent for the United States as a whole. As one source noted in 1958, "For each two people living in the City of San Diego in 1940 there are now five." Irving B. Tebor and Helen L. Larrabee, *Background for Planning for Social Welfare in San Diego County* (San Diego: Research Department, Community Welfare Council, 1958), 1, 3.

80. Laurence I. Hewes Jr., with the assistance of William Y. Bell Jr., *Intergroup Relations in San Diego: Some Aspects of Community Life in San Diego which Particularly Affect Minority Groups, with Recommendations for a Program of Community Action* (San Francisco: American Council on Race Relations, 1946), 17, 26; see also Beatrice Griffith, *American Me* (Boston: Houghton Mifflin, 1948).

81. The African American population, concentrated in the integrated, overcrowded, and economically depressed interracial neighborhood of Logan Heights, measured around fifteen thousand in the late 1940s. Estimated to be larger than the black population, the Mexican American community in San Diego was not measured by census figures because Mexican Americans were counted as "white." Approximately 3.1 percent of the population in 1940, nonwhite minorities made up 6.5 percent of the city's population in 1950; Mexican Americans in San Diego numbered approximately thirty-eight thousand in 1950, and African Americans numbered around twenty-eight thousand by 1957. Hewes with Bell, *Intergroup Relations,* 11–12; Tebor and Larrabee, *Planning for Social Welfare,* 11–12. For a personal account of racial dynamics in the city, especially with regard to the police force, see Gene Sylvester Muehleisen, interview by Sally West, transcript, San Diego, California, 1 December 1933, San Diego Historical Society, San Diego, California.

82. Logan principal [Farnum] to parents, in G. Gage Wetherill, *Human Relations Education: A Program Developing in the San Diego City Schools* (New York: American Social Hygiene Association, 1946), 41.

83. Hewes with Bell, *Intergroup Relations,* 12.

84. "Sex Education . . . San Diego Pioneers," *Ladies' Home Journal,* April 1948, 23, 273, 275–77, quotations on 275.

85. "Sex Education . . . San Diego," 273.

86. Evelyn L. Dowdy, "Social Hygiene," *Parent-Teacher Courier* 12 (October 1937): 10.

87. William J. Lyons, "Sex Education in Our Public Schools," *Parent-Teacher Courier* 12 (January 1938): 5, 12, quotation on 5.

88. G. Gage Wetherill, "Accepting Responsibility for Sex Education," *Journal of School Health* 30 (March 1960): 107–10, quotation on 108.

89. Wetherill, "Accepting Responsibility," 108. For a similar observation see Lloyd S. Van Winkle, "The Teaching of Sex Education in the Elementary School," Ed.D. diss., Colorado State College of Education, 1949, 40.

90. Wetherill, *Human Relations Education,* 13; see also Gloyd Gage Wetherill, "Developing a Program of Integrative Health Instruction for the Secondary Curriculum," master's thesis, Stanford University, 1943.

91. Will C. Crawford, "How R We Doing?" *California Parent-Teacher* 29 (November 1952): 9, 18, quotations on 9.

92. The superintendent admitted to "starting with the point of view that every girl is a potential homemaker" but also claimed that the school district's homemaking education was "forward-looking" and "goes far beyond the old concept of 'food' and 'clothing.'" Crawford, "How R We Doing?" 18. Such innovations included a section for eighth-grade girls on "good grooming," coinciding with "a time when they are increasingly conscious of appearance and are seeking guidance." Rhea Black, "Teaching Good Grooming," *Curriculum Digest: San Diego City Schools in Action* 15 (March 1955): 6. "Home mechanics" for ninth-grade homemaking students was another in-

novation undertaken at Horace Mann Junior High. "Girls Enjoy Experimental Shop Activity," *Curriculum Digest: San Diego City Schools in Action* 16 (March–April 1956): 5.

93. G. Gage Wetherill, "Sex Education in the Public Schools," *Journal of School Health* 31 (September 1961): 235–39, quotation on 235.

94. Wetherill, *Human Relations Education*, 8.

95. Hewes with Bell, *Intergroup Relations*, 20.

96. Few people of color held teaching and administrative positions in San Diego public schools during this period, as in the United States in general, and presumably the sex educators in San Diego were white, middle-class, and Protestant Christians. Greta Willis Slater, "An Historical Study of the Social Health Program in the San Diego City Schools, 1937–1966," master's thesis, University of California, Los Angeles, 1966, 38–39; see also Hewes with Bell, *Intergroup Relations*, 18–19, 23. A photograph from Logan Elementary School in 1953, however, shows an apparently African American first-grade teacher. *Curriculum Digest: San Diego City Schools in Action* 14 (November–December 1953). Other classroom photographs revealed integrated student populations, but in every other instance the teachers appear white.

97. For parents' interest in boys' classes, see Slater, "Study of the Social Health Program," 41; see also Viola I. Lampe, "Growing Up: Lessons in Health and Human Relations for Sixth Grade Boys and Girls," in Wetherill, *Human Relations Education*, 42.

98. The revised version of "Growing Up" omitted the section called "Reason for Offering Instruction," which listed "the abnormal home conditions caused by the war": two working parents and fathers' absence. This section had also included mention of poor housing and minimal privacy as contributing to a reduction of "family unity and the close ties of normal family living." Lampe, "Growing Up," 39; cf. Viola I. Lampe, "Growing Up: Lessons on Social Hygiene for Sixth-Grade Boys and Girls," in Wetherill, *Human Relations Education*, 2d ed., 40.

99. Lampe, "Growing Up," 44.

100. Ibid., 44–45. The sample first lesson for boys expressed a similar concern about "trouble" and "serious difficulties" that might have arisen in the war environment for boys who did not carefully choose their friends, but it did not link such adversity to interactions with girls or women. Nor did the boys' lesson express the teacher's concern "to protect you all." Ibid., 51.

101. Farnum in ibid., 41. Lampe suggested an alternate plan of using the material over five lessons. Lampe, "Growing Up," in ibid., 58–59. The five-lesson format appeared as standard in the second edition of *Human Relations Education*, although again noting variations. Lampe, "Growing Up," 2d ed., esp. 49, 57, 64, 67.

102. Wetherill, "Sex Education," 237.

103. Lampe, "Growing Up," 46.

104. Karl de Schweinitz, *Growing Up: The Story of How We Become Alive, Are Born and Grow Up* (1930; reprint, New York: Macmillan, 1928).

105. De Schweinitz, *Growing Up,* 103, 104. The book sustained multiple printings and several revisions but kept the same focus. The text's second edition, from 1947, rephrased the first sentence quoted and deleted the second. Only marginally more specific, this version claimed, "Men and women know that when the sperm joins the egg a baby will start growing, and when they mate, each wants to mate with the person he or she loves." Karl de Schweinitz, *Growing Up: The Story of How We Become Alive, Are Born and Grow Up,* 2d ed. (New York: Macmillan, 1947), 88–89. Both the original and revised bibliography for the San Diego curriculum listed a 1945 version. Lampe, "Growing Up," 60; Lampe, "Growing Up," 2d ed., 73.

106. Lampe, "Growing Up," 47. Ordinarily in such exercises students did not have to sign their names.

107. Lampe, "Growing Up," 2d ed., 54.

108. G. Gage Wetherill to Harriet A. Scantland, 27 June 1951, box 82, file 9, ASHA Papers.

109. Wetherill, *Human Relations Education,* 2; see also Avery, "Toward an Understanding," 21–22; and Force, *Teaching Family Life,* 35.

110. Available films included *From Flower to Fruit,* 16 mm, 16 min., Eastman Teaching Films and Encyclopedia Britannica Films, Chicago, Ill., 1933; and *The Sunfish,* 16 mm, 11 min., Encyclopedia Britannica Films, Chicago, Ill., 1941; *The Snapping Turtle,* 16 mm, 12 min., Encyclopedia Britannica Films, Chicago, Ill., 1940; and *Snakes Are Interesting,* 16 mm. 12 min., Murl Deusing Film Productions, Milwaukee, Wis., 1947. *The Miracle of Reproduction* and *Human Growth* were added to the expanded lesson plans in the 1950s and 1960s. Lampe, "Growing Up," 2d ed., 49, 53; and Slater, "Study of the Social Health Program," 80.

111. According to Brown Trust records, San Diego Unified School District purchased sixteen prints of *Human Growth* with slides between 12 September 1950 and 7 April 1958. Receipts register, June 1950–October 1958, 1, 7, 10, 11, 16, 24, 26, 27, 28, 33, box 1, E. C. Brown Foundation Papers, Division of Special Collections and University Archives, University of Oregon, Eugene. By 1951 *Human Growth* was part of the printed curriculum for sixth-grade students. Lampe, "Growing Up," 2d ed., 41.

112. Wetherill, *Human Relations Education,* 2d ed., 55–59. The terms above and below correspond to the titles of sections in the lesson plan.

113. Ibid., 60–66.

114. Sue Ernest, "Know Yourself and Others—Experiment at Roosevelt Junior High," *Parent-Teacher Courier* 18 (May 1944): 4.

115. Ernest, "Know Yourself and Others."

116. Wetherill, *Human Relations Education,* 2d ed., 10.

117. Wetherill, *Human Relations Education,* 10.

118. Ibid., quotation on 10; Slater, "Study of the Social Health Program," 46–49.

119. Wetherill, *Human Relations Education,* 10–11, quotations on 10.

120. Ibid., 10. On Freud, psychoanalysis, and mother blaming, see Kathleen W. Jones, *Taming the Troublesome Child: American Families, Child Guidance, and the*

Limits of Psychiatric Authority (Cambridge: Harvard University Press, 1999), esp. chap 7. On the oedipal complex, see Sigmund Freud, *A General Introduction to Psychoanalysis* (Garden City: Garden City Publishing, 1943).

121. Wetherill, *Human Relations Education*, 2d ed., 10.

122. G. Gage Wetherill, "A Community Social-Hygiene Program (San Diego, California)," *Journal of Educational Sociology* 22 (March 1949): 468–74, quotation on 471.

123. Wetherill, "A Community Social-Hygiene Program," 471; Wetherill, "Sex Education," 239.

124. Alfred C. Kinsey et al., *Sexual Behavior in the Human Female* (Philadelphia: W. B. Saunders, 1953); Alfred C. Kinsey, Wardell B. Pomeroy, and Clyde E. Martin, *Sexual Behavior in the Human Male* (Philadelphia: W. B. Saunders, 1948).

125. Richmond Barbour, "Intriguing Ideas," *California Parent-Teacher* 30 (November 1953): 12–13, quotation on 13; see also Richmond Barbour, "Sex Education," *California Parent-Teacher* 29 (November 1952): 4.

Chapter 4: The Facts of Life

1. Ruth Strang, *The Adolescent Views Himself: A Psychology of Adolescence* (New York: McGraw-Hill, 1957), 221.

2. Herbert M. Kleibard, *The Struggle for the American Curriculum, 1893–1958,* 2d ed (New York: Routledge, 1996), 106–8. By 1960, 82.4 percent of secondary school students attended schools that had some type of junior high school. Harl R. Douglass, *Trends and Issues in Secondary Education* (Washington: Center for Applied Research in Education, 1962), 67.

3. Viola I. Lampe, "Growing Up: Lessons on Social Hygiene for Sixth-Grade Boys and Girls," in G. Gage Wetherill, *Human Relations Education: A Report,* 2d ed. (New York: American Social Hygiene Association, 1951), 52, 50, quotation on 50.

4. Joan Jacobs Brumberg, *The Body Project: An Intimate History of American Girls* (New York: Random House, 1997), 4.

5. Helen Kitchen Branson, "Sexual Protection for Young Girls," *Sexology* 19 (March 1953): 516–21, quotation on 520.

6. On teenagers and bras, see Brumberg, *The Body Project,* 108–18.

7. "Teen-Age Sex Hysteria," *Science News Letter,* 1 January 1955, 4.

8. Estelle B. Freedman, "Uncontrolled Desires: The Response to the Sexual Psychopath, 1920–1960," *Journal of American History* 74, no. 1 (1987): 83–106. For an earlier perspective, reprinted from a 1953 pamphlet, see Lester A. Kirkendall and Thomas Poffenberger, "Parents, Children, and the Sex Molester," in Lester A. Kirkendall, *Kirkendall on Sex Education* (Eugene: E. C. Brown Center for Family Studies, 1970).

9. In her research on "troublesome" children of the early twentieth century, Jones found that within the child guidance clinics of the 1930s sex education was more often a remedy for troubled boys than troubled girls in spite of the fact that it was girls' sexual behavior—and not boys'—that caused them to be labeled delinquent. Child

guidance professionals, trained as experts in mental hygiene, believed that knowledge about heterosexual reproduction could steer boys away from masturbation and same-sex sexual activity, but for girls, professionals felt that knowledge was part of what led to rebellion. Kathleen W. Jones, *Taming the Troublesome Child: American Families, Child Guidance, and the Limits of Psychiatric Authority* (Cambridge: Harvard University Press, 1999), 162–68.

10. For feminist critiques of objectivity, see, for example, Sandra Harding, "Rethinking Standpoint Epistemology: What Is 'Strong Objectivity'?" in *Feminist Epistemologies*, ed. Linda Alcoff and Elizabeth Potter (New York: Routledge, 1993), 49–82.

11. Russell. B. Babcock, "A Seventh Grade Course in Sex Education," *Progressive Education* 13 (May 1936): 374–82, quotation on 379. Winnetka public schools, situated in a high-income, residential suburb of Chicago, were well known for their progressivism. Lawrence Cremin, *The Transformation of the School: Progressivism in American Education, 1876–1957* (New York: Knopf, 1962), 295–99.

12. Eva Kirby, "Family Life Education in Biology," *California Journal of Secondary Education* 25 (January 1950): 34–37, quotation on 35.

13. Professionals at the Fifteenth International Congress of Hygiene and Demography in 1900 disapproved of the use of visual aids in sex education. Wallace H. Maw, "Fifty Years of Sex Education in the Public Schools of the United States (1900–1950): A History of Ideas," Ed.D. diss., University of Cincinnati, 1953, 37, 68.

14. Alice V. Keliher, with the Commission on Human Relations, *Life and Growth* (1937; reprint, New York: D. Appleton-Century, 1938), 162–63, 166–67.

15. Dickinson's three-dimensional models of reproductive anatomy appeared at the 1938–39 World's Fair in New York and were donated to the Cleveland Health Museum in 1945, to be viewed by students on field trips there during the 1940s and 1950s. Bruno Gebhard, "The Birth Models: R. L. Dickinson's Monument," *Journal of Social Hygiene* 37 (April 1951): 169–174; Robert Latou Dickinson and Abram Belskie, *Birth Atlas* (New York: Maternity Center Association, 1940). On Dickinson, see Jennifer Terry, *An American Obsession: Science, Medicine, and Homosexuality in Modern Society* (Chicago: University of Chicago Press, 1999), esp. 143–56.

16. "Correct information" helped build "wholesome attitudes." Lampe, "Growing Up," 2d ed., 40. Although the precise source of the Dickinson drawings printed in *Human Relations Education* is unclear, they closely resemble drawings printed in Robert Latou Dickinson's *Human Sex Anatomy: A Topographical Hand Atlas,* 2d ed. (Baltimore: Williams and Wilkins, 1949), fig. 13, 105.

17. Lloyd S. Van Winkle, "The Teaching of Sex Education in the Elementary School." Ed.D. diss., Colorado State College, 1949), 119; G. Gage Wetherill, *Human Relations Education: A Program Developing in the San Diego City Schools* (New York: American Social Hygiene Association, 1946), 9.

18. G. Gage Wetherill to Jean B. Pinney, 18 January 1950, box 82, folder 9, American Social Hygiene Papers, Social Welfare History Archives, Minneapolis, Minnesota (hereafter ASHA Papers). Wetherill was no doubt speaking from the experience of using *Human Growth* in San Diego schools.

19. Babcock, "Seventh Grade Course," 380.

20. Keliher, *Life and Growth,* 162–63, 166–67.

21. Although they had Dickinson's drawings at their disposal, San Diego instructors used charts prepared by Alice Creelman, a nurse, and made them into filmstrips and slides. Greta Willis Slater, "An Historical Study of the Social Health Program in the San Diego City Schools, 1937–1966," master's thesis, University of California, Los Angeles, 1966, 79. I was unable to locate Creelman's charts.

22. Lampe, "Growing Up," in Wetherill, *Human Relations Education,* 46.

23. Ibid.

24. Lampe, "Growing Up," 2d ed., 52.

25. Ibid.

26. Ibid.

27. Lillian L. Biester, William Griffiths, and N. O. Pearce, *Units in Personal Health and Human Relations* (Minneapolis: University of Minnesota Press, 1947), esp. 43, 96, 138–39, 148. For evidence of use elsewhere, see Judith Rabak Wagener, "A Social Epistemology of Sex Education in the Milwaukee Public Schools: 1910–1960," Ph.D. diss., University of Wisconsin-Madison, 1991, 205; Kenneth Gray Hale, "An Inquiry into the Sex Education Knowledge, Needs, and Interests of 1,390 Twelfth-Grade Students," master's thesis, San Diego State College, 1952, 21; and R. S. Cartwright, "Marriage and Family Living," *National Education Association Journal* 45 (February 1956): 92–93.

28. The drawings are attributed to the Medical Art Shop of the University of Minnesota, initialed JEH, and dated 1943 and 1944, respectively. Biester, Griffiths, and Pearce, *Personal Health and Human Relations,* 41, 43.

29. The diagram of a male resembles Dickinson's work in the proportion and placement of organs, whereas that of a female apparently followed the model of another designer, indicated by the phrase following the artist's signature "after Spalteholz." Ibid.

30. Michelle Fine, "Sexuality, Schooling, and Adolescent Females: The Missing Discourse of Desire," *Harvard Educational Review* 58, no. 1 (1988): 29–53; Ruth Hubbard, *The Politics of Women's Biology* (New Brunswick: Rutgers University Press, 1990), 131; Robert Eberwein, *Sex Ed: Film, Video, and the Framework of Desire* (New Brunswick: Rutgers University Press, 1999).

31. Biester, Griffiths, and Pearce, *Personal Health and Human Relations,* 138–39.

32. Lampe, "Growing Up," 2d ed., 60. Fashion and health advisers alike, in such periodicals as *Seventeen* and *Parents' Magazine,* endorsed the idea that bras (especially made of nylon) gave needed support to breasts—even for adolescents. Brumberg, *The Body Project,* 108–18.

33. Bert Y. Glassberg, "The St. Louis Board of Education Program on Personal and Family Living," [March 1957,] grade 9, lecture 4–Boys, 7, box 7, folder 183, Bert Y. Glassberg Papers, Becker Medical Library, Washington University School of Medicine, St. Louis, Missouri (hereafter Glassberg Papers).

34. [Lester F. Beck,] *Human Growth: Film Guide for Teachers and Discussion Leaders* (Portland: E. C. Brown Trust, [1949]), photo captions, n.p.

35. Beck, *Film Guide,* "Complete Text of the Film Story," n.p. This is not at all what the book says, but apparently the filmmakers had the authors' permission. Beck, *Film Guide,* acknowledgments, n.p.; T. M. N. Lewis and M. Kneberg, *Hiwassee Island* (Knoxville: University of Tennessee Press, 1946), 188.

36. According to Richard A. Littman, an associate of the film's creator during the 1950s, Beck was "brilliant," interested in cultural anthropology, and had a Native American half-brother; in spite of the outcome, Beck's intentions would not have been to reify cultural differences or objectify others. Richard A. Littman, telephone communication with author, 18 October 2001.

37. Patricia Penn Hilden's analysis of representations of Indians in American culture suggested that naked dark bodies featured in *National Geographic* were "emblems of American liberalism." Patricia Penn Hilden, *When Indians Were Nickels: An Urban Mixed-Blood Story* (Washington: Smithsonian Institution Press, 1995), esp. 94, 104; see also Catherine A. Lutz and Jane L. Collins, *Reading* National Geographic (Chicago: University of Chicago Press, 1993).

38. Ann Sullivan, "Touchy Sex Subject Handled Objectively in New Film: Bird, Bee Tint Out of Vogue," *Portland Oregonian,* 15 February 1948, 24. Slides were available for loan or purchase along with the film, using images from the movie. The series of twenty slides featured images of the body that could be discussed in greater detail. Beck, *Film Guide,* "Structure and Theory of the Film," n.p. The guide praised the effectiveness of slides as a teaching tool, and E. C. Brown Trust records indicate that most purchases of the movie included the slides. Receipts register, June 1950–October 1958, box 1, E. C. Brown Foundation Papers, Division of Special Collections and University Archives, University of Oregon, Eugene, Oregon.

39. Lester F. Beck, with Margie Robinson, *Human Growth: The Story of How Life Begins and Goes on, Based on the Educational Film of the Same Title* (New York: Harcourt, Brace, 1949), 45–48.

40. Beck, *Human Growth,* 13.

41. Ibid.

42. Littman, who accompanied Beck on screenings of the film, confirmed that students voiced concerns about masturbation during question-and-answer sessions. Littman, telephone communication.

43. Curtis E. Avery and Lester F. Beck, "History of a Film: 'Human Growth,'" *Audiovisual Instruction,* March 1964, quoted in Michael E. Pajot, "Guiding Principles for the Revision of *Human Growth,*" [1974], 4, box 1, "Human Growth" folder, E. C. Brown Trust Papers, Division of Special Collections and University Archives, University of Oregon, Eugene

44. Biester, Griffiths, and Pearce, *Personal Health and Human Relations,* 30, 145, 152; Howard Whitman, *Let's Tell the Truth about Sex* (New York: Pellegrini and Cudahy, 1948), 104–10; Edith Hale Swift, *Step by Step in Sex Education* (1938; reprint, New York: Macmillan, 1950), 170–73.

45. Babcock, "Seventh Grade Course," 381; Lampe, "Growing Up," 55–56.

46. Evert R. Pearcy, "Sex Education in the Senior High Schools of New Jersey," master's thesis, West Virginia University, 1940, 38, 41. The girls' lesson also noted "Use Meagher's Conclusions," which were not indicated. Such sources as the curriculum outlines included in Pearcy's thesis are disappointingly cryptic.

47. Lampe, "Growing Up," 2d ed., 57, 64; c.f. Lampe, "Growing Up," 55–56.

48. Lampe, "Growing Up," 64.

49. Ibid., 57.

50. Glassberg, "St. Louis Program," grade 9, lecture 6 [—Boys], 4, Glassberg Papers. Although not labeled for boys, such passages suggest that a male audience was intended. A corresponding girls' lecture was not preserved in this collection.

51. Ibid., 5.

52. Ibid., 6–11, quotation on 6.

53. Glassberg, "St. Louis Program," Grade 9, lecture 5—Girls, 2, Glassberg Papers.

54. Ibid., 3.

55. Ibid., 3–7.

56. Ibid., 7–8.

57. Lampe, "Growing Up," 2d ed., 64. She offered the same kind of advice for boys.

58. Ibid., 64–66, quotation on 64.

59. Biester, Griffiths, and Pearce, *Personal Health and Human Relations*, 29–30.

60. Ibid.

61. Ibid., 32.

62. Ibid., 30, emphasis added.

63. Brumberg, *The Body Project*, 49.

64. Margot Elizabeth Kennard, "The Corporation in the Classroom: The Struggles over Meanings of Menstruation Education in Sponsored Films, 1947–1983," Ph.D. diss., University of Wisconsin-Madison, 1989.

65. Brumberg, *The Body Project*, chap. 2.

66. Ibid., 46–47.

67. *The Story of Menstruation*, 16 mm, 10 min., Walt Disney Productions, 1946; Kennard, "Corporation in the Classroom."

68. Kennard, "Corporation in the Classroom," 36.

69. Evidence that boys watched *The Story of Menstruation* comes from the teachers' guide, where comments are reprinted from boys. Kimberly-Clark Corporation Educational Department, *A Practical Guide for Teaching Menstrual Hygiene* (Neenah: Kimberly-Clark Corporation, 1961), 14–15, box 45, Ed—Family Life—Sex Educ. Teach Aids—Elem & HS-Comb. file, National Council on Family Relations Papers, Social Welfare History Archives, Minneapolis, Minnesota (hereafter NCFR Papers). See also Kotex advertisement, *Educational Screen*, September 1947, 382–83; and Augustine Escamilla, *Guide for Secondary Social Health Education* (San Diego: San Diego City Schools, 1966), 24.

70. Lampe, "Growing Up," 2d ed., 63. Although San Diego City Schools did not show *The Story of Menstruation* to sixth-grade students, the 1948 pamphlet appeared in the 1951 teachers' manual as a free, recommended resource for girls. Ibid., 74.

71. Kotex advertisement, 382–83.

72. Kimberly-Clark Educational Department, *Practical Guide*, 6, NCFR Papers.

73. Ibid., 8. Tampons were available, but there was disagreement about whether it was advisable for girls to use them.

74. Glassberg, "St. Louis Program," grade 9, lecture 4—Boys, 5.

75. Ibid.

76. Ibid., 6.

77. Lampe, "Growing Up," 48. The wording was rephrased in the revised edition but essentially conveyed the same point. Lampe, "Growing Up," 2d ed., 61.

78. Kimberly-Clark Educational Department, *Practical Guide*, 4, NCFR Papers.

79. "New Biology Film," *Educational Screen* 26 (April 1947): 218.

80. Lampe, "Growing Up," 48; Lampe, "Growing Up," 2d ed., 60–61.

81. Ibid.

82. Excerpts from the film's narration are from Kennard, "Corporation in the Classroom," 95–96.

83. On the factory model, see ibid., 101; and Emily Martin, *The Woman in the Body: A Cultural Analysis of Reproduction* (Boston: Beacon Press, 1987), 37–47. On metaphors in science, see Nancy Tuana, *Feminism and Science* (Bloomington: Indiana University Press, 1989); Nancy Tuana, ed., *The Less Noble Sex: Scientific, Religious, and Philosophical Conceptions of Women's Nature* (Bloomington: Indiana University Press, 1993); and Nancy Stepan, "Race and Gender: The Role of Analogy in Science," in *The "Racial" Economy of Science: Toward a Democratic Future*, ed. Sandra Harding (Bloomington: Indiana University Press, 1993), 359–76.

84. Lampe, "Growing Up," 55.

85. Ibid.

86. Ibid., 48.

87. Lampe, "Growing Up," 2d ed., 61.

88. Payton Kennedy, *A Source Book for Teachers of Family Life Education*, rev. ed. (San Antonio: San Antonio Independent School District, [1951]), 65.

89. Ibid., 64–65.

90. Ibid., 66.

91. Emily Martin, "The Egg and the Sperm: How Science Has Constructed a Romance Based on Stereotypical Male-Female Roles," *Signs* 16, no. 3 (1991): 485–501.

92. Karl de Schweinitz, *Growing Up: The Story of How We Become Alive, Are Born and Grow Up* (1930; reprint, New York: Macmillan, 1928), 103, 104. For classroom use of the book see Babcock, "Seventh Grade Course," 380; Lampe, "Growing Up," 60; and Lampe, "Growing Up," 2d ed., 73. See also Julian B. Carter, "Birds, Bees, and Venereal Disease: Toward an Intellectual History of Sex Education," *Journal of the History of Sexuality* 10, no. 2 (2001): 213–49, esp. 233–41.

93. Reuben D. Behlmer, "Family Life Education in a Large High School," *Marriage and Family Living* 21 (August 1959): 284–86, quotation on 286.

94. Kennard, "Corporation in the Classroom," 191.

95. Kimberly-Clark Corporation Educational Department, *Practical Guide,* 8, NCFR Papers.

96. Mildred Morgan, "The Hillsborough Study: A Grass Roots Development of a County-Wide Family Life Program Which Includes Sex Education," unpublished manuscript, 1962, box 12, "Florida—Hillsborough" folder, ASHA Papers.

97. Beck with Robinson, *Human Growth,* 86.

98. Ibid.

99. Lampe, "Growing Up," 2d ed., 68, 70–71.

100. Ibid., 68.

101. Ibid., 70.

102. Ibid., 71.

103. Ibid.

104. Biester, Griffiths, and Pearce, *Personal Health and Human Relations,* 98. I have seen no other discussion of hymens in texts for school sex education from this period.

105. Glassberg, "St. Louis Program," grade 9, lecture 3, 11, box 7, folder 183, Glassberg Papers.

106. Beck, *Film Guide,* n.p.; Lampe, "Growing Up," 2d ed., 72–73; see also Geneva E. Gordon, *Family Life Education Bibliography* (San Diego: San Diego City Schools, Department of Health Education, 1950–51), cited in Hale, "Sex Education Knowledge," 21.

107. Biester, Griffiths, and Pearce, *Personal Health and Human Relations,* 150–51.

108. Ibid., 151.

109. Ibid., 188–209, quotations on 200, 202.

110. Lampe, "Growing Up," 2d ed., 65.

111. Ibid.

112. Gordon, *Family Life Education Bibliography,* cited in Hale, "Sex Education Knowledge," 21.

113. Harold A. Miller and Robert S. Breakey, "Sex Education in the Curriculum," *Education Digest* 5 (February 1940): 39; Behlmer, "Family Life Education," 286; Kenneth E. Oberholtzer and Myrtle F. Sugarman, "Denver Educates for Home and Family Living," *Journal of Social Hygiene* 37 (February 1951): 51–61, esp. 59.

114. Biester, Griffiths, and Pearce, *Personal Health and Human Relations,* 150, 203.

115. Babcock, "Seventh Grade Course," 381.

116. Maude M. Firth, unpublished report to the superintendent of schools, n.d., cited in Joseph K. Folsom, *Youth, Family, and Education* (Washington: American Council on Education, 1941), 100; James A. Michener, "Sex Education: A Success in Our Social Studies Class," *Clearing House* 12 (April 1938): 461–65, esp. 463.

117. John W. Masley and Arthur F. Davis, "Sex Education in Pennsylvania's Public Secondary Schools," *Journal of Social Hygiene* 39 (March 1953): 107–19, esp. 113.

118. Morgan, "Hillsborough Study," ASHA Papers.

119. Ibid.

Chapter 5: Gender and Heterosexual Adjustment

1. "The School's Responsibility in Social Hygiene Education: Preliminary Report of a New York Statewide Committee," *Journal of Social Hygiene* 26 (October 1940): 294–304, quotation on 297.

2. Division of Instruction, Department of Family Life Education, Detroit Public Schools, *Family Life Education in the High School: A Source Book for Teachers* (Detroit: Board of Education of the City of Detroit, 1958), 17. The developmental tasks come from Robert J. Havighurst, *Developmental Tasks and Education,* 2d ed. (New York: Longmans, Green, 1952), chap. 5.

3. On connections between race and the sex/gender system, see Sally Markowitz, "Pelvic Politics: Sexual Dimorphism and Racial Difference," *Signs* 25, no. 2 (2001): 389–414.

4. Historian Ellen Herman has argued that the mid-century rise of clinical psychology contributed to the women's movement of the late twentieth century, collapsing sharp distinctions between self/other, psychic/social, and personal/political. Ellen Herman, *The Romance of American Psychology: Political Culture in the Age of Experts* (Berkeley: University of California Press, 1995), esp. chap. 10.

5. For the roots of sexual and social change among college students before the 1960s, see Beth L. Bailey, *Sex in the Heartland* (Cambridge: Harvard University Press, 1999).

6. Judith Butler, *Gender Trouble: Feminism and the Subversion of Identity* (New York: Routledge, 1990).

7. Self-scrutiny and discipline regarding such attributes as body size, configuration, gestures, movements, and ornamentation yield feminine bodies and personas; regulating diet, exercise, posture, gaze, cosmetics, and clothing is fundamental to achieving femininity. Sandra Lee Bartky, "Foucault, Femininity, and the Modernization of Patriarchal Power," in *Feminism and Foucault: Reflections on Resistance,* ed. Irene Diamond and Lee Quinby (Boston: Northeastern University Press, 1988), 61–86. See also Butler, *Gender Trouble;* and Susan Bordo, *Unbearable Weight: Feminism, Western Culture, and the Body* (Berkeley: University of California Press, 1993), esp. 165–84.

8. For a similar argument in an earlier period in Denmark, see Birgitte Søland, *Becoming Modern: Young Women and the Reconstruction of Womanhood in the 1920s* (Princeton: Princeton University Press, 2000).

9. Kathy Lee Peiss, *Cheap Amusements: Working Women and Leisure in Turn-of-the-Century New York* (Philadelphia: Temple University Press, 1986); Joanne J. Meye-

rowitz, *Women Adrift: Independent Wage Earners in Chicago, 1880–1930* (Chicago: University of Chicago Press, 1988).

10. Lester F. Beck, with Margie Robinson, *Human Growth: The Story of How Life Begins and Goes on, Based on the Educational Film of the Same Title* (New York: Harcourt, Brace, 1949), 119, 120.

11. *Human Growth*, 16 mm, 20 min., E. C. Brown Trust and Eddie Albert Productions, Portland, 1947; *The Story of Menstruation*, 16 mm, 10 min., Walt Disney Productions, 1946.

12. Margot Elizabeth Kennard, "The Corporation in the Classroom: The Struggles over Meanings of Menstruation Education in Sponsored Films, 1947–1983," Ph.D. diss., University of Wisconsin, Madison, 1989, chap. 4.

13. Kennard, "The Corporation in the Classroom," 111.

14. Ibid.

15. "New Biology Film Helps Girls," *Educational Screen*, April 1947, 215, 218, quotation on 215.

16. See, for example, Edward H. Clarke, *Sex in Education; Or, A Fair Chance for the Girls* (Boston: J. R. Osgood, 1873).

17. Harold A. Miller and Robert S. Breakey, "Sex Education in the Curriculum," *Education Digest* 5 (February 1940): 37–40, quotation on 38.

18. G. Stanley Hall, *Adolescence: Its Psychology and Its Relations to Physiology, Anthropology, Sociology, Sex, Crime, Religion, and Education* (New York: D. Appleton, 1908).

19. Payton Kennedy, *A Source Book for Teachers of Family Life Education*, rev. ed. (San Antonio: San Antonio Independent School District, [1951]), 26.

20. Viola I. Lampe, "Growing Up: Lessons on Social Hygiene for Sixth-Grade Boys and Girls," in G. Gage Wetherill, *Human Relations Education: A Report*, 2d ed. (New York: American Social Hygiene Association, 1951), 57, 60.

21. Beck with Robinson, *Human Growth*, 44.

22. Ibid., 43.

23. Frances Y. Henthorn, "Personal Hygiene for Adolescents," *Journal of School Health* 29 (January 1959): 15–19, quotation on 16.

24. Beck with Robinson, *Human Growth*, 61.

25. Virginia Milling, "How Do You Rate on a Date?" *Clearing House* 19 (November 1944): 165–66, quotations on 166.

26. Havighurst, *Developmental Tasks*, 38, 37.

27. Ibid., 38, emphasis in the original.

28. Howard Stanley Hoyman, "Basic Issues in School Sex Education," *Journal of School Health* 23 (January 1953): 15.

29. See, for example, Gertrude Burgess, "Development and Results of a Sex Hygiene Course in a Consolidated High School," *Michigan Public Health* 23 (September 1935): 170–77; and Roanoke City Public Schools, *Family Life Education Resource Guide, Grade 1 through 12* (New York: American Social Hygiene Association, 1958), 81.

30. Viola I. Lampe, "Growing Up: Lessons in Health and Human Relations for Sixth Grade Boys and Girls," in G. Gage Wetherill, *Human Relations Education: A Program Developing in the San Diego City Schools* (New York: American Social Hygiene Association, 1946), 44.

31. Lampe, "Growing Up," 45. In the second edition, Lampe made no reference to injury but did maintain the need for support. Lampe, "Growing Up," 2d ed., 60.

32. A medical doctor explained to parents in the early 1950s that a teenaged girl should wear a bra "to prevent sagging breasts, stretched blood vessels, and poor circulation, all of which would create problems in nursing for her future," but he also mentioned the potential to prevent unattractive, saggy breasts. Frank H. Crowell, "When Your Daughter Matures," *Parents' Magazine,* August 1952, quoted in Joan Jacobs Brumberg, *The Body Project: An Intimate History of American Girls* (New York: Random House, 1997), 112.

33. Lampe, "Growing Up," 2d ed., 60. The first edition did not mention the foreskin.

34. Ibid., 57.

35. Lampe, "Growing Up," 51. The second edition lesson plans included cautions to boys and girls in the same lesson, explaining that "Your parents want to protect you" without gendered distinctions. Lampe, "Growing Up," 2d ed., 49.

36. Milling, "How Do You Rate?" 166.

37. Burgess, "Development and Results," 174.

38. An atypical and harsh critique of homosexuality in adolescents appeared in the curriculum guide for San Antonio: "The boy or the girl who is attracted to his own sex and attempts a ridiculous facsimile of man-woman relations is more to be pitied than anything else. He needs psychiatric treatment to be reclaimed for normal living." Kennedy, *Source Book,* 62.

39. Havighurst, *Developmental Tasks,* 37–38.

40. Women in the paid labor force increased from 34 percent in 1950 to 38 percent in 1960, part of a longer twentieth-century trend toward women, especially married women, entering the workforce. Diane Crispell, "Myths of the 1950s," *American Demographics* 14 (August 1992): 38–43, esp. 42; William Henry Chafe, *The Paradox of Change: American Women in the Twentieth Century,* rev. ed. (New York: Oxford University Press, 1991). By the mid-1950s, rates of women's employment matched the artificially high levels attained during World War II. Susan M. Hartmann, "Women's Employment and the Domestic Ideal in the Early Cold War Years," in *Not June Cleaver: Women and Gender in Postwar America, 1945–1960,* ed. Joanne Meyerowitz (Philadelphia: Temple University Press, 1994), 84–100, esp. 86. Hartmann cites Claudia Goldin, *Understanding the Gender Gap: An Economic History of American Women* (New York: Oxford University Press, 1990), 119–58.

41. Elizabeth S. Force, *Your Family, Today and Tomorrow* (New York: Harcourt, Brace, [1955]), 131. The illustration appeared in the unit "Object—Matrimony," which began with a section entitled "Is Marriage for You?"

42. Alfred C. Kinsey, Wardell B. Pomeroy, and Clyde E. Martin, *Sexual Behavior in the Human Male* (Philadelphia: W. B. Saunders, 1948); Alfred C. Kinsey et al., *Sexual Behavior in the Human Female* (Philadelphia: W. B. Saunders, 1953); Estelle B. Freedman, "'Uncontrolled Desires': The Response to the Sexual Psychopath, 1920–1960," *Journal of American History* 74, no. 1 (1987): 83–106; James Gilbert, *A Cycle of Outrage: America's Reaction to the Juvenile Delinquent* (New York: Oxford University Press, 1986), chap. 9; Constance A. Nathanson, *Dangerous Passage: The Social Control of Sexuality in Women's Adolescence* (Philadelphia: Temple University Press, 1991); Jeffrey P. Moran, *Teaching Sex: The Shaping of Adolescence in the Twentieth Century* (Cambridge: Harvard University Press, 2000).

43. On the nineteenth-century origins of the view of men and women as complementary, see Cynthia Eagle Russett, *Sexual Science: The Victorian Construction of Womanhood* (Cambridge: Harvard University Press, 1989).

44. The idea of companionate marriage—based on love and compatibility rather than economic arrangements—grew popular in marriage advice books and in practice during the early twentieth century. Nancy F. Cott, *Public Vows: A History of Marriage and the Nation* (Cambridge: Harvard University Press, 2000).

45. Force, *Your Family,* 108.

46. Wetherill, *Human Relations Education,* 16; Lillian Biester, William Griffiths, and N. O. Pearce, *Units in Personal Health and Human Relations* (Minneapolis: University of Minnesota Press, 1947), 181; Elizabeth S. Force and Edgar M. Finck, *Family Relationships: Ten Topics toward Happier Homes* (Elizabethtown: Continental Press, 1948), 62; Force, *Your Family,* 159–61.

47. Force, *Your Family,* 169.

48. Lester A. Kirkendall, "Sound Attitudes toward Sex," *Journal of Social Hygiene* 37 (June 1951): 241–51, quotation on 251.

49. Kirkendall, "Sound Attitudes," 250.

50. Beck with Robinson, *Human Growth,* 36.

51. Kennedy, *Source Book,* 25. Acknowledgments indicate that the volume was "revised by Mrs. Payton Kennedy in the light of student evaluations and her experience in teaching the course for three terms in the schools to approximately 1,900 students." Ibid., n.p.

52. Ibid., 26.

53. Ibid.

54. Elizabeth S. Force, "What Teen-Agers Want to Know about Sex and Marriage," *American Magazine* 155 (January 1953): 34–35, 103–6, quotation on 104–5.

55. Detroit Public Schools, *Family Life Education,* 17–21.

56. Helen Randolph, "Senior Problems and Family Life," *Journal of Secondary Education* 25 (January 1950): 12–17, quotations on 17.

57. Biester, Griffiths, and Pearce, *Personal Health and Human Relations,* 133.

58. Ibid., 164–87.

59. Mildred Sanders Williamson, "High School Family Life Courses," *Journal of Home Economics* 42 (February 1950): 98–100.

60. Biester, Griffiths, and Pearce, *Personal Health and Human Relations,* 164.

61. Force, "What Teen-Agers Want," 104.

62. Louise Ramsey, "Education for Marriage and Family Life in the High School as a Means of Strengthening National Defense," *Marriage and Family Living* 4 (August 1942): 52–55, quotation on 53.

63. Educators cited girls' frequent questions on this topic; see, for example, Wetherill, *Human Relations Education,* 10.

64. Alma M. Volk, "Rock Island's Program of Sex Education," *School Executive* 65 (May 1946): 53–54, quotation on 54.

65. Mabel Grier Lesher, *Meeting Youth Needs* (Trenton: New Jersey Congress of Parents and Teachers, [1945]).

66. Milling, "How Do You Rate?" 165.

67. World War II, the GI bill, and the Korean War contributed to the trend toward earlier marriage—men were able to support a family at a younger age and departure overseas led many young couples to tie the knot sooner rather than later. Jessica Weiss, *To Have and to Hold: Marriage, the Baby Boom, and Social Change* (Chicago: University of Chicago Press, 2000), 4, 22.

68. Oberholtzer and Sugarman, "Denver Educates"; Marjorie Cosgrove, "School Guidance for Home and Family Living: A Required Course for Seniors in Highland Park, Michigan High School" *Marriage and Family Living* 14 (February 1952): 26–51.

69. Oberholtzer and Sugarman, "Denver Educates," 51.

70. A short outline of this course appeared in John Newton Baker, *Sex Education in High Schools* (New York: Emerson Books, 1942), 120–21.

71. The unnamed student's letter is quoted in Force, *Your Family,* ix.

72. Force, "What Teen-Agers Want," 104.

73. James A. Michener, "Sex Education: A Success in Our Social Studies Class," *Clearing House* 12 (April 1938): 461–65, quotation on 464.

74. Alice Strawn, "A Human Relations Class," *Marriage and Family Living* 11 (Spring 1949): 44–45, quotation on 45.

Chapter 6: Sexuality Education beyond Classrooms

1. Kelly Schrum has identified the origins of adolescent consumer culture—especially involving girls—in the 1920s and 1930s in *Some Wore Bobby Sox: The Emergence of Teenage Girls' Culture, 1920–1945* (New York: Palgrave Macmillan, 2004). For a contemporary source on extracurricular school activities see August B. Hollingshead, *Elmtown's Youth: The Impact of Social Class on Adolescents* (New York: John Wiley and Sons, 1949).

2. William Graebner, *Coming of Age in Buffalo: Youth and Authority in the Post-*

war Era (Philadelphia: Temple University Press, 1990), 6; see also Wini Breines, *Young, White, and Miserable: Growing up Female in the Fifties* (Boston: Beacon Press, 1992).

3. Grace Palladino, *Teenagers: An American History* (New York: Basic Books, 1996); Graebner, *Coming of Age;* Breines, *Young, White, and Miserable;* James Gilbert, *A Cycle of Outrage: America's Reaction to the Juvenile Delinquent in the 1950s* (New York: Oxford University Press, 1986); Thomas Doherty, *Teenagers and Teenpics: The Juvenilization of American Movies in the 1950s,* rev. ed (Philadelphia: Temple University Press, 2002).

4. Amy L. Best, *Prom Night: Youth, Schools, and Popular Culture* (New York: Routledge, 2000).

5. Grace Metalious, *Peyton Place* (New York: Messner, 1956).

6. Brett Harvey, *The Fifties: A Women's Oral History* (New York: Harper Collins, 1993), 13.

7. "People Are More Important than Nuclear Submarine," newspaper clipping, *Atlanta Constitution,* 15 August 1959, box 89, folder 7, American Social Hygiene Association Papers, Social Welfare History Archives, Minneapolis, Minnesota; D. H. Lawrence, *Lady Chatterly's Lover* (New York: New American Library, 1959).

8. Vin Packer, *Spring Fire* (New York: Fawcett Publications, 1952). Vin Packer was the pen name—among several others, including Ann Aldrich—of Marjane Meaker, see http://www.cleispress.com/Meaker_spotlight.html, accessed 21 June 2005.

9. Ann Bannon, introduction, *Odd Girl Out* (1957; reprint, San Francisco: Cleis Press, 2001). The many letters Bannon received from readers, unfortunately, have not survived.

10. Harvey, *The Fifties,* 190.

11. My analysis is based primarily on two sets of yearbooks from two school districts in the 1950s. These were the yearbooks of Carol Ortman, a 1960 graduate of San Diego High School, and Cy Perkins, a 1957 graduate of Webster Groves High School in suburban St. Louis, Missouri. The yearbooks are in the possession of Carol and Cy Perkins. For an analysis of yearbooks and their relationship to youth culture, see Schrum, *Some Wore Bobby Sox.*

12. Breines, *Young, White, and Miserable,* 97; see also Betty Friedan, *The Feminine Mystique* (New York: Norton, 1963); and Joanne Meyerowitz, ed., *Not June Cleaver: Women and Gender in Postwar America, 1945–1960* (Philadelphia: Temple University Press, 1994).

13. *Teddy's Round-up,* Theodore Roosevelt Junior High School yearbook, San Diego, California, 1955; *Gray Castle,* San Diego High School yearbook, 1958, 1959, 1960.

14. Benson and Benson, Inc., *Life with Teena: A Seventeen Magazine Survey of Subscribers and Their Mothers* (New York: Triangle Publications, 1945), 54.

15. Palladino, *Teenagers,* 106.

16. *Echo,* Webster Groves High School yearbook, Webster Groves, Missouri, 1953.

17. Ibid., 1952, 1953, 1954, 1955, 1956, 1957.

18. *Gray Castle,* 1958, 164.

19. Ibid., 1960.

20. William H. Payne, "High School Group Interprets the Meaning of American-ism," *Curriculum Digest: San Diego City Schools in Action* 12 (September 1951): 5.

21. *Gray Castle,* 1960. Carol Ortman Perkins pointed out the deliberate effort to make the boy appear taller. Conversation with Carol Perkins, 1 June 2005.

22. Breines, *Young, White, and Miserable,* 90.

23. Beth L. Bailey, *From Front Porch to Back Seat: Courtship in Twentieth-Century America* (Baltimore: Johns Hopkins University Press, 1988); Helen Moore Priester, "The Reported Dating Practices of One Hundred Six High School Seniors in an Urban Community," master's thesis, Cornell University, 1941; Opal Powell Wolford, "The Dating Behavior and Personal and Family Relationships of High School Seniors with Implications for Family Life Education," Ph.D. diss., Cornell University, 1948; John R. Christ, "High School Dating as a Behavior System," Ph.D. diss., University of Missouri, 1951; Warren Breed, "Sex, Class, and Socialization in Dating," *Marriage and Family Living* 18 (May 1956): 137–44; Russell L. Bliss, "Teen-Age Dating Behavior in Two Eastern Kentucky High Schools," master's thesis University of Kentucky, 1957. Christ and Bliss discovered only minor variations in youth behavior based on region and rural versus urban distinctions.

24. Edna Gillingham, "The Teen-Ager in Search of Recreation," *California Parent-Teacher,* January 1944, 8, 16, quotation on 8.

25. Lois Cullison, "Report of the Discontinuance of Coed Inn at Williams Ave. YWCA Center, May 23, 1956," 14 June 1956, Portland YWCA Archives, http://wom-hist.binghamton.edu/portywca/aawomen/afamdoc2.htm, accessed 21 June 2005.

26. Cullison, "Report of the Discontinuance."

27. *Echo,* 1955, 100.

28. Christ, "High School Dating," 126.

29. Mac Eagle, *Raised in Toms River and Darn Proud of It* (Grand Rapids: Mac Eagle, 1996), 73–74.

30. Social Behavior Classes of 1955, "What Every Pupil Should Know about School Dances," box 2, file 12, Elizabeth Sculthorpe Force Papers, Ocean County Historical Society, Toms River, New Jersey.

31. Ibid., 60.

32. Paladino, *Teenagers,* 124–25; see also John Johnstone and Elihu Katz, "Youth and Popular Music: A Study in the Sociology of Taste," *American Journal of Sociology* 62, no. 6 (1957): 563–68.

33. Breines, *Young, White, and Miserable,* 86–87.

34. Harvey, *The Fifties,* 3–4.

35. Ibid., 5.

36. Ibid., 8.

37. Ibid., 9.

38. Ibid., 13–14.

39. Ibid., 15.

40. Christ, "High School Dating"; Breed, "Sex, Class, and Socialization in Dating."

41. *Teddy's Round-up*, 1955.

42. Ibid.

43. *Echo*, 1952.

44. *Echo*, 1954.

45. *Echo*, 1952.

46. *Echo*, 1953, 1955.

47. Carol Ortman Perkins, a white woman who during high school developed close friendships with black male peers, drew my attention to a photograph of her surrounded by football players on the field following the team's victory. She described the racial dynamics between white and black players in ways not obvious in the image. In particular, her gaze is turned in the direction of a particular black player who is outside the frame of the photograph. Conversation with Carol Perkins, 1 June 2005.

48. Renee C. Romano, *Race Mixing: Black-White Marriage in Postwar America* (Cambridge: Harvard University Press, 2003), 2, 169.

49. Eugene J. Kanin, "Male Aggression in Dating-Courtship Relations," *American Journal of Sociology* 63 (September 1957): 197–204.

50. "Teenage Sex Hysteria," *Science News Letter*, 1 January 1955, 4.

51. See, for example, Melvin J. Williams, "Personal and Familial Problems of High School Youths and Their Bearing upon Family Education Needs," *Social Forces* 27, no. 3 (1949): 279–85.

Conclusion

1. Elizabeth S. Force, "High School Education for Family Living," *Annals of the American Academy of Political and Social Science* 272 (November 1950): 156–62, quotation on 161.

2. Roy E. Dickerson, "Pre-Induction Course for High School Students," *Journal of Social Hygiene* 31 (April 1945): 211–16, esp. 215–16

3. Kelsey Hudleson Ingle, "A Study of the Needs of High School Girls in the Area of Sex Guidance in Family Life Education," master's thesis, University of North Carolina, Greensboro, 1948, 41.

4. Many students used this language, according to Kenneth Gray Hale, "An Inquiry into the Sex Education Knowledge, Needs, and Interests of 1,390 Twelfth-Grade Students," master's thesis, San Diego State College, 1952, 78.

5. Thomas Poffenberger, "Responses of Eighth Grade Girls to a Talk on Sex," *Marriage and Family Living* 22 (February 1960): 38–44, quotations on 42.

6. "Sex in the Classroom," *Newsweek*, 10 August 1959, 84.

7. Ibid.

8. [Questions on Sex Education, Normandy Hi-Y Group,] postmarked 3 March

1958, box 3, folder 70, Bert Y. Glassberg Papers, Becker Medical Library, Washington University School of Medicine, St. Louis, Missouri.

9. "Teen-Age Council Shelves Subway Fare Rise but Votes for a Course in Sex Education," *New York Times,* 27 April 1946, 19.

10. Force, "High School Education," 161.

11. Leora Tanenbaum, *Slut! Growing Up Female with a Bad Reputation* (New York: Seven Stories Press, 2000).

12. For examples of Catholic leaders' occasionally voiced opposition to sex education, see "Harvey Says Reds Sway Rule of City," *New York Times,* 17 May 1937, 11; and "Sex Education Held Unwise in Schools," *New York Times,* 8 February 1939, 24. For examples of passing comments or brief allegations of Catholic opposition in the 1940s, see Harold Isaacs, "Youth: Shall Our Schools Teach Sex?" *Newsweek,* 19 May 1947, 100–102; and "Where Babies Come From: University of Oregon Program of Education on Family Life," *Newsweek,* 22 March 1948, 90. Researcher Howard Whitman explained that Catholics did not oppose sex education but preferred it to take place in homes rather than schools. Howard Whitman, *Let's Tell the Truth about Sex* (New York: Pellegrini and Cudahy, 1948), 14–16.

13. Ruth Farnham Osborne and Lester A. Kirkendall, "Family-Life Education in Illinois High Schools," *School Review* 58 (December 1950): 516–26, esp. 517.

14. Gordon V. Drake, *Is the Schoolhouse the Proper Place to Teach Raw Sex?* (Tulsa: Christian Crusade Publications, 1968); Gloria Lentz, *Raping Our Children: The Sex Education Scandal* (New Rochelle: Arlington House, 1972); John Steinbacher, *The Child Seducers* (n.p.: Educator Publications, 1971). See also Jeffrey P. Moran, *Teaching Sex: The Shaping of Adolescence in the Twentieth Century* (Cambridge: Harvard University Press, 2000), chap. 6.

15. Jack Hyles, *Sex Education Program in Our Public Schools: What Is Behind It?* (Murfreesboro: Sword of the Lord Publishers, 1969), 13.

16. Janice M. Irvine, *Talk about Sex: The Battles over Sex Education in the United States* (Berkeley: University of California Press, 2002).

17. "Sex Education That Teaches Abstinence Wins Support," *New York Times,* 23 July 1997, A19.

18. "Abstinence Is Focus of U.S. Sex Education," *New York Times,* 15 December 1999, A18.

19. "Abstinence Is Focus."

20. *It's Elementary: Talking about Gay Issues in School,* prod. Helen S. Cohen and Debra Chasnoff, 77 min., Women's Educational Media, 1996, videocassette.

21. Dallas Independent School District, *Home and Family Life Education for Secondary Schools and Adults Curriculum Guide* (Dallas: Dallas Independent School District, 1953), 89.

22. Ellen Herman, *The Romance of American Psychology: Political Culture in the Age of Experts* (Berkeley: University of California Press, 1995), 277.

23. Herman, *The Romance of American Psychology,* 280.

Bibliography

Archival Sources

American Social Hygiene Papers. Social Welfare History Archives, Minneapolis.

Department of Education (General) Papers. Oregon State Archives, Salem.

E. C. Brown Foundation Papers. Division of Special Collections and University Archives, University of Oregon, Eugene.

E. C. Brown Trust Papers. Division of Special Collections and University Archives, University of Oregon, Eugene.

Elizabeth Sculthorpe Force Papers. Ocean County Historical Society, Toms River, N.J.

Bert Y. Glassberg Papers. Becker Medical Library, Washington University School of Medicine, St. Louis. Microfilm.

National Council on Family Relations Papers. Social Welfare History Archives, Minneapolis.

Oral History Program, Research Archives, San Diego Historical Society.

Oregon Social Hygiene Society Records. Oregon Historical Society, Portland.

Papers of the NAACP. Microfilm.

Portland (Oregon) YWCA Archives at womhist.binghamton.edu/portywca/.

Records of the San Diego Unified School District. San Diego City Schools Board of Education.

Films

Dangerous Stranger. 16 mm, 12 min. Sid Davis Productions, Los Angeles, 1950.

Family Circles. 16 mm, 31 min. McGraw-Hill, New York, 1949.

From Flower to Fruit. 16 mm, 16 min. Eastman Teaching Films and Encyclopedia Britannica Films, Chicago, 1933.

Human Growth. 16 mm, 20 min. E. C. Brown Trust and Eddie Albert Productions, Portland, 1947.

Human Reproduction. 16 mm, 21 min. McGraw-Hill, New York, 1948.

The Miracle of Reproduction. 16 mm, 15 min. Sid Davis Productions, Los Angeles, 1963.

Name Unknown. 16 mm, 10 minutes. Sid Davis Productions, Los Angeles, 1951.

Palmour Street. 16 mm, 27 min. Georgia Department of Health, [Atlanta,] 1950.

Snakes Are Interesting. 16 mm, 12 min. Murl Deusing Film Productions, Milwaukee, 1947.

The Snapping Turtle. 16 mm, 12 min. Encyclopedia Britannica Films, Chicago, 1940.

The Story of Menstruation. 16 mm, 10 min. Walt Disney Productions, [Burbank], 1946.

The Sunfish. 16 mm, 11 min. Encyclopedia Britannica Films, Chicago, 1941.

Primary Sources

"Abstinence Is Focus of U.S. Sex Education." *New York Times,* 15 December 1999, A18.

American Association of School Administrators. *Character Education.* Tenth Yearbook. Washington, D.C.: Department of Superintendence of the National Education Association, 1932.

Anderson, Wayne J. "Education for Happy Family Living (Utah)." *Journal of Educational Sociology* 22 (March 1949): 450–56.

Applebaum, Stella B. "A School That Prepares for Living: Toms River, N.J. Revamped Its High School Program to Satisfy the Students' Real Needs," *Parents' Magazine* 24 (May 1949): 36–37, 106.

Arnold, Katherine L., and Virginia L. Gleason. "Discussion Methods with New Variations." *Marriage and Family Living* 21 (May 1959): 180–81.

"Audiences Approve Sex Education Film." *New York Times,* 31 March 1949, 23.

Avery, Curtis E. *Meet the E. C. Brown Trust Foundation.* Portland: E. C. Brown Trust, [1969?].

——. "Toward an Understanding of Sex Education in Oregon." In *Sex Education: Concepts and Challenges, A Collection of Readings from "The Family Life Coordinator,"* edited by Curtis E. Avery, with David S. Brody and Margie R. Lee, 17–26. Eugene: E. C. Brown Center for Family Studies, 1969.

——, with David S. Brody and Margie R. Lee, eds. *Sex Education: Concepts and Challenges, A Collection of Readings from "The Family Life Coordinator."* Eugene: E. C. Brown Center for Family Studies, 1969.

——, and Lester A. Kirkendall. *The Oregon Developmental Center Project in Family Life Education.* Portland: E. C. Brown Trust, 1955.

Babcock, Russell B. "A Seventh Grade Course in Sex Education." *Progressive Education* 13 (May 1936): 374–82.

Baber, Ray E. "Youth Can Be Trained for Successful Marriage and Parenthood." *California Parent-Teacher* 19 (February 1943): 6.

Baker, John Newton. *Sex Education in High Schools.* New York: Emerson Books, 1942.

Bannon, Ann. *Odd Girl Out.* 1957; reprint, San Francisco: Cleis Press, 2001.

Barbour, Richmond. "Intriguing Ideas." *California Parent-Teacher* 30 (November 1953): 12–13.

———. "Sex Education." *California Parent-Teacher* 29 (November 1952): 4.

Barclay, Dorothy. "Doctors Give Ideas on Sex Education." *New York Times,* 22 November 1950, 29.

"The Battle over Sex Education Films." *Look,* 30 August 1949, 34–35.

Bautista, Adelaida Teves. "Family Life Education for High School Seniors in the Philippines." Master's thesis, San Francisco State College, 1955.

[Beck, Lester F.] *Human Growth: Film Guide for Teachers and Discussion Leaders.* Portland: E. C. Brown Trust, [1949].

———, with Margie Robinson. *Human Growth: The Story of How Life Begins and Goes on, Based on the Educational Film of the Same Title.* New York: Harcourt, Brace, 1949.

Behlmer, Reuben D. "Family Life Education in a Large High School." *Marriage and Family Living* 21 (August 1959): 284–86.

Bell, Howard M. *Youth Tell Their Story.* Washington: American Council on Education, 1938.

Bellafante, Ginia. "Facts of Life, for Their Eyes Only." *New York Times,* 6 June 2005.

Benefiel, Calvin, and Helen U. Zimnavoda. "Pupil Reaction to Family Life Education." *California Journal of Secondary Education* 28 (November 1953): 363–65.

Benson and Benson, Inc. *Life with Teena: A* Seventeen Magazine *Survey of Subscribers and Their Mothers.* New York: Triangle Publications, 1945.

Bernard, Roscoe George. "An Investigation of the Possibility of Teaching Sex Education as an Integral Part of a Mental Hygiene Program on an Elementary School Level." Master's thesis, Kansas State Teacher's College, 1955.

Biester, Lillian L., William Griffiths, and N. O. Pearce. *Units in Personal Health and Human Relations.* Minneapolis: University of Minnesota Press, 1947.

Bigelow, Maurice A. "The Established Points in Social-Hygiene Education, 1905–1924." *Journal of Social Hygiene* 10 (January 1924): 2–11.

———. "Sex Education in School Programs on Health and Human Relations." *Journal of Social Hygiene* 30 (February 1944): 84–87.

Black, Rhea. "Teaching Good Grooming." *Curriculum Digest: San Diego City Schools in Action* 15 (March 1955): 6.

Bliss, Russell L. "Teen-Age Dating Behavior in Two Eastern Kentucky High Schools." Master's thesis, University of Kentucky, 1957.

"Boys Urge Sex Classes." *New York Times,* 20 June 1949, 16.

Branson, Helen Kitchen. "Sexual Protection for Young Girls." *Sexology* 19 (March 1953): 516–21.

Breed, Warren. "Sex, Class, and Socialization in Dating." *Marriage and Family Living* 28 (May 1956): 137–44.

A Brief History of the E. C. Brown Trust. Portland: E. C. Brown Trust, 1958.

Buck, Ellsworth B. "Our Public Schools and Sex." *American Mercury,* May 1939, 30–36.

Bullis, H. Edmund, and Emily E. O'Malley. *Human Relations in the Classroom, Course I–[III].* 3 vols. Wilmington: Delaware State Society for Mental Hygiene, 1947–1951.

Burgess, Gertrude. "Development and Results of a Sex Hygiene Course in a Consolidated High School." *Michigan Public Health* 23 (September 1935): 170–77.

Cartwright, R. S. "Marriage and Family Living." *National Education Association Journal* 45 (February 1956): 92–93.

"Catholic Boycott of Sex Film Urged." *New York Times,* 5 December 1949, 20.

"Catholic Protest on Film Rejected." *New York Times,* 29 November 1949, 23.

"Catholics Attack School Sex Films." *New York Times,* 14 October 1949, 31.

"Catholics Warned on School Trends." *New York Times,* 9 January 1950, 17.

Christ, John R. "High School Dating as a Behavior System." Ph.D. diss., University of Missouri, 1951.

Clarke, Edward H. *Sex in Education; Or, A Fair Chance for the Girls.* Boston: J. R. Osgood, 1873.

Clyde, Velma. "Sex Education: Oregon Takes Lead over Rest of Nation." *Portland Oregonian,* 4 May 1947.

Committee on Preventive Psychiatry. *Promotion of Mental Health in the Primary and Secondary Schools: An Evaluation of Four Projects.* Topeka: Group for the Advancement of Psychiatry, 1951.

"Companion Poll Question: Do You Favor Special Courses in Sex Education in High Schools as One Means of Reducing Juvenile Delinquency?" *Woman's Home Companion,* November 1943, 32.

Cone, Clara Lee. "A High School Course in Family Living." *Marriage and Family Living* 13 (November 1951): 154–55.

Cosgrove, Marjorie. "School Guidance for Home and Family Living: A Required Course for Seniors in Highland Park, Michigan High School." *Marriage and Family Living* 14 (February 1952): 26–31.

Crawford, Will C. "How R We Doing?" *California Parent-Teacher* 29 (November 1952): 9, 18.

Dallas Independent School District. *Home and Family Life Education for Secondary Schools and Adults Curriculum Guide.* Dallas: Dallas Independent School District, 1953.

de Schweinitz, Karl. *Growing Up: The Story of How We Become Alive, Are Born and Grow Up.* New York: Macmillan, 1928.

———. *Growing Up: The Story of How We Become Alive, Are Born and Grow Up.* 2d edition. New York: Macmillan, 1947.

Dickerson, Roy E. "Pre-Induction Course for High School Students." *Journal of Social Hygiene* 31 (April 1945): 211–16.

———, and Esther Emerson Sweeney, eds. *Pre-Induction Health Education Manual (For Use with High School Seniors)*. New York: American Social Hygiene Association, 1952.

Dickinson, Robert Latou. *Human Sex Anatomy: A Topographical Hand Atlas*. 2d edition. Baltimore: Williams and Wilkins, 1949.

———, and Abram Belskie. *Birth Atlas*. New York: Maternity Center Association, 1940.

Diehl, Harold S. *Textbook of Healthful Living*. 3d edition. New York: McGraw-Hill, 1945.

"District of Columbia: Board of Education Approves Sex Instruction." *Journal of Social Hygiene* 29 (November 1943): 551.

Division of Instruction, Department of Family Life Education, Detroit Public Schools. *Family Life Education in the High School: A Source Book for Teachers*. Detroit: Board of Education of the City of Detroit, 1958.

Douglass, Harl R. *Trends and Issues in Secondary Education*. Washington, D.C.: Center for Applied Research in Education, 1962.

Dowdy, Evelyn L. "Social Hygiene." *Parent-Teacher Courier* 12 (October 1937): 10.

Drake, Gordon V. *Is the Schoolhouse the Proper Place to Teach Raw Sex?* Tulsa: Christian Crusade Publications, 1968.

Dunlop, Maude. "Sex Education in Schools Again Provokes a Debate." *New York Times*, 5 February 1939, sec. 2, 5.

Duvall, Evelyn Millis. *Family Living*. New York: Macmillan, 1950.

Eagle, Mac. *Raised in Toms River and Darn Proud of It*. Grand Rapids: Mac Eagle, 1996.

Edson, Newell W. *Status of Sex Education in High Schools*. Washington: GPO, 1922.

"Education." *Time*, 2 February 1950, 66–72.

Ehrmann, Winston W. "Preparation for Marriage and Parenthood." *Journal of Higher Education* 24 (March 1953): 141–48, 167–68.

Ellis, Grace F., and T. Dinsmore Upton. "Sex Instruction in a High School." *Social Hygiene* 1 (March 1915): 271–72.

Engelhardt, Engelhardt, and Leggett, Educational Consultants. *School Building Needs, Toms River School District, New Jersey*. Trenton: New Jersey Department of Education, 1952.

Ernest, Sue. "Know Yourself and Others—Experiment at Roosevelt Junior High." *Parent-Teacher Courier* 18 (May 1944): 4.

Escamilla, Augustine. *Guide for Secondary Social Health Education*. San Diego: San Diego City Schools, 1966.

Evans, Elva Horner. "Sex Education: It Can Be Taught as a Separate Course." *Health and Physical Education* 17 (May 1946): 268–70.

Everett, Ray H. "Sex Education in Washington." *Journal of Social Hygiene* 40 (June 1954): 222–25.

Ferguson, Donita, and Carol Lynn Gilmer. "Sex Education, Please!" *Coronet,* January 1949, 73–80.

Fink, Kenneth. "Public Thinks Sex Education Courses Should Be Taught in the Schools." *Journal of Social Hygiene* 37 (February 1951): 62–63.

Firth, Maude M. "Teaching Family Relationships to Mixed Classes." *Journal of Home Economics* 29 (March 1937): 151–53.

Folsom, Joseph K. *Youth, Family, and Education.* Washington, D.C.: American Council on Education, 1941.

Force, Elizabeth S. "Family Life Education: Are We Passing the Buck?" *National Parent Teacher Magazine* 53 (February 1959): 24–26, 36.

———. "High School Education for Family Living." *Annals of the American Academy of Political and Social Science* 272 (November 1950): 156–62.

———. *Teaching Family Life Education: The Toms River Program.* New York: Teachers College, Columbia University, 1962.

———. "Toms River Looks Back—1951–1941." *Journal of Social Hygiene* 38 (January 1952): 2–10.

———. "Toms River Meets a Challenge." *Progressive Education,* 24 (April 1947): 202–5.

———. "What Teen-Agers Want to Know about Sex and Marriage." *American Magazine* 155 (January 1953): 34–35, 103–6.

———. *Your Family, Today and Tomorrow.* New York: Harcourt, Brace, 1955.

———, and Edgar M. Finck. *Family Relationships: Ten Topics toward Happier Homes.* Elizabethtown: Continental Press, 1948.

———. *Family Relationships: Ten Topics toward Happier Homes, a Handbook for Administrators and Teachers Who Use the Accompanying Study Guide.* Elizabethtown: Continental Press, [1949].

Foster, William T. "Statewide Education in Social Hygiene." *Social Hygiene* 2 (July 1916): 309–21.

Fox, Kirk. "Sex Education in the Schools." *Successful Farming,* April 1938, 14–15.

Freud, Sigmund. *A General Introduction to Psychoanalysis.* Garden City: Garden City Publishing, 1943.

Friedan, Betty. *The Feminine Mystique.* New York: Norton, 1963.

Funk, Una. "A Realistic Family-Life Program—One Approach to the Problem of Teenage Marriage." *National Education Association Journal* 44 (March 1955): 163–64.

Gebhard, Bruno. "The Birth Models: R. L. Dickinson's Monument." *Journal of Social Hygiene* 17 (April 1951): 169–74.

Gillingham, Edna. "The Teen-Ager in Search of Recreation." *California Parent-Teacher* 20 (January 1944): 8, 16.

Gilmore, Bob. "Sex Goes to School in Oregon." *Better Homes and Gardens,* September 1947, 41.

"Girls Enjoy Experimental Shop Activity." *Curriculum Digest: San Diego City Schools in Action* 16 (March–April 1956): 5.

Glatthorn, Allan Adale. "Family Life Education in the Public High Schools of Pennsylvania, 1957–1958." Ed.D. diss., Temple University, 1960.

Goldberg, Jacob A. "Arousing Teacher Interest in New York City." *Journal of Social
Hygiene* 25 (October 1939): 340–45.

———. "Sex Education or Social Hygiene Education in Schools in Forty Cities." *Journal of Social Hygiene* 33 (December 1947): 437–44.

Gould, Jack. "Programs in Review." *New York Times,* 7 December 1947, section 2, 13.

Gray, Linda Ann. "Family Life Education: A Survey of Selected High Schools of Illinois." Master's thesis, Illinois State Normal University, 1955.

Greulich, William Walter. *Handbook of Methods for the Study of Adolescent Children.*
Washington: National Research Council, 1938.

Griffith, Beatrice. *American Me.* Boston: Houghton Mifflin, 1948.

Griffiths, William. "An Investigation of the Present Status of Social Hygiene Education
in the Minnesota Public Schools." *Research Quarterly* 12, no. 2 (1941): 189–97.

Gruenberg, Benjamin C., with the assistance of J. L. Kaukonen. *High Schools and Sex
Education.* Washington: GPO, 1939.

Hale, Kenneth Gray. "An Inquiry into the Sex Education Knowledge, Needs, and
Interests of 1,390 Twelfth-Grade Students." Master's thesis, San Diego State College, 1952.

Hall, G. Stanley. *Adolescence: Its Psychology and Its Relations to Physiology, Anthropology, Sociology, Sex, Crime, Religion, and Education.* 2 vols. New York: D. Appleton,
1908.

Harris, Marcille Hurst. "Parent-Teacher Attitudes toward Sex Education and the Film
Human Growth." Master's thesis, University of Oregon, 1949.

———, Berlan Lemon, and Lester F. Beck, "Sex Instruction in the Classroom." *Educational Leadership* 6 (May 1949): 519–24.

"Harvey Says Reds Sway Rule of City." *New York Times,* 17 May 1937, 11.

Havighurst, Robert J. *Developmental Tasks and Education.* 2d edition. New York:
Longmans, Green, 1952.

Henry, Nelson B., ed. *The Thirty-Third Yearbook of the National Society for the Study
of Education, Part 1: Adolescence.* Chicago: National Society for the Study of Education, 1944.

Henthorn, Frances Y. "Personal Hygiene for Adolescents." *Journal of School Health*
29 (January 1959): 15–19.

Hewes, Laurence I., Jr., with the assistance of William Y. Bell, Jr. *Intergroup Relations
in San Diego: Some Aspects of Community Life in San Diego which Particularly Affect Minority Groups, with Recommendations for a Program of Community Action.*
San Francisco: American Council on Race Relations, 1946.

"Hi-Y Rejects Ban on Minors' Liquor." *New York Times,* 10 December 1939, 36.

Hickey, Margaret. "Parents Want Help." *Ladies' Home Journal,* April 1948, 23.

"High School Graduates by Sex: 1870 to 1970." Series H 598–601. *Historical Statistics
of the United States, Colonial Times to 1970.* Part 1. Washington: GPO, 1975.

Hill, Gladwin. "Hearing Is Ended on Sex Teaching." *New York Times*, 9 August 1959, 63.

Hill, Wendell P. "A Study of a High School Marriage and Family Course." Master's thesis, University of Michigan, 1952.

Hollingshead, August B. *Elmtown's Youth: The Impact of Social Class on Adolescents.* New York: John Wiley and Sons, 1949.

Hoyman, Howard Stanley. "Basic Issues in School Sex Education." *Journal of School Health* 23 (January 1953): 14–22.

———. *Health-Guide Units for Oregon Teachers, Grades 7–12.* Portland: E. C. Brown Trust, 1945.

———. *Health-Guide Units for Oregon Teachers, Grades 7–12.* Revised edition. Portland: E. C. Brown Trust, 1948.

Human Growth. [Promotional pamphlet.] 3d edition. Highland Park: Perennial Education, 1976.

Hyles, Jack. *Sex Education Program in Our Public Schools: What Is Behind It?* Murfreesboro: Sword of the Lord Publishers, 1969.

"Information Please! E. B. Buck Thinks Instruction in Sex Ought to be Introduced into High School Courses." *Collier's,* 17 June 1939, 82.

Ingle, Kelsey Hudleson. "A Study of the Needs of High School Girls in the Area of Sex Guidance in Family Life Education." Master's thesis, University of North Carolina, Greensboro, 1948.

Isaacs, Harold. "Youth: Shall Our Schools Teach Sex?" *Newsweek,* 19 May 1947, 100–102.

It's Elementary: Talking about Gay Issues in School. Produced by Helen S. Cohen and Debra Chasnoff. 77 min. Women's Educational Media, 1996. Videocassette.

Jennings, Dean. "Sex in the Classroom." *Collier's,* 15 September 1945, 22–23, 51.

Johnstone, John, and Elihu Katz. "Youth and Popular Music: A Study in the Sociology of Taste." *American Journal of Sociology* 62, no. 6 (1957): 563–68.

Jones, Catherine Marsman. "A Resource Guide for the Establishment of a Social Health Program at the Secondary Level." Master's thesis, San Diego State College, 1960, 52.

"'Jury' of 350 Mothers Approves Sex Education Films in Schools." *New York Times,* 22 March 1949, 27.

Kanin, Eugene J. "Male Aggression in Dating-Courtship Relations." *American Journal of Sociology* 63 (September 1957): 197–204.

Keliher, Alice V., with the Commission on Human Relations. *Life and Growth.* New York: D. Appleton-Century, 1937.

Kennedy, Payton. "Family Life Education in San Antonio." *Journal of Social Hygiene* 39 (April 1953): 156–64.

———. *A Source Book for Teachers of Family Life Education.* Revised edition. San Antonio: San Antonio Independent School District, [1951].

Kigner, Elliott E. "Girls in Junior High School Analyze Their Problems." *Clearing House* 31 (April 1957): 466–69.

Kinsey Alfred C. et al. *Sexual Behavior in the Human Female.* Philadelphia: W. B. Saunders, 1953.

———, Wardell B. Pomeroy, and Clyde E. Martin. *Sexual Behavior in the Human Male.* Philadelphia: W. B. Saunders, 1948.

Kirby, Eva. "Family Life Education in Biology." *Journal of Secondary Education* 25 (January 1950): 34–37.

Kirkendall, Lester A. *Sex Education as Human Relations: A Guidebook on Content and Methods for School Authorities and Teachers.* New York: Inor, 1950.

———. "Sex Education in 9 Cooperating High Schools, Part 1." *Clearing House* 18 (March 1944): 387–91.

———. "Sound Attitudes toward Sex." *Journal of Social Hygiene* 37 (June 1951): 241–51.

———. "Values and Premarital Intercourse—Implications for Parent Education." *Marriage and Family Living* 22 (November 1960): 317–22.

———, and Curtis E. Avery. "Ethics and Interpersonal Relationships." *Coordinator* 3 (March 1955): 1–7.

———, and Mark Fleitzer. "Recent Findings on Sex Behavior: The Facts Speak for Sex Education." *Clearing House* 22 (September 1947): 27–31.

———, and Thomas Poffenberger, "Parents, Children, and the Sex Molester," in Lester A. Kirkendall, *Kirkendall on Sex Education.* Eugene: E. C. Brown Center for Family Studies, 1970.

Kline, Richard. "Should Sex Education Be Taught in Schools?" *Los Angeles Examiner,* 2 August 1959, section 1, 2.

Knepp, Thomas H. "The Need for Sex Education in the High School." *The Science Teacher* 19 (March 1952): 60–63.

Kohrs, Karl. "They Study How to Live: Toms River Youngsters Face the Problems of Living in a Special—and Significant—High School Course." *Parade,* 9 May 1948, 5–7.

Lampe, Viola I. "Growing Up: Lessons in Health and Human Relations for Sixth-Grade Boys and Girls." In G. Gage Wetherill, *Human Relations Education: A Program Developing in the San Diego City Schools.* New York: American Social Hygiene Association, 1946.

———. "Growing Up: Lessons on Social Hygiene for Sixth-Grade Boys and Girls." In G. Gage Wetherill, *Human Relations Education: A Report.* 2d edition. New York: American Social Hygiene Association, 1951.

Landis, Judson T., and Mary G. Landis. *Personal Adjustment, Marriage, and Family Living: A High School Text.* New York: Prentice-Hall, 1950.

Landis, Paul H. *Your Marriage and Family Living.* New York: McGraw-Hill, 1946.

Laton, Anita D. "Approaches to Sex Education in the Schools." *University High School Journal* 16 (April 1938): 147–55.

———, and Edna W. Bailey. *Suggestions for Teaching Selected Material from the Field of Sex Responsiveness, Mating, and Reproduction.* New York: Teachers College, Columbia University, 1940.

Lawrence, D. H. *Lady Chatterly's Lover.* New York: New American Library, 1959.

Lentz, Gloria. *Raping Our Children: The Sex Education Scandal.* New Rochelle: Arlington House, 1972.

Lesher, Mabel Grier. "Education for Family Life (New Jersey)." *Journal of Educational Sociology* 22 (March 1949): 440–49.

———. *Meeting Youth Needs.* Trenton: New Jersey Congress of Parents and Teachers, [1944].

Levine, Milton L. "What Do Our Adolescents Really Want to Know about Sex?" *Ladies' Home Journal,* September 1955, 68–69, 194, 197–98.

Lewis, Thomas M. N., and Madeline Kneberg. *Hiwassee Island: An Archaeological Account of Four Tennessee Indian Peoples.* Knoxville: University of Tennessee Press, 1946.

Littman, Jeanne, and Mildred Robinson, eds. *History of Pioneers: Reminiscences and Personal Histories of the Jews of Toms River.* Toms River: Council of Jewish Organizations, 1976.

Lyons, William J. "Sex Education in Our Public Schools." *Parent-Teacher Courier* 12 (January 1938): 5, 12.

Manley, Helen. "Sex Education in the Schools." *Journal of School Health* 21 (February 1951): 62–69.

———. "Sex Education: Where, When, and How Should It Be Taught?" *Journal of Health, Physical Education, and Recreation* 35 (March 1964): 21–24.

Marland, S. P., Jr. "Placing Sex Education in the Curriculum." *Phi Delta Kappan* 43 (December 1951): 132–34.

Masley, John W., and Arthur F. Davis. "Sex Education in Pennsylvania's Public Secondary Schools." *Journal of Social Hygiene* 39 (March 1953): 107–19.

Masten, Fannie B. "Family Life Education at Central High School, Charlotte, North Carolina." *Marriage and Family Living* 15 (May 1953): 105–8.

———, as told to Jack Harrison Pollack. "What I Teach Teen-Agers about Love, Sex, and Marriage." *Woman's Home Companion,* February 1955, 87–88.

"The Matter and Methods of Sex Education." *Social Hygiene* 2 (October 1916): 573–81.

Metalious, Grace. *Peyton Place.* New York: Messner, 1956.

Michener, James A. "Sex Education: A Success in Our Social Studies Class." *Clearing House* 12 (April 1938): 461–65.

"Michigan Adopts Law Proving for Social Hygiene Education." *Journal of Social Hygiene* 35 (October 1949): 346.

Miller, Frances S., and Helen H. Laitem. *Personal Problems of the High School Girl.* 2d edition. New York: John Wiley and Sons, 1945.

Miller, Harold A., and Robert S. Breakey. "Sex Education in the Curriculum." *Education Digest* 5 (February 1940): 37–40.

Milling, Virginia. "How Do You Rate on a Date?" *Clearing House* 19 (November 1944): 165–66.

"More Candid Attitude toward Sex Education." *The Nation,* 24 December 1949, 607.

Murch, Betty A. "Educational Notes." *Journal of Social Hygiene* 34 (November 1948): 392–94.

———. "Rhode Island Offers Lecture Series on 'Love and Marriage Today.'" *Journal of Social Hygiene* 24 (December 1948): 438–40.

National Congress of Parents and Teachers. *Proceedings: Forty-Eighth Annual Convention,* New York, 22–24 May 1944. Chicago: National Congress of Parents and Teachers, 1944.

"New Biology Film Helps Girls." *Educational Screen* 26 (April 1947): 215, 218.

New Jersey Department of Education's Advisory Committee on Social Hygiene Education, "An Approach in Schools to Education for Personal and Family Living." *Journal of Social Hygiene* 38 (February 1952): 63.

New Jersey Department of Education. *A Guide for Health Education in the Secondary School.* Trenton: New Jersey Department of Education, 1955.

New Jersey Secondary School Teachers' Association. *The Family Relationships Primer for Secondary Schools.* [Trenton:] New Jersey Secondary School Teachers' Association, 1949.

"Notes on Recent State Activities Relating to Sex Education." *Journal of Social Hygiene* 31 (April 1945): 220–27.

Oberholtzer, Kenneth E., and Myrtle F. Sugarman. "Denver Educates for Home and Family Living." *Journal of Social Hygiene* 37 (February 1951): 51–61.

"Ohio—Sex Education in Cleveland Secondary Schools." *Journal of Social Hygiene* 27 (November 1941): 412.

Osborne, Ruth Farnham, and Lester A. Kirkendall, "Family-Life Education in Illinois High Schools." *School Review* 58 (December 1950): 516–26.

Packer, Vin. *Spring Fire.* New York: Faucett Publications, 1952.

Paddack, Cecil Thomas. "Public Opinion of the People of Washington Regarding the Teaching of Sex Education in the Public Schools." Master's thesis, State College of Washington, 1951.

"*Palmour Street* Film Discussion Guide." *Coordinator* 4 (September 1955): n.p.

"Parents Demand Sex Education in Schools." *Family Life* 6 (September 1946): 1–2.

"Parents Held Lax in Sex Education." *New York Times,* 5 December 1948, 77.

Payne, William H. "High School Group Interprets the Meaning of Americanism." *Curriculum Digest: San Diego City Schools in Action* 12 (September 1951): 5.

Pearcy, Evert R. "Sex Education in the Senior High Schools of New Jersey." Master's thesis, West Virginia University, 1940.

Pierce, Wellington G. *Youth Comes of Age.* New York: McGraw-Hill, 1948.

Pigg, Ewell G. "Sex Education in High School Science." *Science and Mathematics* 41 (December 1941): 851–54.

Poffenberger, Thomas. "Family Life Education in This Scientific Age." *Marriage and Family Living* 21 (May 1959): 150–54.

———. "A Lesson for Group Leaders from *Palmour Street*." *Coordinator* 4 (December 1955): 5–11.

———. "Responses of Eighth Grade Girls to a Talk on Sex." *Marriage and Family Living* 22 (February 1960): 38–44.

———. "A Technique for Evaluating Family Life and Mental Health Films." Ed.D. diss., Michigan State College, 1954.

Priester, Helen Moore. "The Reported Dating Practices of 106 High School Seniors in an Urban Community." Master's thesis, Cornell University, 1941.

"Public Opinion Polls." *Public Opinion Quarterly* 7, no. 4 (1943): 748.

"Pupils Run City Council." *New York Times,* 3 April 1948, 16.

"Purposeful Education for Tomorrow's Citizens." *Annual Report of the Toms River Schools, 1949–1950.*

Putnam, Rex. "Social Hygiene in Oregon Schools." *Phi Delta Kappan* 29 (March 1948): 303–4.

———, and Dorotha Massey. "Social Hygiene Education in the Oregon Schools." *National Education Association Journal* 37 (November 1948): 498–99.

Ramsey, Louise. "Education for Marriage and Family Life in the High School as a Means of Strengthening National Defense." *Marriage and Family Living* 4 (August 1942): 52–55.

Randolph, Helen. "Senior Problems and Family Life." *Journal of Secondary Education* 25 (January 1950): 12–17.

Reeve, Mildred E. "Gifts of Spring." *Journal of Social Hygiene.* 12 (March 1926): 136–43.

Reiss, Ira L. *Premarital Sexual Standards in America: A Sociological Investigation of the Relative Social and Cultural Integration of American Sexual Standards.* Glencoe: Free Press, 1960.

Roanoke City Public Schools. *Family Life Education Resource Guide, Grade 1 through 12.* New York: American Social Hygiene Association, 1958.

Robinson, Margie C. "Measuring the Sex Knowledge of Junior High School Pupils." Master's thesis, University of Oregon, 1949.

Robbins, Samuel Tubbe. "Education for Responsible Parenthood (Mississippi)." *Journal of Educational Sociology* 22 (March 1949): 468–74.

Schilling, Margaret. "Evaluation in a Family Life Education Program." *Marriage and Family Living* 23 (August 1961): 297–99.

"The School's Responsibility in Social Hygiene Education: Preliminary Report of a New York Statewide Committee." *Journal of Social Hygiene* 26 (October 1940): 294–304.

"Sex Education Has Place in Junior, Senior High Schools." *Nation's Schools* 65 (March 1960): 94.

"Sex Education Held Unwise in Schools." *New York Times,* 8 February 1939, 24.

"Sex Education: Oregon Film Provides New Approach to Delicate Problem." *Life,* 24 May 1948, 55, 58–62.

"Sex Education Put Forward as Public Problem." *San Diego Union,* 4 November 1937, 6.

"Sex Education Question up to S.D. Round Table." *San Diego Union,* 2 November 1937, 12.

"Sex Education . . . San Diego Pioneers." *Ladies' Home Journal,* April 1948, 23, 273, 275–77.

"Sex Education That Teaches Abstinence Wins Support." *New York Times,* 23 July 1997, A 19.

"Sex Education Urged in City High Schools." *New York Times,* 18 May 1937, 25.

"Sex in the Classroom." *Newsweek,* 10 August 1959, 84.

"Sex in the News." *Sexology,* January 1948, 328.

"Sex in the Schoolroom in Oregon." *Time,* 22 March 1948, 71–72.

"Sex Lectures Assailed: Wilmington Bishop Bars Them to Catholics in Public Schools." *New York Times,* 12 February 1945, 21.

"Sexological News." *Sexology* 17 (April 1951): 609.

"Sexological News." *Sexology* 19 (October 1952): 200.

Shenehon, Eleanor. "Colorado: State PTA Favors Social Hygiene Instruction in Schools." *Journal of Social Hygiene* 32 (June 1946): 264–65.

Slater, Greta Willis. "An Historical Study of the Social Health Program in the San Diego City Schools, 1937–1966." Master's thesis, University of California, Los Angeles, 1966.

Snow, William F. *Social Hygiene in Schools: Report of the Subcommittee on Social Hygiene in Schools, White House Conference on Child Health and Protection.* New York: Century, 1932.

"Some Say Toms River Is Next Objective of Ku Klux Klan." *Toms River, New Jersey Courier,* 22 June 1923, 1.

Southworth, Warren H. "A Study in the Area of Family Life Education: The Nature of Sex Education Programs in Wisconsin High Schools." *High School Journal* 38 (December 1954): 77–116.

"Spectacular Visit of Ku Klux at Toms River M.E. Church." *Toms River, New Jersey Courier,* 23 August 1923, 1.

Spock, Benjamin. *The Pocket Book of Baby and Child Care.* New York: Pocket Books, 1948.

Stearns, Myron M. "The ABC's of Happy Marriage." *Today's Woman,* February 1948, 32–33, 131–35.

Steinbacher, John. *The Child Seducers.* n.p.: Educator Publications, 1971.

Stohlman, Mary Helen. "Sex Education in the Public Schools of the District of Columbia." *Journal of Social Hygiene* 25 (October 1939): 330–39.

Strain, Frances Bruce. *The Normal Sex Interests of Children from Infancy to Childhood.* New York: Appleton-Century-Crofts, 1948.

———. "Sex Education at Different Ages." *Parents' Magazine,* April 1945, 34–35+.

———, and Chester Lee Eggert. "Framework for Family Life Education: A Source

Book." *Bulletin of the National Association of Secondary-School Principals* 40 (December 1955): 1–117.

Strang, Ruth. *The Adolescent Views Himself: A Psychology of Adolescence.* New York: McGraw-Hill, 1957.

Strawn, Alice. "A Human Relations Class." *Marriage and Family Living* 11 (May 1949): 44–45.

Sullivan, Ann. "Touchy Sex Subject Handled Objectively in New Film." *Portland Oregonian,* 15 February 1948, 24.

Sweeney, Esther Emerson, and Roy E. Dickerson, eds. *Preinduction Health and Human Relations.* New York: American Social Hygiene Association, 1953.

Swift, Edith Hale. *Step by Step in Sex Education.* 1938; reprint, New York: Macmillan, 1950.

Tebor, Irving B., and Helen L. Larrabee. *Background for Planning for Social Welfare in San Diego County.* San Diego: Research Department, Community Welfare Council, 1958.

"Teen-Age Council Shelves Subway Fare Rise but Votes for a Course in Sex Education." *New York Times,* 27 April 1946, 19.

"Teen-Age Sex Hysteria." *Science News Letter,* 1 January 1955, 4.

"Third Annual State-Wide Conference on Social Hygiene." 4 February 1944. *Oregon Health Bulletin,* 2 February 1944, 6–7.

Torrey, Harry Beal. *Biology in the Elementary Schools and Its Contribution to Sex Education.* New York: American Social Hygiene Association, 1928.

"Urge More Sex Teaching." *New York Times,* 26 June 1947, 17.

"Use of Sex Films in Schools Urged." *New York Times,* 12 May 1949, 26.

Usilton, Lida J., and Newell W. Edson. *The Status of Sex Education in Senior High Schools of the United States in 1927.* Washington: GPO, 1928.

Van Winkle, Lloyd S. "The Teaching of Sex Education in the Elementary School." Ed.D. diss., Colorado State College of Education, 1949.

Vickery, William E. "Ten Years of Intergroup Education Workshops: Some Comparisons and Contrasts." *Journal of Educational Sociology* 26 (March 1953): 292–302.

Volk, Alma M. "Rock Island's Program of Sex Education." *School Executive* 65 (May 1946): 53–54.

Walker, Dollie R. "The Need of Sex Education in Negro Schools." *Journal of Negro Education* 14 (Spring 1945): 174–81.

Wertman, Dorothy. "Our Successful Lecture Series on Sex Education." *Clearing House* 19 (November 1944): 174–76.

Wetherill, Gloyd Gage. "Accepting Responsibility for Sex Education." *Journal of School Health* 30 (March 1960): 107–10.

———. "A Community Social-Hygiene Program (San Diego, California)." *Journal of Educational Sociology* 22 (March 1949): 468–74.

———. "Developing a Program of Integrative Health Instruction for the Secondary Curriculum." Master's thesis, Stanford University, 1943.

———. *Human Relations Education: A Program Developing in the San Diego City Schools.* New York: American Social Hygiene Association, 1946.

———. *Human Relations Education: A Report.* 2d edition. New York: American Social Hygiene Association, 1951.

———. "Sex Education in the Public Schools." *Journal of School Health* 31 (September 1961): 235–39.

———. "Who Is Responsible for Sex Education?" *Journal of School Health* 29 (December 1959): 361–64.

"What about Sex Instruction?" *Nation's Schools* 33 (June 1944): 49.

"What Are Some Promising Administrative Practices in the Junior High School?" *Bulletin of the National Association of Secondary-School Principals* 42 (April 1958): 227–29.

"Where Babies Come From: University of Oregon Program of Education on Family Life." *Newsweek,* 22 March 1948, 90.

Whitman, Howard. *Let's Tell the Truth about Sex.* New York: Pellegrini and Cudahy, 1948.

Williams, Melvin J. "Personal and Familial Problems of High School Youths and Their Bearing upon Family Education Needs." *Social Forces* 27, no. 3 (1949): 279–85.

Williamson, Mildred Sanders. "High School Family Life Courses." *Journal of Home Economics* 42 (February 1950): 98–100.

Wimmer, Nancy C. "Trends in Family Life Education in the Schools." *Journal of Social Hygiene* 19 (February 1953): 69–78.

Wolf, Anna M. W. *When Children Ask about Sex.* New York: Child Study Association of America, 1943.

Wolford, Opal Powell. "The Dating Behavior and Personal and Family Relationships of High School Seniors with Implications for Family Life Education." Ph.D. diss., Cornell University, 1948.

Wylie, Philip. *Generation of Vipers.* New York: Holt, Rinehart, and Winston, 1942.

"Youth 'Legislate' on Varied Lines." *New York Times,* 10 December 1944, 52.

Secondary Sources

Adams, Mary Louise. *The Trouble with Normal: Postwar Youth and the Making of Heterosexuality.* Toronto: University of Toronto Press, 1997.

Alcoff, Linda, and Elizabeth Potter, eds. *Feminist Epistemologies.* New York: Routledge, 1993.

Bailey, Beth L. *From Front Porch to Back Seat: Courtship in Twentieth-Century America.* Baltimore: Johns Hopkins University Press, 1988.

———. *Sex in the Heartland.* Cambridge: Harvard University Press, 1999.

Bartky, Sandra Lee. "Foucault, Femininity, and the Modernization of Patriarchal Power." In *Feminism and Foucault: Reflections on Resistance,* edited by Irene Diamond and Lee Quinby, 61–86. Boston: Northeastern University Press, 1988.

Best, Amy L. *Prom Night: Youth, Schools, and Popular Culture.* New York: Routledge, 2000.

Bordo, Susan. *Unbearable Weight: Feminism, Western Culture, and the Body.* Berkeley: University of California Press, 1993.

Brandt, Allan M. *No Magic Bullet: A Social History of Venereal Disease in the United States since 1880.* Expanded edition. New York: Oxford University Press, 1987.

Breines, Wini. "Postwar White Girls' Dark Others." In *The Other Fifties: Interrogating Midcentury American Icons,* edited by Joel Foreman, 53–77. Urbana: University of Illinois Press, 1997.

———. *Young, White, and Miserable: Growing Up Female in the Fifties.* Boston: Beacon Press, 1992.

Brumberg, Joan Jacobs. *The Body Project: An Intimate History of American Girls.* New York: Random House, 1997.

Burnham, John C. "The Progressive Era Revolution in American Attitudes toward Sex." *Journal of American History* 59, no. 4 (1973): 885–908.

Butler, Judith. *Gender Trouble: Feminism and the Subversion of Identity.* New York: Routledge, 1990.

Carter, Julian B. "Birds, Bees, and Venereal Disease: Toward an Intellectual History of Sex Education." *Journal of the History of Sexuality* 10, no. 2 (2001): 213–49.

Chafe, William Henry. *The Paradox of Change: American Women in the Twentieth Century.* Revised edition. New York: Oxford University Press, 1991.

Cook, James R. "The Evolution of Sex Education in the Public Schools of the United States, 1900–1970." Ph.D. diss., Southern Illinois University, 1971.

Coontz, Stephanie. *The Way We Never Were: American Families and the Nostalgia Trap.* New York: Basic Books, 1992.

Cott, Nancy F. *Public Vows: A History of Marriage and the Nation.* Cambridge: Harvard University Press, 2000.

Cremin, Lawrence. *The Transformation of the School: Progressivism in American Education, 1876–1957.* New York: Knopf, 1962.

Crispell, Diane. "Myths of the 1950s." *American Demographics* 14 (August 1992): 38–43.

De Ras, Marion, and Mieke Lunenberg, eds. *Girls, Girlhood, and Girls' Studies in Transition.* Amsterdam: Het Spinhuis, 1993.

Diamond, Irene, and Lee Quinby, eds. *Feminism and Foucault: Reflections on Resistance.* Boston: Northeastern University Press, 1988.

Doherty, Thomas. *Teenagers and Teenpics: The Juvenilization of American Movies in the 1950s.* Revised edition. Philadelphia: Temple University Press, 2002.

Douglas, Susan J. *Where the Girls Are: Growing Up Female with the Mass Media.* New York: Times Books, 1995.

Eberwein, Robert. *Sex Ed: Film, Video, and the Framework of Desire.* New Brunswick: Rutgers University Press, 1999.

Fausto-Sterling, Anne. *Sexing the Body: Gender Politics and the Construction of Sexuality.* New York: Basic Books, 2000.

Fine, Michelle. "Sexuality, Schooling, and Adolescent Females: The Missing Discourse of Desire." *Harvard Educational Review* 58, no. 1 (1988): 29–53.

Foreman, Joel, ed. *The Other Fifties: Interrogating Midcentury American Icons.* Urbana: University of Illinois Press, 1997.

Foucault, Michel. *The History of Sexuality,* vol. 1., *An Introduction.* Translated by Robert Hurley. New York: Pantheon, 1978.

Freedman, Estelle B. "'Uncontrolled Desires': The Response to the Sexual Psychopath, 1920–1960." *Journal of American History* 74, no. 1 (1987): 83–106.

Gilbert, James. *A Cycle of Outrage: America's Reaction to the Juvenile Delinquent in the 1950s.* New York: Oxford University Press, 1986.

Goldin, Claudia. *Understanding the Gender Gap: An Economic History of American Women.* New York: Oxford University Press, 1990.

Graebner, William. *The Engineering of Consent: Democracy and Authority in Twentieth-Century America.* Madison: University of Wisconsin Press, 1987.

Harding, Sandra, ed. *The "Racial" Economy of Science: Toward a Democratic Future.* Bloomington: Indiana University Press, 1993.

———. "Rethinking Standpoint Epistemology: What Is 'Strong Objectivity?'" In *Feminist Epistemologies,* edited by Linda Alcoff and Elizabeth Potter, 49–82. New York: Routledge, 1993.

Hartmann, Susan M. "Women's Employment and the Domestic Ideal in the Early Cold War Years." In *Not June Cleaver: Women and Gender in Postwar America, 1945–1960,* edited by Joanne Meyerowitz, 84–100. Philadelphia: Temple University Press, 1994.

Harvey, Brett. *The Fifties: A Women's Oral History.* New York: HarperCollins, 1993.

Herman, Ellen. *The Romance of American Psychology: Political Culture in the Age of Experts.* Berkeley: University of California Press, 1995.

Higonnet, Margaret Randolph et al., eds. *Behind the Lines: Gender and the Two World Wars.* New Haven: Yale University Press, 1987.

Hilden, Patricia Penn. *When Indians Were Nickels: An Urban Mixed-Blood Story.* Washington: Smithsonian Institution Press, 1995.

Hubbard, Ruth. *The Politics of Women's Biology.* New Brunswick: Rutgers University Press, 1990.

Imber, Michael. "Analysis of a Curriculum Reform Movement: The American Social Hygiene Association's Campaign for Sex Education, 1900–1930." Ph.D. diss., Stanford University, 1981.

———. "Toward a Theory of Curriculum Reform: An Analysis of the First Campaign for Sex Education." *Curriculum Inquiry* 12, no. 4 (1982): 339–62.

———. "Toward a Theory of Educational Origins: The Genesis of Sex Education," *Educational Theory* 34, no. 3 (1984): 275–86.

Inness, Sherrie A., ed. *Delinquents and Debutantes: Twentieth-Century American Girls' Culture.* New York: New York University Press, 1998.

Irvine, Janice M. *Sexuality Education across Cultures: Working with Differences.* San Francisco: Jossey-Bass Publishers, 1995.

———. *Talk about Sex: The Battles over Sex Education in the United States*. Berkeley: University of California Press, 2002.

———, ed. *Sexual Cultures and the Construction of Adolescent Identities*. Philadelphia: Temple University Press, 1994.

Jones, Kathleen W. *Taming the Troublesome Child: American Families, Child Guidance, and the Limits of Psychiatric Authority*. Cambridge: Harvard University Press, 1999.

Katz, Jonathan Ned. *The Invention of Heterosexuality*. New York: Penguin, 1995.

Kennard, Margot. "The Corporation in the Classroom: The Struggles over Meanings of Menstruation Education in Sponsored Films, 1947–83." Ph.D. diss., University of Wisconsin-Madison, 1989.

Kett, Joseph F. *Rites of Passage: Adolescence in America, 1790 to the Present*. New York: Basic Books, 1977.

Klein, Lawrence D. "Three Areas of Contention in Sex Education: The Policy Problem for American Public Schools." Ed.D. diss., Indiana University, 1971.

Klein, Susan Shurberg, ed. *Sex Equity and Sexuality in Education*. Albany: State University of New York Press, 1992.

Kliebard, Herbert M. *The Struggle for the American Curriculum, 1893–1958*. 2d edition. New York: Routledge, 1995.

Kline, Wendy. *Building a Better Race: Gender, Sexuality, and Eugenics from the Turn of the Century to the Baby Boom*. Berkeley: University of California Press, 2001.

Kunzel, Regina G. *Fallen Women, Problem Girls: Unmarried Mothers and the Professionalization of Social Work, 1890–1945*. New Haven: Yale University Press, 1995.

Ladd-Taylor, Molly, and Lauri Umanski, eds. *"Bad" Mothers: The Politics of Blame in Twentieth-Century America*. New York: New York University Press, 2000.

Lesko, Nancy. *Act Your Age! A Cultural Construction of Adolescence*. New York: RoutledgeFalmer, 2001.

Lutz, Catherine A., and Jane L. Collins, *Reading* National Geographic. Chicago: University of Chicago Press, 1993.

Markowitz, Sally. "Pelvic Politics: Sexual Dimorphism and Racial Difference." *Signs* 25, no. 2 (2001): 389–414.

Martin, Donald F. "A History of the Public Schools of Dover Township, New Jersey, from 1900 through 1955." Ed.D. diss., Rutgers University, 1957.

Martin, Emily. "The Egg and the Sperm: How Science Has Constructed a Romance Based on Stereotypical Male-Female Roles." *Signs* 16, no. 3 (1991): 485–501.

———. *The Woman in the Body: A Cultural Analysis of Reproduction*. Boston: Beacon Press, 1987.

Maw, Wallace H. "Fifty Years of Sex Education in the Public Schools of the United States (1900–1950): A History of Ideas." Ed.D. diss, University of Cincinnati, 1953.

Meyerowitz, Joanne. *How Sex Changed: A History of Transsexuality in the United States*. Cambridge: Harvard University Press, 2002.

———. *Women Adrift: Independent Wage Earners in Chicago, 1880–1930.* Chicago: University of Chicago Press, 1988.

———, ed. *Not June Cleaver: Women and Gender in Postwar America, 1945–1960.* Philadelphia: Temple University Press, 1994.

Michel, Sonya. "American Women and the Discourse of the Democratic Family in World War II." In *Behind the Lines: Gender and the Two World Wars,* edited by Margaret Randolph Higonnet et al, 154–67. New Haven: Yale University Press, 1987.

Mintz, Steven and Susan Kellogg. *Domestic Revolutions: A Social History of American Family Life.* New York: Free Press, 1988.

Moran, Jeffrey P. "'Modernism Gone Mad': Sex Education Comes to Chicago, 1913." *Journal of American History* 83, no. 2 (1996): 481–513.

———. *Teaching Sex: The Shaping of Adolescence in the Twentieth Century.* Cambridge: Harvard University Press, 2000.

Nathanson, Constance A. *Dangerous Passage: The Social Control of Sexuality in Women's Adolescence.* Philadelphia: Temple University Press, 1991.

Nelson, Claudia and Michelle Martin, eds. *Sexual Pedagogies: England, Australia, and America, 1879–2000.* New York: Palgrave Macmillan, 2004.

Oudshoorn, Nelly. *Beyond the Natural Body: An Archaeology of Sex Hormones.* London: Routledge, 1994.

Palladino, Grace. *Teenagers: An American History.* New York: Basic Books, 1996.

Peiss, Kathy Lee. *Cheap Amusements: Working Women and Leisure in Turn-of-the-Century New York.* Philadelphia: Temple University Press, 1986.

Prescott, Heather Munro. *A Doctor of Their Own: The History of Adolescent Medicine.* Cambridge: Harvard University Press, 1998.

Rich, Adrienne. "Compulsory Heterosexuality and Lesbian Existence." *Signs* 5 (Summer 1980): 631–60.

Romano, Renee C. *Race Mixing: Black-White Marriage in Postwar America.* Cambridge: Harvard University Press, 2003.

Russett, Cynthia Eagle. *Sexual Science: The Victorian Construction of Womanhood.* Cambridge: Harvard University Press, 1989.

Schrum, Kelly. *Some Wore Bobby Sox: The Emergence of Teenage Girls' Culture, 1920–1945.* New York: Palgrave Macmillan, 2004.

Sears, James T., ed. *Sexuality and the Curriculum: The Politics and Practices of Sexuality Education.* New York: Teachers College Press, 1992.

Sethna, Christabelle Laura. "The Facts of Life: The Sex Instruction of Ontario Public School Children, 1900–1950." Ed.D. diss., University of Toronto, 1995.

Simmons, Christina. "'Marriage in the Modern Manner': Sexual Radicalism and Reform in America, 1914–1941." Ph.D. diss., Brown University, 1982.

Smith, Ken. *Mental Hygiene: Classroom Films, 1945–1970.* New York: Blast Books, 1999.

Søland, Birgitte. *Becoming Modern: Young Women and the Reconstruction of Womanhood in the 1920s.* Princeton: Princeton University Press, 2000.

Solinger, Rickie. *Wake Up Little Susie: Single Pregnancy and Race before* Roe v. Wade. New York: Routledge, 1992.

Stepan, Nancy. "Race and Gender: The Role of Analogy in Science." In *The "Racial" Economy of Science: Toward a Democratic Future,* edited by Sandra Harding, 359–76. Bloomington: Indiana University Press, 1993.

Strong, Bryan. "Ideas of the Early Sex Education Movement in America, 1890–1920." *History of Education Quarterly* 12, no. 2 (1972): 129–61.

Tanenbaum, Leora. *Slut! Growing Up Female with a Bad Reputation.* New York: Seven Stories Press, 2000.

Terry, Jennifer. *An American Obsession: Science, Medicine, and Homosexuality in Modern Society.* Chicago: University of Chicago Press, 1999.

Tolman, Deborah L. *Dilemmas of Desire: Teenage Girls Talk about Sexuality.* Cambridge: Harvard University Press, 2002.

Trudell, Bonnie Nelson. *Doing Sex Education: Gender Politics and Schooling.* New York: Routledge, 1993.

Tuana, Nancy. *The Less Noble Sex: Scientific, Religious, and Philosophical Conceptions of Women's Nature.* Bloomington: Indiana University Press, 1993.

———, ed. *Feminism and Science.* Bloomington: Indiana University Press, 1989.

Tyack, David B. *Seeking Common Ground: Public Schools in a Diverse Society.* Cambridge: Harvard University Press, 2003.

Wagener, Judith Rabak. "A Social Epistemology of Sex Education in the Milwaukee Public Schools: 1910–1960." Ph.D. diss., University of Wisconsin-Madison, 1991.

Weis, Lois, and Michelle Fine, eds. *Construction Sites: Excavating Race, Class, and Gender among Urban Youth.* New York: Teachers College Press, 2000.

Weiss, Jessica. *To Have and to Hold: Marriage, the Baby Boom, and Social Change.* Chicago: University of Chicago Press, 2000.

Whatley, Mariamne. "Male and Female Hormones: Misinterpretations of Biology in School Health and Sex Education." In *Women, Biology, and Public Policy,* edited by Virginia Shapiro, 67–89. Beverly Hills: Sage Publications, 1985.

Index

SUSAN K. FREEMAN is an assistant professor of women's studies at Minnesota State University, Mankato. Her current research explores the history of gay and lesbian studies courses in the 1970s and 1980s.

The University of Illinois Press
is a founding member of the
Association of American University Presses.

Composed in 10.5/13 Minion Pro
with Meta display
by Jim Proefrock
at the University of Illinois Press
Manufactured by Thomson-Shore, Inc.

University of Illinois Press
1325 South Oak Street
Champaign, IL 61820-6903
www.press.uillinois.edu